RAINBOW DIARY

DIARY

A Journey in the New South Africa

John Malathronas

summersdale

Summersdale Publishers Ltd
46 West Street
Chichester
West Sussex
PO19 1RP
UK

www.summersdale.com

Printed and bound in Great Britain

ISBN: 1-84024-445-3
ISBN 13: 978-1-84024-445-8

Map by Rob Smith

Steve Biko quote from 'Black Consciousness and the Quest for a True Humanity' in *Steve Biko: Black Consciousness in South Africa*, edited by Millard Arnold (1979) reprinted courtesy of Random House Inc, 1540 Broadway, New York, NY 10036, USA.

Nelson Mandela quotes from his book *Long Walk to Freedom* (Abacus, 1994) reprinted courtesy of Little Brown and Co, 1271 Avenue of the Americas, New York, NY, 10020, USA.

Quote from Amnesty International Report 2003, AI Index POL 10/003/2003, section on Swaziland, courtesy of Amnesty International, 99–119 Rosebery Avenue, London, UK.

Disclaimer

Acknowledgements

I would first like to thank the people who lent me their life stories and made this book possible – although some of the names have been changed, they should be able to recognise themselves easily. Even if they are not mentioned in the book, there are many people who made my sojourn in South Africa so unforgettable; I want to single out Philip Uys, Peter Dayson and Irma Kruger. A big thank you also to Michael Boy and Martin McHale of Club 330 who were responsible for one of my best nights out *ever*.

This book started life as a website, and I am grateful to all those who followed its growth with encouragement, in particular: Matthew Malthouse, Lyn David Thomas, Lionel Barnett, Richard MacDonald, Andrew Hollo and Norman Coyne. I owe many thanks to Mark Hawthorne Richardson, T. J. de Klerk and Peter H. M. Brooks for their comments and corrections. I am also indebted to Dr Rupert Thompson's assistance during my research in the Cambridge University library.

Special thanks are due to the ever-patient Moira de Swardt who helped me with so many questions after I left South Africa and who has been an unwavering friend throughout; to Errol Uys who first saw a book where there was none; and to everyone in Summersdale, especially my editors, Jennifer Barclay and Carol Baker, both of whose spot-on suggestions and professional advice have been invaluable.

To Victor

CONTENTS

Prologue..11

One   Tina Turner: Pretoria...14

Two   Cruising in the Kruger: The Kruger Park..............................43

Three   The Taliban in the Transvaal: Klein Drakensberg...................70

Four   The Baz Bus: Johannesburg to Mbabane.................................92

Five   Swazi Sleaze: Swaziland...111

Six   The Maid from Mozambique: St Lucia.......................................135

Seven   Mad Max IV – Tamin' Durban: Durban.....................................163

Eight   Garden Rout(e) Port Elizabeth to Knysna.............................198

Nine   Ostrich Operetta: Oudtshoorn, Klein Karoo..........................220

Ten   African Drama: Cape Town, Robben Island, Cape Flats......253

Eleven   A Shrimp Learns to Whistle: The Cape.....................................292

Epilogue..331

SOUTH AFRICA
Limpopo River
Kruger National Park
Lebombo Mountains
Moholoholo
Blyde River Reserve
Pilgrim's Rest
Nelspruit
Johannesburg
Pretoria
SWAZILAND
Mbabane
Manzini
Vaal River
The Battle of Blood River
Orange River
Orange River
Tugela River
St Lucia
Gingindlovu
LESOTHO
Stanger
Durban
Valley of 1000 hills
Swartberg Mountains
Addo Elephant National Park
Prince Albert
Cango Caves
Motherwell
Oudstshoorn
Tsitsikamma
Cape Town
Cape Flats
Stellenbosch
Swellendam
George
Knysna
Port Elizabeth
Cape of Good Hope
Cape Agulhas
ATLANTIC OCEAN
INDIAN OCEAN

Prologue

I don't consider myself a backpacker. I find the whole world of backpackerdom a bit incestuous. You move from hostel to hostel meeting the same kind of people (anarcho-alternatives, stinky students or healthstrong hikers), you follow the same rules (*'Please take a beer and write your name in the book'*; *'Do not force the lock on the pool table'*; *'We do not lend pens – in fact we do not lend anything'*), and you are encouraged to stay away from the locals. Backpacker hostels are a perfect breeding ground for tomorrow's megacoach family tourist: self-contained (sleep, cook, eat, drink and socialise under the same roof), self-important (*'You're only spending five weeks in South Africa? We're here for six months'*) and finally self-defeating – are you really visiting a foreign country if you hang around with like-minded young Westerners? So I don't consider myself a backpacker. I hang around in the bars and the clubs of a new town, drink with the locals and make them tell me their stories. And on top of that I am a dorm's nightmare. Put me in the lower bunk and I'll knock my head on the top bed. Put me in the top bunk, and I'll want to go to the toilet four times in the course of the night. Oh, and I drag dry hides, as the Zulu say. This means I snore heavily. Dorms inspire my adenoids.

Plus in South Africa I tasted luxury. I was forced by circumstances to stay in a four-star hotel in Durban and what did it cost me? Twenty quid. I expected to rough it in the Kruger Park and I had a huge, superbly decorated three-man hut for myself. For the first time I started looking at the better hotels in the Lonely Planet guide. Could I really afford to stay at the Edward Hotel in Port Elizabeth? I called. I could. I did. Luxury is like a drug: if I hadn't missed the occasional sociability of the backpacker's bus, who knows – I might have crammed my credit card with bills from luxurious, yet inexpensive, hotels. The exchange rate rocks.

It is perhaps because luxury *is* like a drug that the problems plaguing South Africa were generated and have persisted to this day. More than a hundred years ago, gold and diamonds started providing the elite of the country with a lifestyle which has to be lived in order for outsiders to comprehend why it was defended so ruthlessly. And many a time, since the larger, disadvantaged population of South Africa lives outside the cities, it was easy to forget how this high standard of living was attained.

Crime is therefore a big problem, which will not surprise anyone who knows that sharp divisions in a society create stress. But it does seem to surprise white South Africans. 'Perpetrators of crime act with impunity in the new South Africa,' they told me. One could argue, of course, that perpetrators of crime have *always* been able to act with impunity in South Africa, but a prologue is not the place for such arguments. It is, however, a place for creation myths.

It was Unkulunkulu, the ancestor of all ancestors, who broke off mankind from the reeds of the eastern swamps where the Indian Ocean meets the African continent. Unlike the version in Genesis, a man emerged simultaneously with a woman, for how could there have ever existed a male without his partner?

Unkulunkulu sent off two animals to greet mankind. He first dispatched a chameleon to bestow immortality to humans by announcing 'Let men not die!' Then, after granting the chameleon a good handicap, He sent a gecko with an opposite message of death. But the chameleon loitered on the way to eat the fruit of some bush; thus the gecko arrived first with the dreaded curse that has befallen the human race: 'Let men die.' By the time the chameleon arrived, it was too late.

Although the gecko is merely feared as a harbinger of death, the chameleon has been squarely blamed for mankind's mortality. Even today black Africans will avoid touching a chameleon and many a shepherd has killed one from a distance by blowing smoke at its open mouth.

It seems blind prejudice has deep roots in this land.

The reason I travelled to South Africa is to celebrate the 'New' and to understand what happened during the times of the 'Old', expecting to argue politics and meet obnoxious individuals. I don't know if they've all emigrated, but I didn't encounter a single white South African who was not friendly, hospitable, polite and, well, *nice* in an old-fashioned, Agatha-Christie-novel-without-the-hemlock kind of way. If anything came as a shock to me, it was how many friends I made and how much I enjoyed the company of even the ones with whom I disagreed fundamentally. The new South Africa is a reality they all seem to accept, many with fervour, some with a newly-found guilt and others with a mixture of apprehension, excitement, shock and, yes, pride. There may be crime and punishment in this life, but there is also redemption, and it's only around the corner for white South Africans, albeit disguised as a cheque-book.

This brings me to the title. If anything, this is less a travelogue and more a series of vignettes of the people I met and grew to like a lot. I must add that any similarity to persons, hotels, or even places is purely coincidental. (Is there really a town called Oudtshoorn? Is there really a club in Durban called 330?) I, myself, do not really exist. I never really travelled in South Africa.

And I never, *ever*, take drugs.

Chapter One

Tina Turner: Pretoria

My feelings for you, Hank, are like a bowl of fish-hooks
Meryl Streep to Leonardo DiCaprio in Marvin's Room

1. A long, drowsy Thursday

The South African Airways pilot on the Tannoy was one of these Afrikaners who speak in paragraphs, not sentences: *And now we leave the realm of the stars and descend to Johannesburg International where the temperature is twenty-five degrees. Remember I predicted twenty-five? Well, I was right! We are landing in the glowing sun having made a crossing from the cold and windy Europe over the whole of the continent of Africa, and the crossing was good. I hope the last bit of turbulence did not disturb too much that Indian lady who was terrified earlier. I hope she feels better...'*

'A few of my drivers are like this,' said Jane, my next-seat neighbour. 'Once they start, they can't finish. They like the sound of their own voices.'

'... *you can see the patches of blue amongst the green grass of the gardens below. It's swimming pools. Johannesburg has a greater concentration of swimming pools per square kilometre than Los Angeles...*'

Jane was an ex-English teacher from Derby who had settled in the Western Cape, leading specialised flower-photography tours, and I was a drunk and dozy British tourist. During the overnight flight, Jane had suggested I tried Amarula liqueur which is a bit like Baileys with berries. 'Elephants love it,' she'd said. 'They eat the semi-decomposed fruit of the marula tree and turn tipsy.' Hell, if it can finish off an elephant, I'll have five, please.

'... *but it's time to land. I always ask for the music from the* Chariots of Fire *or one of Beethoven's symphonies to play while we are descending, because this is what we all deserve.*'

When our pilot finally paused for breath, the passengers applauded.

'Is this the end of your trip?' Jane asked as the low Cs in Beethoven's Fifth made the plane doors rattle more than any turbulence we had experienced so far. I hope our Indian lady had a strong constitution.

'Sort of,' I said. 'I'm staying in Pretoria. I'm being picked up at Jo'burg airport. And you?'

She made a long face. 'I won't be home for another eight hours. I have a connection with another flight to Cape Town and then I have to drive to the Karoo.'

The Karoo?

'I live in a small town called Prince Albert, quite, quite far from Cape Town.'

I couldn't hide my surprise. They named a town after a penile piercing?

Jane thought I was impressed. 'I love the Karoo. It's so quiet, so empty, so clear. Try to make it there, at least to Oudtshoorn. It's the centre of the ostrich trade.'

I yawned. If all had gone according to plan, Jaco would be waiting for me outside.

When I decided to go to South Africa, everyone and his guidebook was against the idea. At best I would be robbed upon arrival; at worst I would be ritually sacrificed and my entrails used for witchcraft. I'd have to carry an Uzi on my shoulder to walk about and drive a Challenger tank to avoid carjacking. I laughed off the first warning, but by the time I read *The South African Handbook*'s comment on Johannesburg safety (*'We recommend you stay in Pretoria'*), I thought, 'Dammit, they might be right,' and followed their advice.

After passing through customs brandishing my bar-coded visa (they have computerised immigration in South Africa), I spotted the sign with my name on it. The guy who was holding it was Jaco, agent for Ulysses Tours: tall, blond and horribly, horribly healthy.

'Where are we going?' I asked as we found ourselves driving on a busy motorway, more of a German autobahn than the usual Third-World, unmaintained – and frequently, because of Nature, unmaintainable – B-road.

'Brooklyn,' Jaco said.

I tried to find Brooklyn on my map of Pretoria. It wasn't in the centre. It was far to the right. If it was further to the right, it would bump into Pik Botha himself.

'Is there public transport?' I asked innocently.

Jaco looked at me unmistakably in the negative. I cowered.

'It's one of the best 'burbs,' he said. 'You'll like it.'

By then we had reached Pretoria which consists of miles and miles of avenues of flowering jacarandas, all 70,000 of them imported from Rio de Janeiro in 1888. In October they were in full bloom, shading the street with their branches and cloaking the pavement with their exquisite mauve flowers. In the colour spectrum of this new Rainbow Nation, Pretoria must occupy the magenta end.

My B&B was on Duncan Street and nothing had prepared me for the sight. I said goodbye to Jaco and greeted the owner, Martin, a softly-spoken, silver-haired Afrikaner; he had turned on Maria Callas who was singing 'Casta Diva' in the living room. Bellini's marvellous aria matched the ambience: a central, hexagonal, domed hall was surrounded by doorways which led to the kitchen, the office, the veranda, the garden and the living room. On the sixth side, an art deco spiral staircase led upstairs to the three guest rooms. In my London flat you can just about swing a cat around; in my double bedroom in Brooklyn you could swing a medium giraffe. I nearly pinched myself, but I thought that would wake me up and I didn't want to. I explored my environment: parquet floors, thick stinkwood furniture and a balcony overlooking the garden, where stone fish and amoretti spewing fresh water decorated the 35-foot swimming pool. Below me, in the *stoep,* there were four tables and fourteen wicker chairs under colonnades covered by large red velvet curtains.

Martin was keen to chat and offered me a drink. I declined as politely as I could. I needed to sleep and within minutes of lying down I was gone.

I woke up still drowsy. It was four o'clock in the afternoon. I looked around in a daze. The colonial furniture still appeared as fantastic as five hours ago.

I rubbed my eyes and went for a wash.

Damn! I thought I'd brought everything: Imodium tablets (as this, after all, was Africa), turbohalers for those unaccustomed-to tropical flower allergies, hydroperiodide pills for water purification (with neutralising tablets to remove the taste of iodine), Trust underarm anti-perspirant (as perfected by the Israeli army, who must know a thing or two about itches and rashes), an anti-blister kit for feet (since this is the country of Great Treks), pills against malaria, insect repellent… *but no shampoo*!

I looked around in despondency and noticed the pictures hanging on the wall. As if to reinforce South African stereotypes, they were antique illustrations of, wait for it, 'The Races of the World'. Here was a drawing of black Africans: from the Ashanti to the Zulu, they were all there, annotated with a key for explanation. Another sketch depicted the 'American Races', North to South: from a Labrador Eskimo to a Tierra del Fuego Indian. Opposite hung another – 'Asian Races': Yukagir, Ostiak, Mongolian Kalmuk...

I stopped. Why this overwhelming need to classify people? OK, point taken, these antique prints were designed when phrenology was the rage and the dimensions of your skull were the blueprint of your innermost characteristics; they were drafted during a bygone period when science was used to reinforce prejudices about the superiority of the European; but what were they doing here and now? Decorations like these seemed to provide the confirmation a tourist would expect from South Africa: here's a country fostering an unhealthy obsession with race and its classification.

I didn't know Martin well enough to bring up the subject. Plus I was having a bad hair day, and I had to walk to the Brooklyn Plaza Shopping Centre for a bottle of shampoo.

Pretoria is where shopping malls go to die. There is a sort of centre that harbours businesses where one can stroll during the day but, after work hours, it is deserted. The white residents retire to their villas behind barbed wire and the black ones disappear out of sight in the remote townships or sleep roughly in the darkened corners. Brooklyn is typical of this shopping-mall-and-cellphone white culture of South Africa which is suburbia in a big, American, Spielberg kind of way. No one walks: one drives a car from the fenced-off 24-hour-armed-response house to the mall with its police-patrolled, restricted-access pedestrian areas in order to shop, eat or simply post a letter and returns home, cellphone attached to belt, shopping in the boot, infrared garage door opener in the hand. I could easily see how tourists are recognised and mugged: they are the white ones who walk. If they also have a small daypack they have been positively identified. What can there be in that daypack? It sure ain't their lunch.

Shampooed and cleansed, I opened my door – no key – and waltzed down the grand spiral staircase. Martin and Elben, his male housekeeper, were waiting patiently in the living room; they had turned the music off so as not to disturb me. Martin offered me a beer. As an introduction to the Afrikaners, he was the perfect specimen: he had the manners of Cary Grant combined with the charm of Bryan Ferry.

'Amazing place,' I said.

'You like it?' Martin asked and his face lit up. 'It's a famous house. It was designed by a famous architect in the nineteen-thirties. His name was Gerhard Moerdijk.'

I jumped. 'As in the architect of the Voortrekker monument?'

'The very same.'

'Who did the house belong to, then?'

Martin took a deep breath. 'It belonged to Jimmy Kruger.'

'Who?'

'Jimmy Kruger. He was the South African Minister of Police when Steve Biko died.'

Oh, *that* Jimmy Kruger. I winced. Martin smiled. 'I've had the place exorcised properly, don't you worry. Ritual upon ritual.'

'How much did the house cost, if I may ask?'

'About 1,400,000 rand,' Martin said.

My mouth dropped. At ten rand to the pound, this was £140,000.

'My poxy London flat cost more than that,' I retorted.

Elben, Martin and I looked at each other in mutual incredulity.

'I suppose to you this is cheap with the rand so low,' Martin said sheepishly.

He was right: I'd had a peek in the shopping mall – I could have a restaurant meal for the price of a takeaway kebab in Hackney. The falling rand must have had a more devastating effect on the insularity of South Africans than sanctions ever did.

'You're the second-ever guest in my B&B,' Martin said. 'I call it the Blue Angel.'

'As in the Dietrich movie?' I asked.

'Exactly.' Martin clapped his hands and turned to Elben triumphantly. 'I told you they would get the reference.' He looked back at me. 'Elben said it was too obscure.'

Elben gracefully acknowledged his mistake. I examined him closely for the first time: blond and healthy, he was a carbon copy of Jaco from Ulysses Tours – his prominent arm tattoos camouflaging an easy-going temperament.

A movement outside caught my attention. I expected a black gardener, but not – what? – one, two... *eight* construction workers packing up to go home.

Martin followed my gaze. 'I'm building an extension,' he said. 'It will be an antique shop. Do you know anywhere in the world for buying cheap antiques?'

'Not in Europe,' I said. 'The way the rand is going... try Buenos Aires. These grand Argentinian families are selling the family silver because they found themselves living in a Third World country.'

'Like South Africa,' the duo said in unison and with not a little glee.

Aha, political discourse already! I was ready to take off but pangs of hunger made me realise I had eaten nothing since my in-flight meal. Plus it was getting dark outside.

'I'm starving,' I said to Martin. 'I'm off. Do I get a key to my room?'

He was taken aback. 'A key? But there will be someone here all the time.'

I was taken aback in return. 'Yes, but other residents...'

'There are no other residents,' he said and then added innocently: 'Do you think I should provide keys for my guests?'

'I suppose, it's customary,' I said apologetically.

'I see.' I could sense he was lost for words. 'I'll call a locksmith tomorrow.' And after a pause: 'Where are you going to eat?'

'I thought I'd walk to Hatfield Square.'

'*Walk?*' exclaimed Martin. '*Walk?* It's night, and this is South Africa. I'll take you there in my car.'

We left immediately through the back door.

'You see this *ficus* plant?' asked Martin.

'What about it?'

Martin put his finger across his lips with a conspiratorial grin. 'Sssh,' he said and buried the house keys among the *ficus* roots. 'Now you know how to get in.' I shook my head in disbelief: a crime-ridden society and a hamlet's vicarage mentality.

As the garage door opened, it revealed several shadows lurking beside the car. Something stirred. A dog?

This was much bigger than a dog.

'There's someone there!' I shouted. 'Martin, there are people in your garage!'

'Are there?' Martin seemed nonplussed.

'It's the construction workers!' I exclaimed. I looked at Martin with astonishment. 'Is that where they sleep? With no facilities?'

'Oh, I don't know,' protested Martin. 'Some don't want to go home during the week and they're welcome to sleep here. I only have dealings with one contractor. I don't even know how many he sub-contracts to.'

I knew. I had counted them.

Martin mistook my silence for disapproval and opened the car door for me with a shy smile. In fact, I was too stunned to register anything other than incomprehension. I got quietly into the car, Martin drove off, and we didn't exchange another word until we reached the Hatfield Plaza.

'Here it's safe to walk around,' he said, with that same timid smile. 'Have a nice dinner. Ask them to call you a taxi back.'

I got out and looked back at the straight road we had driven on. 'But we're only ten blocks up from your house!'

'Ask them to call you a taxi,' Martin repeated softly, waved and left.

I sat at the first fish restaurant I found, 'The Ocean Basket', where Greek *syrtaki* music was blasting out of the speakers.

'Why the Greek music?' I asked, ordering a *kingklip* – a South African fish like Pacific eel – with chips and a bottle of Windhoek, a beer brewed in Namibia by descendants of German settlers. As the label proudly proclaims, it's the only one outside Germany that follows that country's Purity Law, the *Reinheitsgebot*.

The waiter, smiling American-style, informed me that the owners of the restaurant came from Greece. 'There are many Greek immigrants in South Africa,' he said.

I should know. It was my first encounter with apartheid and I was very, very young.

My family was living in Athens. A distant uncle – Uncle T, I shall call him – had arrived from Johannesburg and we had a dinner party. He had emigrated there in his early twenties.

Uncle T was arguing about apartheid. He was claiming, nay, *boasting*, that whole sections of townships had been mined and would be blown to smithereens if there ever was an armed insurrection. His was a condensed account of Graham Greene's 'Uncle Remus' conspiracy in *The Human Factor*: Soweto would become the greatest cemetery in the world, an open grave to feed the vultures. A friend of the family, let's call him D, was about to leave, enraged. My mother tried to defuse the situation; her dinner party was being ruined. Uncle T kept telling us how the black Africans' only purpose in life was to steal, skive off work and try to trick the hard-working whites. He was defending censorship, racial supremacy and what I misheard as the Morality Law: my boy's ears weren't as yet attuned to Immorality.

'What's the Morality Law?' I asked.

Then the miracle happened. Uncle T looked at me and changed the subject. Mr D, however, was not amused. 'Go on, explain what it's all about.'

'Stop it, D,' said my mother. 'It's not a subject fit for a child.'

'I'm not a child,' I protested.

Mr D was in full flood. 'Go on, tell him. If it's about morality, why are you ashamed to explain it to a boy?'

There was silence. Nevertheless, peace was restored. There were no more arguments.

The next I heard from Uncle T was a decade later. He'd had a heart operation in Johannesburg. He was lucky in a sense, for this was a top speciality in South Africa; the country was in such need of heroes it had turned transplant surgeon Christian Barnard into a pop culture icon. Uncle T died not long afterwards, childless and relatively young. I never really knew him, and he never made any impact on my life.

Except that I made it my mission to find out what that intriguing Morality Law was all about.

2. A long, good Friday

'DARRAM!' said Martin and pulled the tablecloth like a magician, unveiling the spread: a bowl of yoghurt and fresh fruit with an assortment of cold meats, cheese and crackers on the ready. Although I'd woken up at noon, he was there waiting for me, so that he could cook me a full English breakfast.

The more I gobbled the food, the more annoyed and insistent the flies became. One landed on my bacon, but Martin was there promptly to shoo it off like my personal swatting fairy.

'Very camp,' I said. 'Do you also have a feather duster?'

'You don't know where these flies have been,' Martin replied. 'This is Africa!' Of course, he didn't say that: in the old Transvaal the unfortunate continent is either *Efrica* or *Ufrica*, but never, ever, *Africa*. The Afrikaner vowels are a mystery to me: in this land a *sheep* is a boat and a *shit* is something you make your bed with.

Martin gave a nod to his building supervisor who waved the workers on. It looked as if the building work had been at a standstill during the time I'd been asleep.

While I was thinking, he gave me a listings magazine. 'It's Friday,' he said. 'I presume you're going clubbing later.'

He presumed right.

Clubbing is not pleasant on an empty stomach, so I dined at Giovanni's in the Brooklyn Plaza, allured by its cold buffet of a thousand antipasti: all you can stuff on a plate, a main course and a bottle of white Graça wine for 25 rand. On the way home afterwards, I crossed pavements to avoid a posse of barefoot black youths. I had been warned: Friday is payday and many a manual worker gets blotto on his weekly wages. As I changed pavements back, a cat darted in front of me and crossed the road – a big, spotted cat.

A very big, spotted cat!

When I told Elben over a scotch, he didn't bat an eyelid. 'A genet, probably,' he said. 'You can find them sometimes in the city. They've become scavengers.'

Some useless facts about genets:
1. *Although small, they are the ultimate natural born killers. Let them loose in a chicken coop and watch them get into a frenzy: they kill a lot more than they can eat; they do it for kicks.*
2. *When they spit and growl they raise the roof; you'd think they had a mike hidden in their lungs.*

Elben was in a talking mood, evidently the norm for Afrikaners. Today he was in khaki shorts, which look silly on the English, baring as they do white shins and red, knobbly knees, but fit the Afrikaners like a uniform, exposing tufts of blond, curly hair on powerful thighs and muscular calves.

'Jaco called,' Elben said. 'He asked if you're interested in a three-day safari in the Kruger.'

'When, though? I want to party in Pretoria over the weekend.'

'You're all right then. It would be for next Monday.'

Cool.

'I'd like to be a wildlife guide,' said Elben. 'I'm talking to Jaco about it. I grew up on a farm in the Eastern Transvaal, and I miss the open spaces. I'd love to show tourists around. It wouldn't be like a job at all.'

'Have you ever been in danger in the bush?' I asked.

Elben smiled. '*Ja* – I came face to face with a lion once.'

Huh?

'We were on a night walk with an armed guide in the Kruger. Three of us. Suddenly, I saw a male lion in front of me. I'm glad I reacted properly. It roared – and the lion's roar once heard is never forgotten – but I stood my ground and crouched a little. The lion roared again and, seeing that I didn't move, left. That is what you have to do. Stay your ground. Crouch and appear insignificant. Else you're prey. If I had run away, it might have attacked me and the guide would have to shoot it.'

I choked on my whisky. 'What are you on about? Of course he'd have to shoot it! It might have mauled you!'

Elben's eyes were fixed in the distance, reliving the experience.

'I don't think about that.'

He gulped back his drink.

'This does not apply to the leopard,' Elben continued. 'If a leopard meets you, it attacks you. A leopard never runs away. One of you will have to die.'

'How dangerous is a genet?' I asked.

Elben sighed politely. 'Very dangerous if you're a chicken.'

The Yearling was a mixed/gay club, always seemingly half-full, oddly situated on the first floor of a pi-shaped mall above a car park, on the site of what looked like an old betting shop; only the security gorilla downstairs was a familiar club sight. Inside, the music was uplifting house on two dancefloors with an outdoor balcony chill-out.

I ordered a whisky with ice.

'Single or double?' asked the barman.

'How much is the single?' I asked back. It was 60p. Sometimes I think that South Africa was created just for me. 'Make it a double,' I said. 'Oh, hell, make it a *triple*. Saves time.'

After much such time-saving, I caught the eye of a dark-haired guy with five-o'clock stubble and a furry grunge hat. He was a half Afrikaner-half Italian chef which is a very good exchange of genes in my book. He wasn't good company, though. He was so out of it he couldn't keep his eyes in focus for longer than ten seconds before he rolled them into the Great Beyond.

'What have you taken?' I asked him.

'A Mitsubishi,' he said.

'Do you have a spare one?'

He looked at me and rolled his eyes. 'Follow me,' he said.

We got our hands stamped at the door, left the club and returned after a slight detour so that my chef could buy something slightly illegal. We danced for the next hour or so, but then I had a rush and felt the urge to converse, so I moved to the balcony and started chatting to two London entrepreneurs with a strong cockney accent. They were in Pretoria with an odd business proposition.

'We're opening bingo halls. We've committed money and three years of our lives to see the project succeed. The South Africans bet like mad and here bingo halls don't carry the Hilda Ogden stigma as in Britain, where working class women, widows and pensioners are their main customers. Research shows that affluent males may indeed be our target clientele.'

Bingo lingo in the bush. Things appeared weirder by the minute. I could almost hear *A flea in heaven – thirty-seven! Duck and dive – twenty-five!'* resonating in those open spaces of the *veld*.

I looked inside. The Yearling crowd was thinning out already. My chef had disappeared.

'I've lost my friend,' I said.

'Maybe he's gone to Club DNA,' said my cockneys. 'That's where people go from here.'

'Where is Club DNA?'

'Not far. It goes on until nine in the morning.'

'Are you two going?'

'No, we're lunching with some investors tomorrow.'

Bang on the drum – seventy-one!

'Can I walk there?'

They looked at me, surprised. *'Walk?* Suppose you can.'

I asked the security gorilla for directions, as my grey cells were exploding one by one in my brain. *Pop!* There goes 22 January 1992. *Pop!* There goes 18 March 1995. I hope the police never ask me what I did on those days.

'You walk left until you see the first robot, then you turn right until you pass two more robots and then do a left at the entrance of Berea Park,' he said.

'Wow,' I said. 'You have *robots* patrolling the streets? Is that because it's too dangerous to have policemen?'

The security guard thought I was taking the piss. I went on: 'You know your country is soooo advanced. I mean, I got a bar code to tag me at immigration and now you have robots – what, they are zapping the cars and...'

'Robots are *traffic lights* in South Africa,' said a voice behind me. I turned around. It was a girl who introduced herself as Bianca, a farmer's daughter from Hazyview out on a night on the town. She was nineteen, and her pretty features were distorted, because she was cross-eyed. This was a bit disconcerting given the state I was in, and I kept turning around to see whether she was staring at someone else.

'You're going to Club DNA? If I show you where it is, will you walk me there?' she asked.

'Yeah, sure,' I said, as my male protector instinct emerged from its cobwebs, double-checking that she wasn't addressing the security guard behind me.

'OK, let's go.'

After a half-hour walk in the dark and deserted streets of central Pretoria ('See? It's so safe. I'd never do this in Jo'burg.') we reached Berea Park. Club DNA was staged in a two-storey rugby pavilion with a central, hard trance dancefloor overlooked by a balcony through an inner atrium. The upper floor had a chill-out room where a huge, bouncing castle was full of resting, tripping bodies. Bianca found her friends, and I went off in search of my chef – there was no sign of him. The walking had made me thirsty, but, thankfully, club water is plentiful in South Africa with jugfuls of the stuff available free at the bar. It was there I met Juan. *Juan?*

'My father is Spanish, my mother Afrikaner,' he explained. 'I live in Jo'burg.'

'And you come here for the clubs?'

'Only Fridays. On Saturday and Sunday everyone converges to Jo'burg. There are big clubs there like Therapy and ESP.'

Juan went on to explain his grand entrepreneurial scheme. He was currently unemployed, but he was thinking *big*. 'I'm going to sell live chickens to the townships,' he said. 'Most of the blacks don't have fridges – I mean, most of them have no electricity – so the only way to keep their food fresh is to keep it alive.'

'Amazingly simple,' I babbled.

'No one has thought of this: buying live chickens from farms and selling them wholesale to the townships. I'll make a fortune.'

'What are you on?' I enquired.

'Nothing,' Juan protested. 'Nothing. Anyway, how do you like this club?'

I pointed at a sign saying '*Check your firearms at reception*'.

'Scary,' I said. 'Checking your guns at reception.'

Juan raised his eyebrows. 'No firearms are allowed in the club,' he said. 'Why, in London you go inside *with* guns?'

'No, *no*,' I said. 'We're not allowed to carry firearms at all.' I noticed incredulity in his face. 'Not even flick-knives. There is a law against carrying offensive weapons. So we don't allow handguns.'

'What – not even small ones?'

'None.'

Juan had never contemplated a gunless society. 'Weird,' he said and bobbed his head in time to the music. 'Wanna dance?'

About time, actually.

We walked down to the dancefloor. We danced and chatted for a few hours about London and South Africa, about hard house and the Jimmy Kruger house, until the chill-out beckoned.

Upstairs we bumped into Bianca again – 'bumped' being the operative word, as she was sitting on the bouncy castle. She waved us over, looking in the wrong direction as usual. I lay down. Tripping on a bouncy surface is fab. I closed my eyes. I rolled over. My thigh touched a body next to me and I moved closer. Was it Bianca? Was it Juan? Was it someone else?

Who cares?

When I next looked at my watch, it was six. Bianca was nowhere to be seen. Could Juan give me a lift home?

'Yes, but I'm staying till the end,' he said.

'When's that?'

'Nine.'

Pass.

When I walked out the light was blinding, for the sun had risen: not golden, but platinum-white and unforgiving. I put on my sunglasses and tried to hitch a lift from the cars leaving Berea Park, but they were all returning to Johannesburg. The security guards would not use their mobiles to call me a cab. The nearest taxi rank was at the railway station. So I walked through the eerily empty streets of post-dawn Pretoria with newly-found alacrity. There were no cars in the streets; only black labourers were about so early, walking to work or sitting at the back of a lorry, facing backwards, legs dangling. With my head held high and my sunglasses reflecting the sun, I moved on purposefully like Keanu Reeves in *The Matrix*, assuming a superior air so that I could be mistaken for a local Afrikaner. When I reached Station Square, I saw three white policemen holding a dishevelled black man on the ground. Next to him was a big mothafucka of a gun.

I had just seen my first AK-47.

3. Hallowe'en

The saying goes that when a jacaranda flower drops on your head you'll be lucky. That afternoon I had a whole bunch rain on mine: too much good fortune for my liking. I was clearly a marked man – better not walk the streets. Time for a museum; the Pretoria Police Museum.

This is where Steve Biko died.

The museum is housed in an old police station on Pretorius Street, two blocks off Church Square, one of the focal points of the city. This square used to be the open expanse in front of Pretoria's first Dutch Reformed Church. The building, like the institution itself, stood at the heart of the town, but don't be confused if you fail to spot it: that original *kirk* was struck by lighting – God presumably scrimping on the brimstone – and its second incarnation was just plainly demolished in 1900. And yet you know instinctively, gazing at the large Kruger statue guarded by four bronze Boer sentries, that this is unquestionably Pretoria's pivot: it dominates a rectangular, well-ordered street grid that pumps traffic from the idyllic holiday resorts of Magaliesberg to the shantytown grime of Mamelodi.

The black guard by the museum door – colour is important in this book – wanted to see my ID. I had none, I was foreign. My passport? I had left it at the B&B. The guard was stunned – for someone required to carry a pass since he was weaned, this was a universe-challenging proposition. 'Go on then,' he said. 'Just sign your name.' Not for the last time in South Africa rules and regulations would be bent for my convenience.

A stuffed dog welcomed me – but this was no ordinary dog. This was a hound to inspire Sir Arthur Conan Doyle: the unsightly result of a stud stallion penetrating a Rottweiler bitch. This was a specially-bred canine trained to go for the extremities in order to break down demonstrations. Ouch! I covered my private parts in trepidation.

Oh, look, the torture instruments! Funny how the Dutch and their descendants have such a piquant fixation: the Amsterdam Torture Museum is much more comprehensive, but here the chill came from the realisation that these contraptions had been used recently. There was a scolding bridle, a mouthpiece to suppress the tongue; heavy handcuffs; flat, pan-like, fingerless mittens...

I moved on.

Some police cases were described in special photographic glory. They stemmed from the apartheid era and much attention was paid to race. Looking at the exhibition, one would conclude that only black Africans committed murders with excessive cruelty. Still, nothing comes close to the horror of *Muti* killings.

From time immemorial, human organs have been used by African natives in magic *Muti* rituals to strengthen one's health, to manufacture essential medicines and to create invincible soldiers; the *assegais* of the Zulu were said to have been smelted using human fat. There supposedly existed a class of people called *unswelaboyas*. They wore animal tails on their faces and were said to be secret abductors of children who provided the fat for those *assegai* blacksmiths. *Unswelaboyas* ('those who lack hair') rode hyenas with one leg to the ground, the rubbing action on the animal removing any hair on the inside of the leg. It was this feature that made them most repulsive; not that the Zulu are hirsute, mind you, but I presume they are proud of the little bodily hair they can muster.

In a celebrated serial killer case during the late seventies, several girls aged eight to twelve were found whose throats had been slit, tongues had been cut and flesh from the thighs removed. Lurid photographs and gory commentary accompanied the exhibition. A witch doctor, Phoku John Kpabi was arrested and convicted of these murders in 1978. I checked: there was no information about the extent of his bodily hair – but there was a reconstruction of his hut. I shivered as I went in. It was like entering the house of Leatherface from the Texas Chainsaw Massacre – the closest one can get to a real-life slasher movie. John Carpenter eat your heart out, if I may use the expression.

Muti still accounts for one or two murders a month in South Africa: hands are buried in shop thresholds to make customers spend money; sexual organs are consumed to enhance sexual prowess. Mutilation occurs when the victims are still alive, since their screams are thought to enhance the potency of the magic. Organised gangs in the townships go on the prowl harvesting human organs: the BBC newshounds found and interviewed a 16-year-old teenager who had been castrated with a butcher's knife by such a gang in 1998 – the last he had heard of his tormentors was that they were selling his genitals at a premium. The price? Well, a human head goes for 10,000 rand in Mpumalanga. This is how much a man requested in May 2002 for the head of a 52-year-old victim, slain solely for that purpose. Police were tipped and caught the culprit, who had preserved his trophy in a Krugersdorp abattoir.

The apartheid era itself was reflected in another room with an exhibition of pass books, pictures from the Sharpeville massacre, and a special corner for Steve Biko. A small wax effigy of the man himself, like a sacred voodoo doll, was displayed in a glass cage as he was found: naked, with his arms twisted behind his back. Peter Gabriel's eponymous song was playing in a loop in the background.

When I read for the first time Steve Biko's *Black Consciousness* book, it became very clear, very quickly why he was such a threat to the government. Call the National Party leaders what you like, stupid they were not. They hand-picked the best minds of the opposition and silenced them, because they knew the power of rhetoric. Steve Biko's book, for those who haven't read it, is a compelling case for Black Power Without the Help of Whites. It uses race to defy racism: '*For the liberals the thesis is apartheid, the antithesis is non-racialism, but the synthesis is very feebly defined. They want to tell the blacks that they see integration as the ideal solution. Black Consciousness defines the situation differently. The thesis is in fact, a strong white racism, and therefore, the antithesis must, ipso facto, be a strong solidarity amongst the blacks on whom the white racism seeks to prey. Out of these two situations we can therefore hope to reach some kind of balance – a true humanity where power politics will have no place.*' Very incisively, Steve Biko saw the situation as one of a political power struggle rather than a racial conflict. His presence in South Africa, along with that of Nelson Mandela and Desmond Tutu, begs the question: if the white minority were so superior why did they produce no great men?

Steve Biko died in Pretoria, but only in the sense of 'expired', because he ceased to exist long before that. He was arrested in Grahamstown, in the Eastern Cape, on 12 August 1977 and held in solitary confinement in Port Elizabeth until 6 September, naked and unwashed. Even at night he was left handcuffed and shackled with leg irons attached to the walls. On 7 September he was interrogated once more and somehow 'developed' a stroke which slowly overtook him. It is not clear whether the morning shift (Major Snyman, Captain Siebert, Officer Marx, Officer Beneke, Sergeant Nieuwoudt) or the night shift (Officer Coetzee, Officer Fouché or Lieutenant Wilken) was in charge when a doctor diagnosed '*a lumbar puncture revealing blood-stained cerebrospinal fluid indicating possible brain damage*'. Half-dead and naked, Steve Biko was transported in the back of a car more than 1,000 km away to Pretoria, where he died five days later in this very same police station by what was described in his inquest as '*brain injury, followed by contusion of the blood circulation, disseminated intravascular coagulation as well as renal failure with uraemia'*. To add insult to injury, two days after Biko's death Jimmy Kruger – the Minister of Police in whose converted house I was staying – was addressing the Transvaal Congress of the National Party. He mentioned Steve Biko. He famously said: *'I am not glad and I am not sorry about Mr. Biko. It leaves me cold.'*

At the inquest, the magistrate (Martinus Prins) delivered his verdict on 2 December 1977: *'The available evidence does not prove that the death was brought about by any act or omission involving or amounting to an offence on the part of any person.'* No one was charged and no one was tried.

There is a list in the police museum in Pretoria of black detainees who died while in custody. 'S. Biko' is listed at number 44. I noticed that on the same day 'S.Biko' died, a certain 'B. Malaza' died too.

Let's hear it for B. Malaza.

Hallowe'en at the Yearling promised a great line-up: besides the regulars, there was Derek the Bandit, South Africa's most famous DJ. There was a fancy dress competition and there were many in the crowd who sported Hallowe'en attire: skeletons, witches, werewolves, devils. The music was once more house of the highest standard, but the place looked again half-empty – most obviously in the circle around the small black guy on the dancefloor. No one danced with him, no one seemed to know him and no one made an effort to befriend him.

I hung around the barman a lot: Tristan, blond and muscle-toned, had a coterie of admirers. I described to him how I walked to Pretoria railway station after Club DNA in order to impress him. He was horrified.

'I tell you,' he said, 'last month I was walking home in Hatfield at night and suddenly I heard a click behind me. There were two blacks with cocked guns, pointing them at me. They wanted my cellphone. I said, "Hey, there's my cellphone and here's my wallet, you can have that, too."'

I listened, appalled.

'It was quite civilised. They refused my credit cards. They knew they'd be useless.'

Tristan paused. 'I thought this shit happened in Jo'burg, not Hatfield. But I was wrong.' And then, shrugging his shoulders, he went off to serve another client; I had monopolised him for too long.

Outside it had started to rain. I spoke to a Grim Reaper who was counting droplets into a glass of water.

'What's that?' I asked.

The Grim Reaper winked. I stood there looking.

'Do you want some?' he asked.

I nodded.

'Bring some water.'

I filled my glass in the toilet wash basins and returned. The Grim Reaper counted five droplets into the water. A more apt symbolic scene I could not have concocted if I'd wanted to.

I drank the water and almost immediately my mind left my body and twirled around like a model showing off a new dress on a Milan catwalk.

'Take care,' said the Grim Reaper and left.

Where did those Klieg lights come from?

I spread myself on a sofa, my brain spinning like a damaged propeller. And thus it was that I was transported underneath the Strijdom Dome monument in central Pretoria. How ironic that the monument to J. G. Strijdom, one of apartheid's master planners and South Africa Prime Minister from 1954 to 1958 (apogee of foreign diplomacy: his characterisation of India a 'coolie republic') is now surrounded by an all-black market. It is remarkable that, unlike those Lenin busts in the former Soviet Union, it still stands – I don't know whether it is magnanimity and forgiveness or the old fear of white authority. But suddenly a mob emerged and attacked me because they thought I was guarding it. I started to run away. I was stark naked as normally happens in these dreams. Tristan was there.

Trick or treat?

Tristan, with his new mobile, called me a cab. By then I knew enough people in Pretoria to ask for favours.

When Steve Biko died, it did not escape the attention of the medical profession that two doctors had signed the certificates allowing his transportation to Pretoria which sealed his fate: Dr Benjamin Tucker, chief district surgeon of Port Elizabeth, and his second-in-command Dr Ivor Lang. In the resulting inquiry the South African Medical and Dental Council (SAMDC) exonerated them. But Frances Ames, the head of neurology at Groote Shuur Hospital, disagreed. She and four other doctors demanded a full disciplinary inquiry. The SAMDC refused. Frances Ames and her team went to the Supreme Court and demanded a decision. Her determination caused friction in the hospital; she was threatened with the sack. Her colleagues at the University of Cape Town where she was teaching implored her to stop – the apartheid government, they claimed would cut the grants; they would lose their jobs. Yet Frances Ames went ahead, prepared to mortgage her house to pay for the legal costs.

In 1985, after several countries – including the UK – threatened not to recognise South African medical degrees, the SAMDC found Dr Benjamin Tucker guilty of improper and disgraceful conduct on three counts and Dr Ivor Lang guilty of improper conduct on five counts. Dr Tucker was struck off the medical register, Dr Lang was suspended for three months and the SAMDC was awarded the trial costs. It was only a moral victory – Dr Tucker was reinstated to the medical register some years later and Dr Lang was subsequently promoted to chief district surgeon in Port Elizabeth to fill Dr Tucker's place – but as far as moral victories go, it counted nine on the Richter scale: Christian Barnard's successors were revealed to be corrupt bully boys.

Next day I felt sorry for Martin. He was patiently waiting for me to wake up so that he could cook my breakfast. I plunged into the pool and convinced him that a coffee would do.

Where was *he* last night?

'In Jo'burg. There was a Mr South Africa contest,' Martin said. 'It was crap.'

'Mr South Africa and it was crap?'

'These people are not very intelligent,' Martin complained. 'Brawn and no brains. They were not even good-looking!'

'Oh – was it a *straight* Mr South Africa contest?' I asked.

It was.

'Well,' I shrugged my shoulders, 'what do you expect?'

Martin smiled. 'So what did *you* do?'

I spared no detail: the Police Museum, Club DNA, the Yearling...

'You seem to know Pretoria better than I do,' Martin admitted when I finished.

'All in the interests of research,' I countered bashfully.

'Your liver must be working overtime.'

'I know. If alcohol is a preservative, I will live forever.'

I felt pleased to see Martin in good spirits. This had been a tough twelve months for him. That's how long it had been since he split with his partner of many years.

'He was also my partner in a restaurant,' he said. 'Our businesses were so entwined, lawyers upon lawyers are eating up our money trying to separate them.'

Like a complicated divorce case.

'Don't laugh. I sympathise completely with divorcing couples. I saw my ex last week for the first time in months. I felt nothing. It's odd when you meet someone you used to know so well, and it feels like you're meeting a stranger.'

He sat down.

'Six months ago, I gave up the restaurant for good, bought this house and started the B&B.'

New venture, new life?

'You could say that. I brought my eighty-year-old mother next door. I built a large fence so that she can't peek in. Who knows what she might see. I don't want her to have a heart attack.'

So the money he paid was for a *bigger* house?

'Oh, yes. This is only half of the converted Jimmy Kruger villa,' Martin said. 'You don't think he lived in a house this small?'

I giggled nervously.

Thus it was on the day after Hallowe'en, as I relaxed in the sun by the pool, that I came to realise I was amongst friends. I never brought up the subject of the bathroom race pictures because I finally understood that, although I had encountered a mentality I could not penetrate, I was faced with artless innocence, not sinister malevolence.

'What was it like being gay during apartheid?' I asked Martin.

'What do you think?' he asked back. 'It was illegal. No one spoke about it, and everyone pretended. There were no gay bars. There were certain 'houses' in the country where you would be 'entertained' – more unlicensed brothels than clubs.'

It was worse than that. The strategy developed to avoid the 'total onslaught' the apartheid regime was facing from the 1960s to the 1990s included the ruthless employment of a politicised police force to suppress the enemy within and an army permanently engaged to fight the enemy without. Unity and clarity of purpose were the weapons for survival and citizens with a 'behavioural disorder' (*gedragsafwyking*) such as homosexuality were as much of a threat to the cohesion of society as the bombs of the ANC. Nowhere was this doctrine more entrenched than in the Army. As late as the 1960s, one of the capital offences you could be executed by a court martial for was homosexuality. During conscription, official bullying ranged from humiliation and verbal abuse during training to sexual coercion during service. No avenue was spared: in compulsory religious instruction you learned that the hottest spot in hell was booked under your name tag; the threat of public outing hung over you; and if you persisted in getting stiffies in the shower, the South African Army used its final, well, *solution*.

Between 1971 and 1978 soldiers with 'psychiatric disorders' were held in isolation, pumped with drugs and subjected to hormonal treatment under conditions of forced labour in a notorious farm in the Northern Transvaal, called Greefswald. (In 1980 a new centre started in Magaliesoord.) In both camps homosexual inmates were sedated and subjected to aversion therapy. One inmate disclosed that he had been subjected to more than two hundred sessions during one year alone. Electrodes were strapped to his arms, and wires were connected to a continuous voltage source. Black and white pictures of naked men were projected and the inmate was asked to fantasise. The current would then gradually increase, causing muscle contraction, resulting in great pain. Only after the inmate began screaming and pleading would the machine be switched off and a *Playboy* centrefold projected instead – in colour. Hey, we *are* subtle.

Many of those who were subject to such aversion therapy committed suicide. Those who did not take their own lives still suffer from migraines, photosensitivity and malfunction of the prostate and genitals. If you thought that only black people were mistreated under apartheid, think again. A social system which depends on blind conformity for its survival – be it Nazi Germany, South African apartheid or, indeed, religious fundamentalism of many a tint and cast – abhors any living examples of non-compliance (they don't dress like we do, they don't pray like we do, they don't fuck like we do) because they are witnesses to an alternative to some all-flattening doctrine.

'There was no nudity as such,' said Martin, disturbing my nightmare. 'Magazines required stars on girls' nipples. There were hardly any foreign *films,* let alone pornography. There were no performances on Sunday. No late night drinking, especially for blacks. They didn't allow them bars. That's how shebeens started. They were illegal drinking dens in the townships. They were raided all the time. There was a strong Puritan Calvinist streak going through the regime as well as the repression. The Dutch Reformed Church dictated behaviour.'

Like the Taliban. The Taliban in the Transvaal.

'That's why everyone went to Sun City to have fun,' added Elben. 'It was situated in Bophuthatswana, in a black 'homeland' where South African law supposedly did not apply, although it was only a few hours away. Hypocrites, all of them.'

'The strangest thing is that after that speech by F. W. de Klerk,' said Martin, 'the one which conceded white rule – when was that? 1990? 1991? Whatever – within six months you had porn videos and gay clubs and late drinking hours and drugs and everything.'

I see. Progress.

'It was as if something had given in, and there was this explosion, and we were free. Black prejudice against homosexuals is strong – look at Robert Mugabe – and the ANC rode in the face of their supporters on a principle, and they delivered. They understood that prejudice is prejudice no matter whom it is directed to.'

I thought that after Magaliesoord and Greefswald South African gays might have actually *earned* it.

'The ANC went against the grain and put gay rights in the constitution,' Elben said. 'This new South Africa isn't perfect, and it's become very violent and crime-ridden, but then people should ask themselves: *what would have happened otherwise?* Imagine apartheid continuing to the year 2000. Imagine Mandela not having been released. Would the crime and the bombings and the terror not have been worse?'

Very eloquently stated.

'What frightens me,' Elben continued, 'is people like Winnie Mandela. She has a lot of appeal amongst the uneducated young. There are many among them who would like the white man exterminated. Look at what's happening in Zimbabwe.'

'Did you vote ANC?' I asked.

'Yes, I did. Many gays voted ANC and look: we have a constitution which is the most liberal in the world. I can walk in the street and kiss my boyfriend and hold him – the things straight couples take for granted. We might get beaten up in parks, but that's not the point is it? It is individual prejudice rather than state prejudice.'

I couldn't have put it better myself.

Or perhaps I can, for nothing better summed up my days in Pretoria than what I saw in the Bull's Eye that same evening.

The Bull's Eye bar is on Schoeman Street – pronounced as in 'school' – in a setting mirroring the Yearling: first floor club by a car park. Extremely popular, it was as camp as a Christmas Number One – especially on that Sunday night when a drag show was on. Anyone I knew? Yes, the Londoners who wanted to open the bingo halls. At this rate they'd spend their loan money clubbing rather than delight the locals with two little ducks, 22. I kept these comments to myself since they had a mobile and my taxi call for the night was in the can.

We watched the cabaret: the familiar glamour of the drag queens miming to songs – hell, if there is such a thing as a universal culture, it ain't Coca Cola. We heard the laughter when a sketch took the piss out of a stupid South African suburban family who put a VCR in the washing machine to erase a tape. But then came the sight that made us wince and look at each other with mute incomprehension. Everyone else laughed and cheered, as we were left startled but certain that we had chanced upon an unexpected, visceral glimpse of the complex fabric that weaves the Afrikaner mentality. For in front of us, in full drag splendour, facing an adulatory crowd and moving sensuously while miming to 'Goldeneye', was a Tina Turner impersonator.

A *white* Tina Turner impersonator.

Chapter Two

Cruising in the Kruger: The Kruger Park

The purpose of our lives is to celebrate the grandeur of the cosmos
William Kotzwinkle in Dr Rat

4. Weird people

I woke up around the time I normally go to sleep, but hey, sacrifices have to be made for a safari. Martin was in worse shape than me, muttering an assortment of Boer curses as he dutifully cooked me breakfast. Afrikaans is surprisingly inventive when it comes to swearing: *Sit jou kop in die koei se kont en wag tot die bul jou kom holnaai* ('Shove your head in a cow's arsehole and wait until a bull rams it up your own') being one of the kinder offerings.

The doorbell rang.

I expected a minibus. It was a sports Mercedes. I expected a male, rough-hewn Boer guide. In his stead, a feisty, fortyish female stood in front of me in safari shorts and a discernible North American accent.

'Hello, I'm Laura,' she said curtly. 'And you are Dylan.'

'No, I'm John,' I said, bewildered.

She turned to her companion in the Mercedes who was about to leave. 'You told me it was Dylan,' she said in an accusing voice.

'It's John, believe me,' I said.

'It *is* John,' said a befuddled Martin beside me.

Something clicked almost audibly as Laura's brain locked into thought. 'You're not the guide for the Kruger!'

I was flattered. Did I look so butch?

'I'm Laura,' said the woman again. 'Nice to meet you. I'll be touring the Kruger with you.' She pointed at her backpack which sported a big maple leaf. 'I'm Canadian. Winnipeg, to be precise.'

I took that to mean 'Don't mistake me for an American or I'll sock it to you.'

'It's OK,' I said. 'I can handle that.'

Laura had decided on a last minute safari; she'd arranged it the previous night and had been given the B&B's address as a pick-up point.

'What do you do for a living, Laura?' I asked her to make conversation.

'I'm a vet,' she said brusquely.

More like a Vietnam vet, I thought, looking at her, but kept it to myself. 'Good, you'll enjoy the animals then,' I said instead.

She stared at me as if I had just crawled out of a Boer curse's cow's bottom. 'It's only a *job*,' she said. 'I don't have to *enjoy* it...'

I shrugged my shoulders.

'... but yes, I do. How did you guess?'

I looked up in frustration. Laura was *so* high maintenance.

'Is it your first time in South Africa?' I asked.

'Yes and no,' she answered.

I sighed. If this book were a symphony, this chapter might well be the scherzo.

An eight-seater minibus pulled by and saved me. The driver was a genial old Afrikaner ('of Welsh stock,' he said proudly) whose name was, indeed, Dylan. I sat next to him to avoid Laura.

From Johannesburg airport we picked up Frank and Gabi, a thirty-something couple from Germany. Dresden, to be precise, as Laura might say. Gabi was a dentist (I pretended to smile and said, 'Nice') and Frank had a business selling dentists' chairs and implements. I presume they fell in love under a drill. Dylan and I exchanged glances. In the popularity stakes, let's say that if our van was a *Big Brother* household, they'd be evictees number one and two. We'd most certainly keep Laura for the crankiness.

The last two passengers we picked up were also German: Patricia and Marcus, a handsome couple in their mid-twenties, from Frankfurt this time. Patricia was blonde, and Aryan-looking; Marcus was tall, dark and a semi-professional volley-ball player. In our make-believe Big Brother household he would only have to smirk at the camera to win those millions of female votes without any further effort.

Everyone had to answer the same questions: yes, it was our first time in South Africa. Where had we been and where were we off to next? Frank and Gabi were returning to Germany immediately afterwards, having spent ten days in Cape Town, which they pronounced cold and wet. This sent a chill down the spines of Patricia and Marcus who were flying there next. As I was not due there for another month, I smiled smugly.

And Laura? Was this her first time in South Africa?

'Yes and no,' she said again cryptically.

Thankfully, ambiguous or illogical statements are simply not acceptable in Germanic small talk. 'Excuse me,' said Marcus, 'I did not understand. Did you say yes and no? My English is not good.'

Laura had to explain herself at last.

'Yes, I've been to South Africa before,' she said, with a self-satisfied grin. 'But not like this, not as a tourist. I spent five years doing a postgraduate degree at Pretoria University back in the mid-seventies. During my studies I never left Pretoria. Now I'm doing what I couldn't back then. I'm travelling all over southern Africa.'

The question hanging in the air was unequivocal, though unspoken.

'It's difficult to believe it,' she offered, unprompted, in what could be construed as an apology, 'but people during apartheid were duped and brainwashed. Soweto was a riot gone wrong. Nobody had heard of Nelson Mandela. It was all dressed up as Western civilisation versus Communism. Race and racial divisions and the resulting...' she paused for a word, '*stratified* ways of living were perfectly legitimate, natural even. Apartheid had its own strange logic, which I accepted because everyone else did.'

With that she stopped and continued reading her book.

Dylan – who, with his amiable face and red alkie's nose, could easily have passed as a barman in *Coronation Street* – started recounting how he used to work with Telekom, the South African state communications company.

'Until, that is, I started living. Never again will I sit behind a desk in an air-conditioned office. I took voluntary early retirement at fifty-five, bought this minivan and became an official tour guide.' His chest swelled with pride. 'Passed the state exams,' he said and showed us a badge.

Suddenly Laura spoke out of nowhere.

'I tell everyone I'm a tourist now. You see, a tourist can ask questions whereas a resident can't. I met some Dutch Reformed Church ministers the other day who were so self-righteous about condemning apartheid at last and I asked them, "Do you have any black ministers then?"'

She laughed alone at her own banal effrontery.

The worst drive in the whole of South Africa is the eastbound N4 from Pretoria to Nelspruit. It is a flat, industrial plateau full of petrol stations and tourist shops. When I tell you that the most interesting feature in the highway was an open coal mine, then you'll know what depths of boredom we were plunging into. We had to stop at every service station because Marcus had the metabolism of a horse. He'd eaten breakfast in his hotel and had a quick hamburger and chips on the sly while we were checking out the woven baskets. Hell, I thought, mentally calculating the fat totals, who wants to live for New Year's Eve?

Dylan was bored the most, so when we encountered the roadworks after Belfast ('You can tell elections are coming up when they start spending money on public works,' he said. 'This is the main route from Jo'burg to Maputo.') he took the more scenic, northern route via Schoemaskloof where we could see some trees and hills at last.

'Australia rules the world,' I said, observing the flora. 'Eucalyptus trees, wattle trees, gum trees. Everywhere I go I see Australian trees turned native.'

'They grow quickly,' said Dylan. 'And you make cheap chipboard from them.' As if to reinforce our driver's remark, a copse of black wattles showed up next. This tree was introduced to Natal from Australia and from there to the rest of South Africa in the 1860s, a reminder that the greatest ecopolluter was not the twentieth century consumer, but the nineteenth century trader.

Soon we left the plateau and by Montrose we had descended into the low-lying grasslands where more native species such as marulas, acacias and bushwillows dominate the landscape. This transition, sudden and spectacular, is one of South Africa's distinctive geographical characteristics: a *lowveld*, extending from the coast into the interior, rising up sharply to a high plateau called the *highveld*. Pretoria stands at an altitude of 4,200 feet; Johannesburg at nearly 5,900 feet; the town of Belfast, which we had passed, stands at 6,500 feet above sea level, higher than Denver, Colorado. This escarpment dominates the eastern section, littered with views towards the Kruger Park.

Ah, at last, the Kruger Park. Even *it* is not immune from domestic politics in the new South Africa. The Makuleke, a Tsonga-speaking community, have lived in the Pafuri triangle between the Limpopo and the Luvuvhu on the north edge of the park throughout their history, but the creation of the park precipitated their displacement in the interests of conservation. The first attempt to remove them was made in 1931 with the advent of extensive road-building. Offers of relocation were repeated in 1950 and in September 1969 the apartheid government sent a magistrate and a fleet of trucks to uproot the ten remaining Makuleke villages and snatch 50,000 acres from the tribe. They were driven with typical cruelty out of their ancestral homes; when the magistrate was met with kids throwing stones, he said: 'If you are too tough and recalcitrant, we shall just start shooting one of you. Then you will agree to move.'

Now, it's true that the Kruger suffers from poaching, even today. Sad photographic stories of ensnared and bloodied animals exist in the reserves for visitors with strong stomachs: antelopes are hunted for food, elephants for ivory and rhinos for their horns. Animal welfare organisations in the US and Europe push for animal protection – but can conservation survive if the locals don't benefit from it? One can protect endangered wildlife by putting up fences and banishing people, but ultimately it has to win their consent. White South Africans shake their heads. They don't trust the locals and they cannot envisage a reserve with human inhabitants – though they accept unquestioningly the existence of private reserves and estates adjoining the Kruger. But across the Atlantic, in South America, the concept is not alien; in the Eduardo Avaroa reserve on the altiplano, the slender, gazelle-like vicuña – the rarest of the Andean camelids – are making a comeback, because the Quechua Indians realised that tourists make the trek to observe such wildlife and they have benefited accordingly. Remember: Africans have looked after their wildlife pretty successfully for centuries. It was the colonialist white hunters who drove most animals to near extinction.

In May 1998, the Mandela government made the admirable gesture of a partial restitution of the wrongs committed by the *ancien régime* upon the Makuleke: they gave them back 12,500 acres of their land to exploit ecologically and control economically. The tribe now collectively sublets and contracts out the tourist operations in their park section in what seems to be a blueprint for such settlements in the future. Sadly the Pafuri triangle is out of the way for the mainstream tour crowds, but even if a trickle of the tourists visiting the Kruger every year reaches the tribe's lands, their future is secure.

International politics have also left their mark in the park. Although bounded by the Crocodile River in the South, the Limpopo in the North and by the barbed wire of the private reserves in the West, wildlife used to move freely through the Lebombo mountains which formed the frontier with Mozambique. This was the route of elephant migration moving to the wetlands of the East during the Kruger dry season. Until, that is, a high security fence was built in 1975 after the apartheid regime feared that the revolution in the old Portuguese colony might spread over to the Transvaal like an all-trampling herd of wildebeest on an incessant gallop. The fence – a kind of bestial Berlin Wall – sealed the fate of animals who found themselves on either side: almost every elephant on the Mozambique side was hunted and killed for ivory in exchange for weapons, and the rest of the fauna was killed for meat by the jungle-bound rebels. On the South African side, the elephants prospered and multiplied well above sustainable numbers and culling began.

With the advent of majority rule on both sides, it was not long before the fence came down. In December 2002, a new superpark was created during a signing ceremony in the Mozambican resort of Xai-Xai: the Great Limpopo Transfrontier Area, comprising the Kruger, Zimbabwe's Gonarezhou and Mozambique's Limpopo parks. The final complex totals 13,500 square miles, an area larger than Belgium. The rangers hope the migrations can begin again unhindered after a quarter of a century.

Let's see how well elephants can remember.

We approached the Kruger from the south, crossing the Crocodile River at the Malelane gate. We were going to stay at camp Berg-en-Dal, whose big thermometer was showing 37 °C. As our huts weren't ready yet, we had a quick lunch in the cafeteria: another sandwich for Marcus and a kudu pie for me – after the kingklip, the second new species I had consumed since I arrived.

Then we saw our 'huts'.

I thought that after the Blue Angel nothing would surprise me any more when the words 'lodgings' and 'opulence' were spoken together in a South African accent, but I was wrong. I was expecting an old-fashioned tent, maybe a luxury one. What I got in the Kruger was a three-bed, self-contained, air-conditioned jungle chalet, complete with bathroom, a fully-equipped kitchen, a living area with armchairs and sofas plus a porch with a *braai* – a South African barbecue. Still, the strangest thing about it was that, like my room in Pretoria, there was no lock on the door.

'No one steals anything from Berg-en-Dal,' said Dylan. 'Don't worry.'

Wasn't this the most crime-ridden society on the planet? I shook my hand in disbelief: those English village values were popping up in the *veld* again! There was an underlying, touching innocence in white South African mentality that sought to live according to how things ought to be rather than how they were. The steep rise in crime must seem ever so exaggerated to the Afrikaners compared to the apartheid *Pax Boerana*. It is true, of course, that government by iron hand does wonders for crime. Ask Mussolini who even made Italian trains run on time. Ask the Incas with their crime-free kingdom and the death penalty for everything.

Ask the Taliban.

5. Weird facts

The count may have changed since I last checked (and it's more likely that some have disappeared rather than new ones discovered), but with 147 species of mammal, 507 species of bird, 114 species of reptile and 33 species of amphibian, the Kruger Park – itself the size of Wales – does not disappoint. I had brought my small Practica binoculars and my *Game Spotter* picture book, this pursuit being infinitely more interesting than the train variety. I was to tick every animal I saw next to its picture, with a space for comments: 'Number seen / Sighted at / Remarks'. It included a serious note in bold that if I happened to spot the rare oribi antelope, I should report its location to the rangers immediately – probably to take the animal into protective custody.

'If there is reincarnation, I wouldn't like to be one of those in any of my future lives,' said Dylan, pointing at a herd of impala antelope. 'They're really low in the food chain.'

Indeed, the impala (and there are 140,000 of them in the park) are preyed upon by lions, leopards, cheetahs, wild dogs, hyenas, jackals, servals, pythons and crocodiles. Some life! The reason they are still prospering despite being the fast-food equivalent for several species of carnivores is because they pool their resources into a team organism with dozens of eyes and ears.

'A dominant male has a harem of about twenty to thirty,' said Dylan. 'The other males hang around together trying to catch him out. Often a few males will lure him into combat as a diversion while the rest try to mate with his harem.' I averted my eyes as one such act of impala intercourse took place so, so *unashamedly* in front of us, because I want to make this a family read. An uphill task, I know, because it was springtime in the Kruger, and the whole park was a shagging shop.

A herd of four zebras traversed the road in front of us. No, I didn't shout 'zebra crossing', though I was tempted.

'Zebra meat is supposed to be disgusting,' said Dylan. 'Most of them suffer from worms and they stink to high heaven when you slaughter them. It's unsafe to eat zebra meat – and it's fatty, as well.'

Some useless facts about zebras:

1. *Whatever the scarcity of food, they look well-nourished, since they will graze down to the ground and even eat roots.*
2. *The mortality rate of stallions is about twice that of mares. This is because they try to defend their families by facing off the predators.*
3. *The closest relative to the zebra is obviously the horse, but in the Kruger Park it is the rhino.*

Marcus and Patricia wanted out of the car to get a better picture of the zebras.

'It's absolutely forbidden,' said Dylan with that Afrikaner emphasis they adopt – part Schadenfreude, part secret glee – when they are about to stop you doing something. 'Not only are wild animals dangerous – even impalas and zebras – but they should also be left undisturbed as much as possible. They're afraid of man and so they should be. In vehicles, they don't recognise you as a human. When you emerge, they do, and they run away.'

Plus, of course, there were the predators.

'You'd have to be pretty stupid to get out of your car when you see a lion,' Dylan continued, 'but it happens. Recently a Taiwanese party found some lions eating freshly-caught prey and one visitor left the car to take a better picture. He was attacked and mauled to death. Look there, everyone, a common duiker.'

'What happened to the lions?' I asked, taking a snap of the duiker which is really a fancy name for a deer. (You may have heard, though, its African name: *mbambi*.)

'Whenever there's an attack on a human, the beasts involved are chased and killed. Otherwise, they'd realise how easy we are to kill, and they'd attack again. Stupidity puts lives at risk. Not just tourists' lives, but the lives of the people who work here for the welfare of the animals. There are some who travel around by bike and sometimes they've been chased by predators.'

Dylan braked to point at a male kudu antelope browsing gracefully in front, its helical, grooved horns forming a regal tiara over its head.

'Things are worse now. It's the illegal immigrants from Mozambique who are the problem. They decide to walk the border and cross the Kruger Park by themselves. In the last five years more than sixteen thousand illegals have been arrested – alive. There was a famous instance when a five-member family got attacked by a pride of lions. They escaped by climbing up a tree. The lions picked up a boy on the lowest branches and ate him while the rest looked on. Then they thought, "This is easy," and they picked on the second. Over the space of several days they picked the third and the fourth. Eventually, they were spotted by the rangers who came and saved the last one, who was half-crazy with fear. Imagine – up a tree for days, watching the members of your family being eaten one by one, waiting for your turn.'

Everyone in the Kruger talks about the 'Big Five'; they are depicted on the South African currency notes: the 10-rand note is a rhino, the 20-rand an elephant, the 50-rand a lion, the 100-rand a buffalo and the 200-rand a leopard. I wondered if the value sequence reflected the ease of hunting them, since the term stems from the nineteenth century when the great white hunters shot the African wildlife into extinction, burning with desire to complete their trophy collection with a head from the Big Five. It is against this European hunter mentality that President Kruger rebelled and created a safe haven for the hunted animals on 26 March 1898. This was the era of reserves: from the Navajo in New Mexico to the Matabele in Zimbabwe, animals and natives were regarded with the same protect-and-preserve paternalistic condescension. After the Boer War, the British followed President Kruger's conservation policy until the government of the independent South Africa opened the park's gates to the public in 1927. That year, three cars paid to drive in. By the year 2000, annual visitor numbers had swollen to 1.5 million.

'Certainly buffalo and leopard are very difficult to shoot,' answered Dylan. 'Buffaloes because they're so dangerous and leopards because they're so elusive.'

Indeed, although I spent hours looking up trees in the hope of locating a leopard, I failed dismally. The closest I got was to observe leopard scratches on the bark of a tree, marks of its territory.

Some useless facts about leopards:

1. *Not many folk see leopards in the Kruger. You have to be very lucky and make dangerous night walks near rivers or waterholes.*
2. *If you meet a leopard and don't have a gun handy, quickly ask for forgiveness of your sins.*
3. *Even if you do have a gun handy, remember that people have died days afterwards of septicaemia caused by the leopard's scratches. The leopard stores a kill up its tree and the carrion develops poisonous bacteria which multiply under the leopard's claws*
4. *A leopard doesn't have spots. It has rosettes.*

We were passing a bridge on a small river when Dylan stopped.

'Last time I was here,' he said, 'the place was full of wreaths.'

Apparently a ranger had taken a group of tourists on a night drive. He parked the car by this bridge and took the tourists on a night walk. Afterwards, while they were having hot coffee, he leaned on a tree, put his gun down and lit a cigarette. A leopard immediately jumped down and caught him on the neck. The rest of the group didn't know what to do. While the leopard was mauling the ranger, they made their way to the car and drove back to base. When the other rangers arrived and shot the leopard, it had already devoured half his chest and shoulder.

By now the sun was setting fast, and the crepuscular light turned the trail features into shadowy outlines – time for the carnivores to feed. Our first one was a cheetah and, let me tell you, the excitement of seeing a predator for the first time in the wild is hard to describe. You are faced with a hungry animal on the prowl, more powerful than yourself, that you can't beat in its own ground. It cuts you down to size.

The cheetah is a very photogenic animal – read Kate-Moss-like thin. This one was totally blasé about the cars surrounding it. It climbed up a road-marking culvert, had a dump in full view of our cameras and then waltzed lazily amongst the cars.

'Go on, *predate*,' I urged it.

The cheetah yawned for what seemed an eternity. Perhaps it was too early for a kill. Then it did a turn, I blinked, and it had gone.

Some useless facts about cheetahs:

1. *They can't withdraw their claws like other cats. In this respect they are like dogs.*
2. *Although they are the fastest land mammals, cheetahs have no stamina. Despite having an acceleration well above a Ferrari, they run out of breath after 200 or 300 yards.*
3. *As their mouths and teeth are small, they can spend up to 25 minutes killing their prey.*

Dylan was tired of driving by now which is why he nearly hit the hyenas in front of us They laughed collectively and we laughed at their laugh and Dylan thought it was a comment on his driving so he threw a sulk. But no, *no*: we were focused on the animals; big powerful jaws, mouths open with tongues sticking out like dogs, scary green eyes.

Some useless facts about hyenas:

1. *They have the strongest jaw muscles of any predator and they can subsist eating bones, which they crush easily.*
2. *They appear to form a genetic link between dogs and cats.*
3. *Their sex is difficult to spot, because a female's external genitalia are almost as large as a male's scrotum. Because of this, people used to believe that they were hermaphrodites and that they could change sex.*
4. *They are prime witchcraft material. Their tails, ears, whiskers, lips and – no surprises here – their genitals, are extensively used in Muti magic.*

Back at camp, Marcus had a quick snack to sustain him before the big *braai* Dylan was preparing for us outside his hut. The ominous sound of distant thunder and short, sharp flashes of lightning warned us that a storm was brewing up on the *highveld* and coming our way. We brought the *braai* time forward one hour, and I was sent to buy our booze before the camp shop shut. When we next gathered together, it had already started to rain with a vengeance. The *braai* was thankfully covered, and Dylan, Laura and Frank valiantly braved the weather to man it (and I use that expression fully aware that Laura was involved). It rained so much that a pint-sized glass we accidentally left out filled up.

'Jo'burg gets a lot of lightning,' said Dylan. 'More people die there as a result of being hit by lightning than in any other place in the world.'

'Do giraffes get hit by lightning?' I asked.

Laura raised her eyebrows. 'What a silly question,' she said and turned over a sausage.

Well, *do* they? And as no one dared to answer after Laura's interjection, I am still none the wiser.

'Is *braai* the focal point of South African cuisine?' I asked this time and filled my plate with boundless protein that would have delighted Dr. Atkins.

Laura jumped in. After two glasses of Pinotage, I assumed this was her effort to be sociable. 'What do you know about cuisine?' she joked. 'English cooking is terrible.'

'It's a good thing then that you have the French in Canada to teach you,' I snapped back.

Laura brooded imperiously, as Dylan warned the hefty drinkers among us about the dangers of dehydration in the *veld*.

'Beer! One should always drink beer,' Laura interrupted him loudly. 'After a while, even if you are dehydrated you don't care. John here should know. The English drink beer like fish.'

'I'm not English,' I said. 'I'm Greek-British.'

'And pedantic,' she added, and walked away.

Patricia took me aside. 'Sorry, but I must ask you: are you and Laura a couple?'

I was aghast. Whyever would she think that?

'Because you're always at each other's throats,' she replied.

Women, I thought. Next thing I'll find that Laura secretly fancies me.

I wasn't laughing when Laura sat next to me and stretched her legs so as to touch my thigh. I looked around. I was the only unattached male available. I got up as if an electric eel had given me a jolt.

Time to hit the sack.

6. Weird weather

Our morning drive was at 4 a.m. – if you call that 'morning' and not still 'the night before' – but our sleep sacrifice was in vain for the rain fell even harder. There was no question of spotting animals. Like us, they don't like getting wet, so they hide away. We were tired, sleepy, irritable and the brave but foolish souls who had tended the *braai* were sneezing and sniffing. Plus the windows steamed up and any chance of spotting game disappeared like the sun.

'I thought tropical storms didn't persist,' I complained. 'They certainly don't in South America. They have much better behaved weather down there. Thunderstorms last an hour and then they're gone.'

We reached Skukuza camp at about 11 a.m., hungry – by then Marcus could have devoured a hyena by himself – and disappointed: we had been driving for hours, and the only other animals we had encountered were fellow humans looking miserable. No, I lie. We did spot a covey of red-billed hornbills foraging on the ground. These birds get killed because they fight their own reflection on car windows and you can't get more territorial than *that*. We were also rewarded with the sight of a few Natal francolins (capricious turkeys who think they're pheasants); a swimming darter, with its long dark neck protruding out of the water like an aquatic snake, and my favourite bird: the masked weaver. Male weavers were gregariously congregating on trees overhanging a pond, building nests which the female inspects before choosing one to ovulate in. Natural selection has made the masked weaver a master craftsman in nest architecture. There were circular nests, oval nests, nests in the process of construction where the skeleton of the hard twigs was evident, nests with an entrance corridor and nests with a porch. The female checks out the best nest and lays her eggs for the male to hatch and feed the chicks, while she trollops off to mate in another nest proving that in nature promiscuity is not confined to males.

Skukuza camp welcomed us dramatically. As soon as we got out, ready to run into the restaurant for shelter, a flash suddenly struck the flagpole and blinded us. Surprisingly, we did not hear any thunder.

'Wow,' I exclaimed. 'I've never been so close to lightning.' And the most remarkable thing about it was that – that –

'It was *blue*,' mumbled Marcus.

The things you learn in the Kruger Park.

The rain subsided after lunch. The word was that there were lions on the way to Nkuhlu; the Kruger fauna was finally coming out to dry.

We saw the queue of Land Rovers long before we spotted the lions – three males, looking bemused at the mêlée around them. Everyone wants to see lions in the Kruger; it's our instinctive hero worship of celebrity. Or maybe we want to pay homage to the subject of our childhood fantasies, the protagonist of tales and fables that are part of our growing up.

'Has anyone survived an attack by a lion?' I asked, looking through my binoculars, which had made me Mr. Popular, since everyone wanted a peek.

'Don't be silly,' said Laura.

For that she wouldn't have a go.

'Actually yes,' said Dylan. 'There was a celebrated incident in 1904 when a ranger called Harry Wolhuter was attacked on horseback by two lions, but he was lucky: one chased off his horse, and he managed to kill the other one by sticking his knife in its throat. Then he climbed up a tree to avoid the return of the second lion which had left pursuing his horse. The other rangers arrived and saved him in time.'

Some useless facts about lions:

1. *There are many scientific papers on the lion's preferred meal. If you divide the kill frequency by the species abundance you find that lion kill proportionally more waterbuck than any other animal. (But couldn't that mean that waterbuck are simply more stupid?) On the other hand, because of size, giraffe makes up thirty per cent of their diet.*

2. *Lions can swim and climb trees, though typically they are too lazy to bother, spending eighty per cent of their time asleep. How do they keep in shape? Fact number 3 may help.*

3. *Lions leave the pride for up to three days to mate. One researcher reported that a pair copulated 157 times in 55 hours. (That is once every 21 minutes for those without calculators handy.) He went on to report that the lions didn't eat during this period. No wonder, I say!*

On top of the Nkuhlu hill, we could at last stretch our legs and get out to stare at the vast swathe of the savannah below us. An awning sheltered a *braai* which looked as if it hadn't seen fire since it was smelted. I mean, would *you* plan a barbecue party among the pythons and the mambas, the hyenas and the lions, the buffaloes and the baboons? Even finding a quiet corner to relieve yourself in the Kruger becomes a life-threatening prospect. If you ever wondered why men urinate standing up and why women traditionally depend on men for their safety, then try pissing in the bush.

From the hill we could see a range of antelopes below; the gregarious impala herds, ever watchful; the red silhouettes of reedbuck and the grey, graceful waterbuck, brown almond eyes surrounded by a white circle, as if mascara'd for a Venetian masked ball; plus the more familiar sight of a pair of munching giraffes – with the bonus of a small baby not more than two weeks old. 'Giraffe' comes from the Arab *al jarafa*, meaning 'one who walks fast'. I have read in many texts, including the official Kruger guide, that the ancient Greek name reflects the biological thinking of times past: it was called *camelopardalis*, because it was supposedly thought that they were a cross between a camel and a leopard. Let me put a stop to such errors – '*pardalos*' means spotted. A *leopard* is a spotted lion; and a *camelopardalis* is a spotted camel. But while we're at it –

Some useless facts about giraffes:
1. *We still don't know the purpose of those silly horns.*
2. *Giraffes eat leaves from thorny trees unconcerned about their spikes, because their tongues are very thick.*
3. *Giraffes normally sleep standing up. They also give birth standing up, and the calf has to negotiate a hard drop of five feet. Perhaps that's what the horns are for.*
4. *Giraffes can't swim, and no, I can't imagine it, either.*

We were ticking the Big Five quickly: an elephant was head-butting a tree trying to uproot it. No one knows what turns elephants to such acts of mindless vandalism, as such behaviour is not uncommon. We were worried, but Dylan tried to reassure us.

'An elephant has specific signs that it's ready to charge: stomping the ground and putting its tusk on the side. This one's fine. He's concentrating on the tree.'

'And that one?' I asked.

I pointed in the direction of a mother with a newborn calf who was flapping her ears. Although Dylan thought it was just to impress us intruders, we split nevertheless to drive on to the most southern baobab tree – it must be important, it's marked on the map. The baobab tree with its upside-down appearance impresses many, but doesn't cut the mustard with me: it looks like a root vegetable that thinks it's an oak. Or, rather, it's what turnips would mutate into should they survive a nuclear war.

We took a half turn around its massive trunk and found ourselves in the middle of a herd of wild African buffalo. There must have been a hundred of them, looking at us, heads high, nostrils flared, inscrutable and unfathomable. We watched respectfully from inside our cars, on edge, aware that we were being tolerated rather than ignored.

'Buffaloes are very unpredictable,' said Dylan. 'You never know where you stand with them. I've seen one attack a person with his horns and break every bone in his body. The buffalo stamps on you until you are flattened. I mean *really* flattened.'

Some useless facts about African buffaloes:

1. *Hunters fear it more than any other animal; irascible and vicious, it changes its mood from one moment to the next.*
2. *If it charges – at 30 mph – it's hard to kill, because its massive horns shield its head.*
3. *Buffaloes are silent animals. They don't moo except for when they mate.*
4. *When threatened by lions the buffaloes form a circle with their horns sticking out on the perimeter. The lions only have a chance if they lure an animal away from the herd and break the circle, which makes for an interesting strategy game.*

Leaving the buffaloes around the baobab, we inadvertently stepped into a clash among Chacma baboons. I figured soon why the collective noun is a 'troop' of baboons as the two gangs faced each other and started – if I may use the word – a *catfight* which involved biting, scratching, chasing and, yes, kidnapping. It was like Stray Cats v The Jets: New York-style gang warfare to inspire Leonard Bernstein.

Some useless facts about baboons:

1. They live in troops of 30–40 individuals and a very strict hierarchical order is maintained.
2. They can make their hair stand on end to appear bigger.
3. When an infant dies, the mother carries the baby with her well into putrefaction.
4. Baboons with swollen red backsides are females on heat. Male baboons find these deformed bottoms very sexy.
5. They are fierce and they bite, so keep off.

From then on the images blurred in my tiredness into a John-Wayne-*Hatari* kind of movie: a stream with hippos, pink eyes and nostrils protruding from the water; a Nile crocodile basking in the sun; a family of warthogs; a giant African snail as big as a terrapin living dangerously as it slid slowly on the tarmac; and a couple of marabou storks, surely the ugliest birds alive, looking like a dishevelled Cruella DeVil after the final car chase with the 101 dalmatians.

Next I knew we had left the Kruger by the Orpen gate. John Orpen was the great Transvaal nomenclator. He surveyed the open land for Boer homesteads during the land speculation of the 1840s; most of the European-sounding names in the area are his and, since he drew the maps, the indigenous designations perished. It's odd that after all his hard work he ended up as just a Kruger gate.

7. Weird stepchildren

Twenty minutes' drive into the Northern Province we reached a private reserve where we would spend the night. It was called

Moholoholo: the Big, Big One, after a big, big battle between the Pedi and the Swazi in the 1860s.

Our master at Moholoholo was Tony. Short, round and energetic, he was a mining engineer who had spent most of his life in Zimbabwe. Unlike many of his compatriots, he came back two years into the new South Africa with his wife and daughters. The same spirit of the *veld* which imbued Elben in Pretoria and Dylan in Johannesburg affected Tony, too; what they say about that mythical Afrikaner bond with the bush must be true. It's here Tony realised the dream of his lifetime: to work in a hospice and rehabilitation centre for wild animals. The owner of Moholoholo was a rich wildlife enthusiast who donated his farm in 1990 for this very purpose. The centre is sponsored by several companies, happy to be associated with charities in post-apartheid South Africa. The fame of the reserve has spread: the animal hospital has featured in a National Geographic TV series called *Wild Orphans*.

We arrived at seven and were allotted our again luxurious 'huts'. Dinner was at seven-thirty with a night drive at nine. We had been up since four, so showering was a race against time and lying down an impossibility: if my back but touched the mattress, I'd never be able to raise myself again. Ample replenishment of the strength we were lacking came in the form of an enormous buffet, with pride of place given to the nyala stew – it's a delight to visit a country with so many edible species. I stuffed myself on what little cheesecake escaped Marcus; thankfully he spent most of the dessert time in the veranda which overlooked a specially-lit waterhole watching bushpigs drink the water. Our Germans were suckers for bushpigs.

During our night drive we saw more of the ever-grazing but oh-so-boring impala. Did they ever *sleep*?

'Impala sleep either during the day or during the night. Some of the herd is always awake, on the lookout against predators,' answered Tony.

There were plenty of nyala antelopes in the reserve. There were so many that they were being farmed, but *humanely*. What did 'humanely' mean?

'A corridor with bait is first built; nyala get used to it and visit it regularly. On the other side there is a parked lorry. At some point, the farm workers open the door between the corridor and the lorry and nyala enter the vehicle willingly – upon which they are trapped. They travel to their death unstressed,' Tony insisted. Still, I have my doubts: extermination must surely be the mother of all stresses.

By then I was as tired as could be; I dozed off and missed the hare and the thick-tailed bushbaby. Wake me up if there's a leopard.

Fat chance.

In the morning, after a hearty breakfast that made Marcus and Patricia squeal with delight, we had a walk around the reserve. It was inspiring to see a guy like Tony, so enthusiastic about, so involved in a new project late in life. He walked steadily, pointing the trees out to us with teenage ardour and Richard Attenborough thoroughness.

'This here is the umbrella thorn acacia tree, otherwise known as the mimosa tree, the king of the savannah. You have seen pictures of it spreading its flat top branches like an umbrella in every safari guide. It's one of the sturdiest trees in existence: it can live in totally arid grasslands and in areas with high rainfall. It can survive extremes of heat during the day and freezing temperatures at night.'

Very impressive.

'That there is the African quinine tree, the *kinaboom*. Nothing to do with the South American quinine tree.' He showed us its oblong leaves with a striking white midrib. 'Its bitter sap was thought to cure malaria but it's not effective. Its bark, however, contains chemicals used effectively against hypertension'.

Tony pointed at another tree. 'That is a cork tree. It's used for fishing by the natives. They crumble the bark over water; it enters the gills of fish; they choke and rise to the surface. And that one next to it's a marula tree which is used not only for the liqueur but also' – he took a deep breath – 'as an insect repellent!'

This, I admit, put me off my next Amarula slammer.

Tony proceeded to show us the Japanese lantern tree with its distinctive flowers which resemble (no car prizes here) Japanese lanterns and (though I blush to mention it) the Kaffir lime tree – now sensitively renamed the Makrut lime, although its leaves are still branded so politically incorrectly in the Selfridges food hall.

'It's not a native African tree,' explained Tony. 'It comes from South-East Asia. The Malay slaves transported it to the Cape colony. "Kaffir" itself comes from the Arabic: *al Q'afr*, the infidel. In South Africa it signified the Xhosa. The Ciskei – Xhosa territory – was called British Kaffraria in the nineteenth century. It was only during apartheid that the word became a slur.'

Selfridges can breathe out again.

We reached two caged corrals, their electrified edges adorned by fried frogs and seared giant millipedes, which kept three lions at bay.

'There was this circus owner in Mozambique,' said Tony, 'who travelled around performing – except that he was trading in rare animals and used the circus as his cover. He was caught, but the problem was what to do with the circus animals. One couldn't let the lions back in the wild. They smell of man and would be killed by their own kind. So they were given away to zoos or private reserves. Three came here.'

We approached the cage of the lioness Sarah, who was dozing, uninterested, like lions do.

'We used to take visitors inside,' explained Tony, 'because she loves humans and we've brought her up from a small cub. But there was this American woman' – he glanced sideways at

Laura – 'who wanted to *commune* with her like "one female to another". She lay down with Sarah and embraced her and started rolling and wrestling with her and Sarah got a bit miffed and scratched her. Then she sued us. We had to pay her compensation equivalent to one year's earnings.'

He shook his head. 'So, no more visitors inside. But I will show you something.'

His gaze stopped at Gabi, our East German dentist, who had the smallest build in the group. 'Can you please run to the end of the fence and back a few times?' he asked her.

As soon as Gabi started jogging away, Sarah's head shot up. 'You see?' said Tony. 'Gabi's prey now.'

Gabi trotted back.

Then came the unforgettable sight: the lioness suddenly leapt to her feet and with an impossible forward jump reached the fence on the other side of Gabi, startling her. It had all taken place in a split second.

Laura broke the silence.

'By the way, Tony,' she said, 'you know I'm *Canadian*, don't you?'

Sarah was now walking like the proverbial caged lion, which, of course, she was. Tony waved her over, and ordered her to sit down. This she duly did. Tony put his hand through the narrow fence and stroked her back – the electricity was off. Sarah lay down enjoying it. One by one, we put our hands through the fence and stroked her. I was the last one to brave the touch of a lion, but in the end empathy took the best of fear and I, too, stroked her gently.

'There,' said Tony, 'you can tell people at home that you touched a lion and lived to tell the tale.'

A major part of Moholoholo deals with wounded or orphaned raptors. The aviary hospice was the brainchild of Brian, the chief vet: two eagle owls without wings that would die if left in the wild; a brown snake eagle that was stoned off his nest as a chick; a martial eagle with a skin disease. It was harsh to see such proud birds incarcerated but what was the alternative? Certain death. We stopped in front of a cage with a female crowned eagle, named Queen. She's one of the stars of the *Wild Orphans* series and like a proper prima donna she stared at us, aloof and unapproachable. Brian had used an arm glove that looked like an eagle-head to feed her and teach her to eat and drink since her birth. As imprinting is very powerful on birds, she ended up falling in love with him and wanted to mate with him – or, rather, his glove – by turning her back when that time of year arrived. She would even attack other male eagles, poor thing. Brian felt sorry for her and took an egg from a nest of another pair of crowned eagles in the wild and put it underneath her one day. It sounds easy, but it almost didn't happen because crowned eagles are a protected species. Special permissions had to be granted by the Parks Board to remove eggs from a nest and by the time the paperwork had been issued, the chicks had almost hatched. The reason it was allowed at all was that if two eggs are laid by the crowned eagle only one eaglet survives; the chicks engage in a struggle to the death to monopolise the food source in a cruel ritual set piece of survival of the fittest. It ain't Disney out there, you know.

Queen hatched the egg and raised it as her own. In her cage, she taught it how to prey on the live guinea pigs that were bred in the reserve for the raptors. Before Brian's eaglet stepchild could be set free, he had to be sure that it could fend for itself: he separated mother and child and released a mouse, a different species from the one the eaglet had learned to hunt. Would it only look out for guinea pigs? The small eaglet killed the mouse and ate it, all right, thereby earning its passport to freedom. Brian hoped it survived, because it never came back.

'We have gone on breeding eagles in captivity with her,' said Tony. 'She seems quite tame, but when she has offspring, she is dangerous. One of the workers usually takes her on his arm and trains her to do tricks. Once, he entered the cage when her little one had hatched. She attacked him immediately. One talon caught him in the eye, one in the ear and the other in the cheek. It took three men to break them up.'

'Let me show you how we control birds of prey,' he added.

We followed him happy-go-luckily into the vulture cage, where a dozen nasty-looking specimens were perched on high. Tony called on them to sit on his arm which he covered with a shoulder-length glove, but they didn't want to play ball. He goaded the vultures on. Some nictitated nervously; others only changed perching spots. Tony waved at them with frustration. One of them flapped its wings at last. It took off – wingspan as large as a man.

Instead of landing on Tony's hand, it had a go at my face.

I barely had time to duck; I felt the talons touch my hair and ducked even lower. Before it found space to turn around, I was out of the cage, surprised at my own agility. Forget the cheetah, time *me* instead!

I looked at my companions with shock at the unpredictability of the incident but grateful that my eyeballs were still in their sockets and I was still able to see out of them.

'Erm, sorry about that,' apologised Tony with an embarrassed smile, while the rest of our group carefully left the enclosure. 'Erratic sort, those vultures. Perhaps there were too many of us.'

Laura shook her head scornfully. 'You shouldn't have ducked! You should have stood your ground!'

She made no sense, as usual, but I paid no attention; I'd had my own wings clipped. Even inside a cage, my own vulnerability had been dramatically exposed. Deprived of those luxurious chalets and four-wheel-drives, stripped from guns and *assegais* – in short, without all the technology that we have amassed as a species throughout our passage on this Earth – we are still as low on the food chain as the impala herds themselves.

I watched broodily as Tony led our party into a compound that acts as a clearing house for unwanted pets with a difference.

'Here we take unwanted pet servals – you call them lynxes – and breed them. This one was cute while a baby, but then it wouldn't stand for the owner's children's pranks and scratched one's face. That one bit the owner's dog. These animals are ferocious; they'll fight off and kill a German Shepherd. But,' he turned to us, 'they won't hurt you if you want to go in and stroke them.'

I prudently stayed out unwilling to chance my luck for a second time. Still apprehensive, the only animal I chose to caress was a cute, wounded civet; it looked sufficiently small, toothless and weak.

I stroked it, and it snarled at me.

Chapter Three

The Taliban in the Transvaal: Klein Drakensberg

Both thy bondsmen, and thy bondsmaids, which thou shall have, shall be of the heathen that are round about you; of them shall ye buy bondsmen and bondsmaids.
Moreover of the children of the strangers that do sojourn among you, of them shall ye buy, and of their families that are with you, which they begat in your land: and they shall be your possession.
And ye shall take them as an inheritance for your children after you, to inherit them for a possession; they shall be your bondsmen forever.
Leviticus 25: 44–46

The Good Book provides a passage that was used to justify slavery.

8. 'I've never met a nice South African'

My first real job was with a British computer company in the 1980s; it had developed a software product and was marketing it worldwide, including South Africa. My department consisted of about sixty staff; none of us belonged to a union and only one, if I remember correctly, belonged to a political party: a Scottish programmer straight out of *Gregory's Girl*. One day he refused to work on a support request by our South African distributors. This caused a stink. Our manager came around and took names. Each one of us was individually summoned and asked whether he or she was prepared to work on any South African assignments. We arranged no meeting, we had no secret agenda, but an overwhelming majority said 'No', including myself. It was not long after this that the company withdrew from South Africa with the excuse that its product was difficult to support.

My action was hardly grand; I had the advantage that my friends and colleagues were acting in unison. I know people who took a principled stand alone and had to suffer the consequences.

My London flatmate around the same time (let's call him David since his name is, well, David) was employed by a high-powered consultancy. He earned a lot, drove a Mercedes, smoked cigars and was working long hours; he was the bright, young star of the company.

One night he came home drunk and upset. He had been asked to work on the design of a new chemical plant in South Africa.

'So?' I asked him.

'I refused point blank,' he said. 'I'm not doing any work for South Africa.'

'And? They accepted that?'

David shrugged his shoulders.

Next day the managing director called him into his office and asked a straightforward question: was David refusing to work on the task he was given? David said that his conscience prevented him from working on that project. The director shook his head: 'I'm so sorry, David,' he said. 'I'm so sorry.'

My flatmate wasn't sacked. He was frozen out. They thought he didn't fit in the company and frankly, so did he. Within six months he had resigned and taken another job, diametrically opposite to what he had been doing before: a university lecturer. He eventually became the president of his University Teachers' Union.

'Believe me, Dylan,' I said. 'Whatever you may think, opposition to the apartheid regime wasn't an international Communist plot.'

We had been discussing the image of South Africans abroad as we drove 2,000 feet up the Drakensberg Mountains through the Abel Erasmus Pass, possibly the only mountain pass named after a tax collector. Before the white man arrived, the local native tribes were happily living with their livestock in a barter society and were reluctant to adopt wage earner status. To correct this aberration, the Transvaal government imposed a graded hut duty of five shillings in 1870 – unsurprisingly, black workers employed in white farms were exempt. The reasoning was blunt and blatant: we impose a tax to force you to work for it. The only way black Africans could afford five shillings was by toiling in the mines of the Witwaterstrand – an occupation which they abhorred. So they started bribing the tax collectors who, in return, overcharged the homesteads or simply looted their cattle. Abel Erasmus was one of the most famous and feared tax collectors who made a fortune by exploiting his position and by smuggling guns to local chieftains in his free time. We were now just passing the place where he descended to milk the natives dry every winter for twenty-odd years.

Dylan was now against the media.

'I've seen pictures on TV where they showed black workers running behind the garbage truck throwing the sacks in. They said: "Look how they treat the black workers. Running behind, never sitting inside." Hell, that's what they *wanted* – to finish early! It's all propaganda.'

'Dylan,' I said, 'I've never seen a picture on TV of black youths running behind a bin lorry. But I've seen pictures of black youths being shot at in Soweto.'

That photograph of a bloodied schoolboy, Hector Petersen, carried by an unidentified weeping teenager in overalls with Hector's sister Lulu crying hysterically alongside them made the syndication runs around the world. A reporter rushed Hector Petersen to the nearest hospital in his Volkswagen Beetle, but the boy was pronounced dead on arrival, more famous in death than he was in life. The reporter who shot the picture – still the most iconic image of the struggle against apartheid – was Sam Nzima. As he was working for the South African *Star* newspaper, he did not see a rand of the fortune that his picture amassed until 1996 when copyright reverted back to him. His bitterness in seeing his image travel the globe, while he remained poor and powerless, made him abandon photography and join a famine relief aid agency in one of the black homelands.

I told Dylan of the satire directed at South Africa which was such an easy target. Tom Sharpe's *Riotous Assembly* – a book very popular and lethal in its wit – did more than any ANC publicity in destroying the image of the Afrikaners. His putdown of Pietermaritzburg, 'half the size of New York cemetery and twice as dead', is pure Grade A bitchiness. In the 1980s, the TV puppets of the send-up *Spitting Image* show constantly ridiculed the white minority in a series of cutting sketches. One was particularly memorable; people all over the world from Benazir Bhutto and Ronald Reagan to Lord Lucan and Neil Kinnock sang together 'I've never met a nice South African'. The song was released as the flip side of 'The Chicken Song' in 1986 which became a Number One hit. We are talking demolition jobs *par excellence* – no conspiracy could be that effective.

At the other end of the spectrum, Graham Greene's *The Human Factor* exposed the raw brutality of apartheid and the connivance and collusion of the British Secret Services within the maelstrom of the Cold War – for it was ultimately *that* war that propped up the National Party more than its domestic legislation: the regime could not survive so many years in power without its portrayal of the ANC as unreformed Marxists and of itself as a bulwark against the spread of Communism in Africa.

Dylan's carphone rang. It was his wife. His features darkened.

'*What?*' he bellowed. We shut up.

'*Are you serious?*' Dylan looked stunned as the tale unfolded. We couldn't figure out what had happened from his curt grunts, but we could tell it was bad, bad, *bad*.

When he put the phone down, I asked him what was wrong.

'There's a storm in Jo'burg,' he explained. 'We'll probably hit it on the way.'

And?

'Our aerial was hit by lightning, and it travelled down and blew up our TV!'

The Germans asked whether they had heard correctly.

Dylan ignored them. 'I told her to unplug the television during a storm. She just *had* to watch that bloody soap opera!'

'Don't worry,' I tried to comfort him. 'Insurance will pay.'

'No it won't.' Laura's voice sounded merciless behind me. 'It is an act of God and they're exempt.'

Thankfully we had reached the Blyde River Reserve by then, because a distracted Dylan had started taking corners sharply. In this Northern Transvaal reserve, the Blyde River has cut a 20-mile canyon, claimed as one of the largest in the world. The steep incline gives rise to no less than five different *veld* types ranging from subtropical rainforest to high mountain grassland. The view across the edge of the Escarpment to the much-photographed quartzite formations of the Three Rondavels was hazy, yet imposing. The family of the victor of Moholoholo, Chief Maripe of the Mapulana, was commemorated in the three peaks underneath, named after his three principal wives. Behind them, isolated as if protecting the women, rose the magnificent and proud Marieps Kop, the *koppie* of the chief himself 6,415 feet high, guarding the southern entrance of the canyon below. This was just, this was just...

'This is just like the Blue Mountains in Australia,' I murmured.

Dylan nodded. 'That's what Australians say. Same geological processes.'

The rocks we were standing on were some of the oldest on Earth – minimum two billion years old – for the Escarpment is the most ancient subsidence site of the planet. It's also prime Voortrekker country. These were the pioneer farmers who fled the British Cape Colony in the late 1830s and early 1840s in search of new land and who ultimately established the two independent Boer republics: the Orange Free State and the South African Republic of the Transvaal. Why? Because in August 1836, the British decreed – with the aptly named *The Cape of Good Hope Punishment Bill* – that Imperial law applied up to the 25th parallel; the Voortrekkers reached the area where we now were, in order to escape British jurisdiction and, in particular, those new anti-slavery laws. Whatever one's feelings for the Boers, it is impossible to feel anything but deep admiration at the single-mindedness in which they pursued their goals, dismantling their wagons down ravines, reassembling them at the bottom, forever marching towards their Promised Land with a spirit as hard as the hoary rocks surrounding us.

The Escarpment has its own specific flora. The scraggy velvet bushwillow, the corky, coarse mountain cabbage tree and the deep-green wild olive sprout naturally on bosky grassland alternating with thickets of yellowwoods and stinkwoods. Just underneath our vista point we could spot the Transvaal sugarbush, pink and white like strawberry ice cream. Black eagles and jackal buzzards soared effortlessly on the updrafts at eye level, hunting robins, shrikes and louries. In Wonderview, where the panorama was supposed to be at its most sensational and the cliffs rose sharply 3,000 feet over the *lowveld* grasslands, we couldn't see anything below; we were looking down on clouds.

'On a good day you can see the Lebombo mountains in Mozambique,' said Dylan, as we stood there, brooding.

'Have you seen the film *The Gods Must Be Crazy*?' he continued. 'The one where a Coca Cola bottle falls on the head of a Kalahari Bushman from a passing plane?'

Erm, no.

'When it was released in the US in the 1980s, it became the most popular foreign film of its time. If you'd seen it, you'd know that in the end the Bushman returns the bottle to the gods and throws it down an "abyss". This is that abyss. Which is nowhere near the Kalahari – but not many people know that.'

Beyond the scarp, abyss or *koppies*, though, it was the sight of the Bourke's Luck potholes that won us over. These are sheer vertical drops of dolomite rocks at the confluence of the Blyde, the River of Rejoicing and Treur, River of Sorrow. They are criss-crossed by picturesque footbridges over large potholes carved Swiss-cheese-like on the dolomites by the surge of the streams' eddies.

The spectacle has a history to match: not far away was the spot where a crowd of Voortrekkers arrived in 1844 under Andries Potgieter. When they reached the edge of the Escarpment they could go no further, so Potgieter rode off with a small party of Boers to reconnoitre the country beyond the Lebombo mountains they could see on the horizon – it must have been a clearer day than ours. Before he left, he instructed the trekkers to wait for two months exactly, and if he and his men did not come back within that specified time, to withdraw to the safety of the settlement at Potchefstroom. The women and children camped by a river, while Potgieter and his men found their way to the *lowveld*. They reached Delagoa Bay – present day Maputo – but the journey took longer than they thought. When they did not return as expected, the Boer womenfolk thought the men had perished, so they started to retreat from the river they still remember as River of Sorrow. Imagine their elation when Potgieter and his men caught up with them at the next camp by the river they named River of Rejoicing.

And Bourke, he of 'Bourke's Luck' fame? Was he lucky? Did he discover gold?

'Actually, no. He bought this area but the main gold seam was just south of his property,' said Dylan, warming our hearts with Schadenfreude for having missed the *lowveld* views.

We were now well within the Klein Drakensberg, a 100-mile drive of scenic grandeur between the Blyde River Canyon and the city of Lydenburg. This area is mottled with old mining settlements like Graskop and Pilgrim's Rest. These towns have a jaunty charm, all brightly-painted wooden Victorian houses with corrugated iron roofs. The architecture is not dissimilar to their Australian counterparts; Ballarat and Bendigo come to mind.

'Australians get bored when I bring them here,' said Dylan. '"We've seen all that," they say. "We've had our own goldrush." Europeans adore them.'

We adored them.

'Do you want us to go to see the Potgieter Memorial?' asked Dylan.

Marcus and Patricia had started to make noises with their bellies. '*No!*' they answered him.

'You want to have lunch?'

'*Yes!*'

'There is a great crêpe place in Pilgrim's Rest,' Dylan said. 'I'll drive straight there.'

Laura went postal. 'It seems all we do is *eat* on this trip,' she remonstrated. Her eyes met with mine in one rare moment of accord.

'Pilgrim's Rest is an old mining town that was founded by a wandering salesman named Alec "Wheelbarrow" Patterson,' said Dylan, changing the subject tactfully. 'He bought this place and found gold; so he exclaimed: "The pilgrim has come to rest."'

Patterson did, indeed, find gold here back in 1873 during the first South African goldrush by prospecting a tributary of the Blyde river called Pilgrim's Creek. Within three months, fifteen hundred miners were digging around places with Wild West names like Starvation Gully, Poverty Creek and Golden Point. People were still panning gold in the streams around the town until the 1950s. The demand for power to crush the rock was such that the Belvedere power station was constructed in 1911, supplying street lights to Pilgrim's Rest before many European cities installed them, including London.

Those lights were not on to welcome us, for the sky was as blue as could be and the sun as hot as molten gold as we stopped for lunch. I sat back sipping an orange juice, while our Germans were discussing the differences that still exist in their country so long after reunification – the high-speed rail link from Hannover to Berlin had only just been completed and was the main subject of conversation.

I switched off and absorbed the quaint, Victorian atmosphere of Pilgrim's Rest. It's not often you can walk the streets of a South African village and propel yourself into the past, so I dared to take a stroll holding on tight to my camera. I need not have worried – there was no whiff of danger. I passed by the Highwayman's Garage, the town's lovely petrol station, with its carmine-red corrugated iron roof and dark green cast iron posts (a business started by a real highwayman, Tommy Dennison, after he did time for a 1912 coach robbery); the leather shop ('*Shoe sale! From 68 rand!*'); and the Jubilee Potters pub offering snacks of *vetkoek* – a kind of Yorkshire pudding filled with minced meat or cheese – and *koeksisters* – twisted doughnut fingers in flavoured chilli syrup. I breathed deeply: this was the most at ease I'd felt in South Africa so far. The black population was going routinely and matter-of-factly about their daily business with a smile and a nod; mothers and children were eating ice cream on the wooden benches on the rusty veranda of the post office. I wondered how long would pass before jittery Johannesburg becomes as unruffled and serene.

The Germans' comments flashed in my mind. If it took so long to electrify the main railway line from the old West Germany to the new German capital in a state where the people are one nation and where one part is willing to be taxed extra to help the other, how long would it take for an equilibrium to be established between the white haves and the black have-nots in a country where there are several mutually suspicious and hostile ethnic groups? Who will pay, if many white South Africans are loathe to be taxed by a government they don't consider wholly theirs?

The impending storm arrived once we were back on the flat stretch of the N2, blotting out the monotony of the highway with erratic lightning strikes. I snoozed lightly accommodating the prevailing, frequent thunder in my dreams. By the time we arrived back in Pretoria, it was an effort to shake hands with everybody and mumble a 'good holiday' or a 'good journey back'. I did make an effort to shake Dylan's hand with a proper grip, though.

Laura got off the bus with me at the Blue Angel to call her friend and ask her to pick her up. Since I was disappearing straight into my room, Martin was more than pleased to have someone's company for a late night drink. Their loud chatter kept me awake longer than my condition merited. Were they enjoying themselves or were they openly bickering? I couldn't tell.

Did I say goodbye to Laura?
Too late now.

9. *Pretoria reprise*

Once you get used to the size of Pretoria you warm to it. Its low density of cars and excellent road system allows you to cover long distances quickly and the town becomes almost as manageable as Pilgrim's Rest. I realised this as I was being driven around with a Canadian couple by our guide Hendrick, who had a Saff Efrican accent so thick it could be used for bullet-proofing police vests. True to the tradition of Afrikaner loquacious guides, he considered any occasional interstice of silence as an affront to his professional competence; I don't think I even had time to introduce myself to the Canadians.

Hendrick showed us the Pretoria shopping malls and the posh Waterkloof villas with pride: 'You have to be very rich to live in these houses. Look! 24-hour armed response with an exclusive security company! Look, I bet this wire is electrified!' I wanted to pipe up 'I bet the courtyard is a minefield,' but didn't get a break.

From the heights of the Herbert Baker Drive where we stood, Hendrick pointed at a distant township. He was at a loss as to what to call the black citizens of South Africa now that the K-word was out: 'Over there is Mamelodi where the erm... *people of colour* live,' he uttered awkwardly.

Back in the car, maybe lost for sights, Hendrick stopped momentarily by the Minolta-Loftus rugby stadium.

'Last night there was a big match here,' he told us. 'Pretoria versus Cape Town for the Currie Cup. There is big rivalry between the two teams. The Blue Bulls from Pretoria and the Stormers from Cape Town.'

And then with a grin of satisfaction, he added: 'The Bulls won!'

It's not the first or only irony in this herky-jerky country that white South Africans are mad about rugby, a game invented in the school fields of Britain, which, alongside cricket, helped create the ruling class, the imperial arch-enemy of the Boer.

'On your left is the old prison at Salvokop.'

Another odd choice.

'Now it's apartments for the correction officers,' Hendrick informed us.

I interrupted him at last: 'So the prison officers ended up in prison.'

I could almost see Hendrick's brain spinning until he chuckled. 'That's funny,' he said. 'That's *really* funny.'

A better choice for tourists, as far as corrective establishments go, is the prison Winston Churchill escaped from during the Boer War, now a school. Not many people know that the vicissitudes of this particular derring-do shaped Churchill's political fortunes. He arrived in Cape Town in October 1899 as a war correspondent for the *Morning Post* and immediately set off for East London to observe the hostilities, boarding an armoured train to the front line in Colenso. Unfortunately the locomotive was derailed in a Boer ambush (its engine fell off like a Central Line underground train) and Churchill – as he repeatedly claimed later – was captured by General Louis Botha himself.

Churchill was furious with the prospect of inaction and made three requests to be released for being a mere press representative. When his applications were rejected, he climbed the prison fence with typical impatience to make his way to Mozambique. Speaking neither Afrikaans nor any native language, he crossed Pretoria by night – surely an even less appealing prospect than when I walked to Berea Park with Bianca more than a hundred years later – and hopped on a goods train heading eastwards. Next morning he jumped off near Witbank and, after wandering for a whole day, he sought help in a colliery – I suppose one of the many that turned our drive to the Kruger into an exercise in tedium. It was there that his gamble paid off: the mine manager was English and provided him with shelter, food and, yes, cigars, until the intensive search by the authorities had died down. In due time, Churchill hid in a freight train and resurfaced in the Portuguese port of Delagoa Bay in a blaze of triumph. He was hailed as a hero and was given a lieutenant's commission. Ever the self-publicist and quick to strike while the iron was hot, Churchill had a book out in the shops within six months: *London to*

Ladysmith via Pretoria. It sold well. He returned to London in July 1900; ten weeks later, already a household name, he won a by-election in Oldham and entered Parliament.

Prisons aside, Pretoria has its share of interesting sights. Although President Kruger's residence is dull like the man himself, Melrose House is a treat. This is an upper middle class home with history beyond that of the Heys family who built it in 1886 and owned it until 1968 when the municipality of Pretoria bought it and turned it into a museum. It is a perfect example of the Victorians' perverse ideas about style: they had none. Supposedly Queen Anne revival, Melrose House is a hotchpotch of an Elizabethan cottage and a Dutch colonial mansion, its twin-stepped mansard roofs forcing the term 'double-Dutch' to an observer's lips. This was Kitchener's Army HQ during the eighteen-month occupation of Pretoria, and the dining room was the site of the signature of the peace treaty that terminated the Boer War. A plaque informs us that 'The treaty of the peace of Vereeniging was signed on this table at Melrose House Pretoria on May 31 1902'. The table is teak, the armchairs are dressed in red-brown leather, the carpet comes from Smyrna and the atmosphere is muted, as visitors observe the signatures of Generals Milner and Kitchener and the ten Boer representatives: six from the Transvaal and four from the Orange Free State.

The city circuit conveniently brought us along the long straight road that is Church/Kerk Street to the classic revival Presidential Union Buildings in porous pink and smooth yellow sandstone. More than any other architectural complex in South Africa, the Union Buildings are outstanding as a conceptual whole. Curved Italianate structures bisected by clocktowers open up into courtyards in perfect symmetry: the roofs are roman-tiled, the columns delineating, the verandas Ionic, the grounds stone-tiled, the doors arched. Grilled windows and balustraded balconies are reflected in lily-covered ponds next to the terraced, landscaped gardens, a photogenic treat as the city of Pretoria lies below green and jacaranda-mauve. The November spring weather was so perfect and the post-pluvial atmosphere so sharp that you could mistake the Union Buildings for a two-dimensional gigantic tableau for a 1950s gladiator motion picture, a painted backdrop for *Ben Hur* or *Cleopatra*.

'Built by Howard Baker in 1913,' Hendrick said. 'He liked pillars. If you see any building with columns, you can be sure he had something to do with it. He went on to design the government buildings in New Delhi with Edwin Lutyens.'

Hendrick pointed at a plain doorway on the central building. 'This is where the President of South Africa lives, when he's in Pretoria. South Africa's first K... *black* president, Mr Nelson Mandela,' Hendrick swallowed hard, 'addressed the nation here upon his inauguration in May 1994.'

We oo'ed and ah'ed. I noticed out of the corner of my eye that Hendrick seemed pleased at the signs of recognition, interest and awe we displayed at the name of the twentieth century's Last Great. We entered the presidential building for a peek of the lobby, but we could not go beyond the porter, who was sitting under the familiar-yet-still-bizarre sign: *'Please deposit your firearms at reception.'* (A brilliant idea – why hasn't the White House picked it up? *'Please surrender your Semtex at the gate.'*)

From the Union Buildings you can make out the Voortrekker monument in the distance. One can go on and on about its symbolism, its function and its importance to the Afrikaner psyche – one can go on and on like Hendrick did, in fact. But it's time to shut him off.

Time for me to have a word about those Boers.

The Boers spent their time reading the Bible and singing hymns, while the huge quantities of meat roasting over the fires almost extinguished the flames. In their moments of leisure the young men, who were of rather limited intelligence, indulged in trifling games or engaged each other in scuffling matches or attempted to be witty by telling the coarsest of jokes. As they were accustomed to living in the bosom of their isolated families, this great gathering of men was an occasion for merrymaking, particularly as the meat was fat and the daily ration for each man not less than ten pounds.

For these South African Dutch, the ideal existence consists in eating great quantities of grilled meat, drinking hourly cups of coffee and having a woman for the night. It means gazing, for daily recreation, upon the great, shiny, fat herds which adorn their green pastures and engaging, from time to time, in the diversions of the hunt to restore their strength. This is their idea of comfort; what they call lekker leeven.

Adulphe Delegorgue, a French explorer and naturalist, on an expedition with the Boers in 1840.

Nothing in South Africa is as it seems. History is being continuously rewritten, because history is written by the victorious, and the poor country has had its fair share of tumult. The first casualty of war may be truth, but the first casualty of civil strife is history itself. I could spot it in post-perestroika Moscow's Red Square: there was the Kremlin, the Lenin Mausoleum, St Basil's Cathedral and the GUM Department store. But opposite St Basil's stood a little-known elegant red edifice, which was closed 'for refurbishment': it was the Soviet History Museum.

Every major episode and personality in South African history is the subject of heated debate: the Dutch rule, the British takeover, King Shaka Zulu, the Xhosa Cattle Killing, Cecil Rhodes and the Boer War, Gandhi and the Indian immigration, the 1948 election, the ANC, Inkatha, apartheid...

Yet nothing is as controversial as the Great Trek.

In 1952, South Africa celebrated its tercentenary; except that 1652 is not the beginning of Dutch settlement in Cape Town – this was in 1647 (25 March, to be exact) with a merchant called Leendert Jansz. I am not sure whether there has been a consensus amongst historians to ignore the earlier settlement for good reasons or whether we are again in the clutches of propaganda. For by the time the pro-apartheid National Party got elected (1948) the real tercentenary had passed. So, did they decide to celebrate van Riebeeck's 1652 official mission for the Dutch East India Company instead? This would fit perfectly with the Nationalist Party's plans to cement an Afrikaner nationality. Paranoia on my part, maybe. But paranoia is only reality on a finer scale, as William Gibson says in *Strange Days*. The question in South Africa is how paranoid you can become.

The Boers did not always despise the British. When, during the Napoleonic wars, the British captured the Cape to secure the route to India after the Low Countries had fallen to the French, the Boers welcomed them. Proponents of free trade, the British scrapped the Dutch restrictive trade practices: until then, the Boers could only sell their produce to the Dutch East India Company at specified prices. The real turn came about when the British abolished slavery and started introducing laws which protected non-whites against mistreatment. Typically, the British acted with arrogance. Slavery was to be abolished, fine, but compensation would be given – *in London*. Tell that to Paul Kruger's family in Cradock who left the Cape Colony with a party of Voortrekkers in 1835. Dressed in the Dopper coats and *kappies*, Bible in hand, 'God's own people' looked for their illusionary Arcadia beyond the Orange and the Vaal.

The Voortrekkers did not see themselves as a nation (not many peoples did in the early nineteenth century as class ties were stronger), but it was important for their descendants to play up the Great Trek in order to legitimise their position: the white tribe of Africa – just like the Zulu and the Xhosa. After all, they moved into empty land, did they not?

Again history is hotly disputed. The standard history written, as usual, by white scholars is that the Voortrekkers arrived at their destinations during a period when the Zulu kingdom was expanding under King Shaka, causing mass migrations, the famous *mfecane* – the crushing. These were turbulent times indeed, but it wasn't just the Zulu expansion that was the sole reason: the slave trade by Portuguese settlers in Mozambique, the British push in the Cape and, finally, the Great Famine of 1800, sixteen years before Shaka took the reins of power, were equally responsible. Think of recent famine crises that destroyed the ability of nations to defend themselves and made them coalesce around warlords who could offer them survival in return for blind obedience: think of Ethiopia, Sudan and Somalia.

So, the Afrikaner justification goes, all tribes in southern Africa were migrating at that same time, and the Boers were settled in empty lands belonging to no one. This highly controversial conjecture stands right at the centre of South African history. Yet even this assertion seems a matter of faith. When a party of Voortrekkers settled in Natal in 1838, they estimated the indigenous population to be 11,000 souls. (That is, 11,000 people who didn't 'fill' land that was subsequently occupied by 6,000 Boers who managed to fill it.) When the same area was annexed four years later by the British who provided another guesstimate, the population seems to have irrupted to between 80,000 and 100,000. Hell, many women must have spent a lot of time on their backs breeding octuplets!

We reached the top of the hill where the Voortrekker monument stands – a colossal granite cube of a cenotaph crowned by a dome that stands sentry over Pretoria like a sturdy, demure protector. Sixty-four 15-foot-high sculpted Boer wagons surround it, turning the interior into a *laager*: this is the battle formation the Voortrekkers assumed when fighting the enemy, now a byword for the Afrikaner siege mentality. To compound the symbolism, the gigantic statues of four Great Trek leaders stand guard on each corner, defending the monument, the town, the *Volk*.

'This is a memorial to all the Boer pioneers who lost their lives during the Great Trek,' Hendrick explained.

I switched off; in tune with many false orthodoxies in South African history, there was no single Great Trek. There were six: four under Louis Trichard, Hans van Rensburg, Gert Maritz and Piet Uys; our Potgieter trek of the Blyde and Treur rivers fame; and the Retief trek, the most illustrious because it provided martyrs – Piet Retief and his companions were killed by Shaka's heir, Dingaan, after being invited to the Zulu capital in peace.

A myth, however, was necessary for the Afrikaners to build an identity.

In 1919, a secretive, religious organisation based around the Dutch Reformed Church was started. It was called the Broederbond and it later developed into the fulcrum of what would become the National Party. By the 1930s, there was an agenda: conservative, racist, deeply ethnic. The Broederbond controlled the board of the Cultural Afrikaner Federation which had resolved to build a monument for the Voortrekkers and create a focus of national pride. With typical bluntness, the official guide of the Voortrekker monument originally admitted as much: '*The Monument will arouse the pride of belonging to a nation of heroes who saw the Great Trek through; it will arouse and strengthen a love for the country for those whose sake so much was sacrificed and it will strengthen a faith in God whom the people trust. It will induce them to devote their lives to the duty and the privilege of building a nation.*'

The foundation stone was laid on 16 December 1938. It is one of the ironies of South African history yet again that the then pro-British government subsidised to the tune of eighty per cent a monument to aid its eventual demise. The Voortrekker monument was officially opened eleven years later on 16 December 1949. That day again. Coincidence? No.

As every Afrikaner schoolboy knows, 16 December is the date of the Battle of Blood River in 1838 between the Zulu (under Dingaan) and the Retief group of Voortrekkers (under their new leader Andries Pretorius). The previous day they had taken a vow that if God helped them win and avenge Piet Retief, they would commemorate their victory in future generations with a service of Thanksgiving. In the ensuing battle, only three out of 530 Boers were injured (including Pretorius himself), but 3,000 out of 12,000 invincible Zulu were slaughtered and their whole army routed. The Zulu who tried to escape by diving in the river Ncome were spotted when emerging to breathe and shot in the head; their blood turned its water red and named the battle and the river for posterity. The fact that the Boers had muskets and horses and the Zulu just close-combat spears should provide the rational explanation. In the Boer psyche, however, this proved their chosen status with the Divinity acting as jury, judge and compurgator.

It was thus that the Dutch Reformed Church convinced the Boers that a male, patriarchal God had chosen them as the last bastion of civilisation in a savage land; many quotes in the Bible supported them, for in pro-slavery quotes the Good Book abounds. As if to ram the point home, the churches eventually barred black Africans from full membership: *infidels!* as the Taliban would cry out, interpreting their own Holy Book in their own, peculiar way.

This is where the collateral damage starts.

Three hundred years before Blood River, the superior weaponry of a few hundred Spanish conquistadors defeated thousands of Incas and Aztecs who battled against armoured horses with spears and clubs. There is nothing extraordinary in the Zulu defeat. What is extraordinary to a schizophrenic degree is what followed: a monument in a twentieth century country which commemorated in triumph the defeat of one group of its society by another, while they are both expected to live in harmony. The inflammatory Ulster drum marches spring to mind and we know how peaceful *they* can be.

Hendrick finished his text book narration. The momentary silence that ensued disrupted my thoughts and brought me back to the present. We had entered the memorial chamber.

The Hall of Heroes, as it is called, with its twenty-seven marble panels, is the apotheosis of the Great Trek myth. It merges the six treks into one. It uses real twentieth century people to provide the continuation of the history: the grandchildren of Potgieter and Pretorius were used as models, and Piet Retief's likeness was based on a character in a popular 1916 film. It wipes out the accompanying black slaves rendering the journey an all-white venture. Finally, it transforms the Piet Retief killing and the Blood River revenge into a climactic tour-de-force of an Afrikaner-constructed history.

The Voortrekker monument was designed by Gerard Moerdijk and, although he kept denying it until he died, it is clearly based on the 1913 Leipzig *Völkerschlachtdenkmal* that commemorates Napoleon's defeat one hundred years earlier. Its Renaissance-style friezes, made in Italy, depict scenes from the treks doctored for propaganda purposes. In one panel the British settlers present a Bible to the Voortrekkers, although it was expressly forbidden to leave the Cape Colony without permission; in another, Dingaan's heir, Mpande, becomes king of the Zulu with Andries Pretorius on his side as if installed by the Afrikaners. The Zulu and the Ndebele, stylised like crash dummies with every inch of individuality craftily erased, are represented as warlike savages, whereas the Boers are depicted as serene hunters and farmers, men of peace. Except that as hunters they didn't always hunt – they often raided native villages to abduct children, *inboekselings,* to work in their fields; and as farmers didn't always farm – they used slave or paid native labour. But wait: in a touch worthy of Stone Age worship, Moerdijk has added a *coup de grâce*. An oculus on the left wall lets in a sun ray which, on 16 December every year, shines like a torch on a symbolic hero's grave one floor below, looking much like Napoleon's tomb in Les Invalides. The light falls on the words 'We are Yours South Africa' – '*Ons Vir Jou Suid Africa*'.

The Voortrekker monument is the culmination of a 1930s Aryan myth; it is a Calvinist paradigm part Stonehenge, part Japanese ancestral worship and part Wagnerian opera. As symbols go, it is the most potent in modern South Africa and a piercing alarm bell for the rest of the world. History is not the truth, it is what we remember as the truth – and *that* can be manufactured.

I was as surprised to see a celebration of the routing of a seventeenth century conspiracy against the hated English crown, Guy Fawkes' night, honoured in Pretoria as I was by being served fish and chips with vinegar in a takeaway on the way home. On cue, Hendrick sullenly complained about 'that English party'.

'My dog gets really scared. And you should see my dog. He's a *big* dog,' he said as he dropped me off at the Blue Angel in time for the big fireworks display at the Hatfield Plaza.

Martin, Elben and myself climbed on the roof to watch. Perhaps siding with Hendrick's canine, the skies opened and the clouds doused down the celebrations, but not enough to stop them altogether. I didn't care; I was miles forward in time, pondering anxiously over the next stage of my journey, troubled by the official tourist personal security leaflet I had picked up during our tour.

'*Safety tips when staying at a hotel…*'

Set-piece orange bottle rockets fizzed above us. Shells exploded in the clouds, a multicoloured battle to match the Rainbow Nation's own armed struggle. Kaleidoscopic Catherine wheels and girandoles whistled and set the night alight.

'*How to deal with the public safely…*'

Was that a cherry bomb? The airburst explosion, red, deafening and violent is outlawed in the UK and the US, but not, it seems, in South Africa.

'How to drive safely...'

Sparklers, flashes, flares, pyrotechnic snowflakes, twinkling comets, dramatic croisettes and barrages of roman candles ignited into little stars that lasted for milliseconds.

'My life is being threatened by carjackers...'

Mortars fired bright red canisters and silver rockets soared powerfully only to whizz off with a whimper. The night turned day-glo green and smelled of lycopodium powder and creosote.

'Safety hints when withdrawing money at an automatic teller machine...'

The final firework salute, as Big a Bang as the original (a kind of Moholoholo Bang, if you like) sounded ominous and must have shaken the jacaranda flowers off every tree in town.

'Dealing with rape...'

'You're apprehensive,' Martin said.

I was. From next day on I'd be on the road on my own. I knew by now how dangerous this place was.

'That's good,' said Elben. 'Your eyes will be open.'

'Stop worrying,' said Martin. 'You have my number and if anything, *anything* happens to you –' He left the sentence hanging. 'Don't feel that you're alone here. You're not.'

He gave me a hug.

'Where is your next stop?' Elben changed the subject.

So far I had seen, lived and talked with the white minority only. I had always doubted whether I would ever mix with the black majority. Would I even get a chance?

'Next stop Mbabane, Swaziland,' I said.

Chapter Four

The Baz Bus: Johannesburg to Mbabane

The problem in Beirut is political, not criminal. We don't lock our doors in Beirut. Johannesburg is a jungle. I'm leaving and not coming back. Maybe my government will send someone more courageous.
The Lebanese chargé d'affaires speaking to the press after his Johannesburg home was burgled twice in ten days.

10. War zone

I arrived at Pretoria Backpackers – imbued with that familiar smell of stale sweat, stale cookies and stale dope that permeates hostels – just ten minutes before 7 a.m. when we were due to depart. Martin had gone slo-mo on me that early in the morning and his warped spatial awareness had converted the Pretoria rectangular street grid into an Arabian *souk* maze. He took so many wrong turns I wondered whether he wanted to drive me to Swaziland himself.

The bus was still parked outside. *Phew!*

'I'm on the Baz Bus,' I said anxiously to the lethargic girl at reception. 'Am I late for a seat?'

She looked me up and down. 'I'll wake up the driver,' she said.

The Baz Bus is a daily hop-on, hop-off service that runs between hostels from Pretoria to Cape Town via Durban and back. There are two routes to Durban: the direct one via the Central Drakensberg, and a longer, circuitous one via Swaziland and Northern KwaZulu/Natal, which was the one I was taking. You can stay at a designated hostel, stop as long as you like and catch the bus when it next drives by. In a country where public transport is virtually non-existent and, where it exists, is fraught with danger, the Baz Bus is very popular with backpackers. It's convenient, it's cheap, it's frequent, and you're guaranteed to meet like-minded travellers. And if this sounds like a plug, I don't care.

I waited by the bus – a twenty-odd seater with a luggage trailer – fretting and watching in vain for any signs of life. Fifteen lonely minutes later, I returned to reception.

'The driver?' I ventured.

'He knows you're here,' the girl replied wearily, adding: 'In the TV room there's sport on ESPN.' I obediently watched the telly for another half hour, until a sleepy, freshly-showered, red-eyed Indian emerged from the depths of the hostel. 'Baz Bus?' he asked timidly.

At last. Meet Khamesh.

I sat at the front next to Khamesh and turned the radio on. We started 45 minutes behind schedule which became an hour as we took the N1 to Johannesburg, since every vehicle in Gauteng seemed to be stationary, blocking the highway. This country needs public transport more than it needs Loftus-Minolta rugby stadiums.

We had a melange of nationalities to pick up from six different hostels, not an easy or speedy task, as Johannesburg is rather vast. On the plus side, I got a city tour for free – for this was my first venture into the big, brash city on the Gold Reef; the murder and mugging capital of the world, the carjacking centre of the Universe, the place no one has a good thing to say about except a black entrepreneur I watched on SATV. He reminded the viewers that one man's plight is another man's bargain by commenting on the flight of the Johannesburg Stock Exchange to the suburb of Sandton, a move to avoid the high crime rate of the centre. Our venturesome interviewee liked the fact that white residents and businesses had left, since he bought the empty properties at bargain prices. The shape of things to come? Will Johannesburg turn out to be the first African New York, an international megalopolis with skyscrapers, neon lights, plazas and avenues where a white face is as rare as a black smile at Epsom? The area around Hillbrow Tower, the old bohemian enclave, is already called Little Kinshasa and looks the part.

I know a sprawl when I see one and vast, amorphous Johannesburg fits the bill. I also know fear when I smell it, and at Rosebank – where we picked up Robert and Wendy, a just-married couple from Brisbane – the fences were higher, the razor wire denser, the vicious, barking Alsatians bigger and the 'Keep Off/Beware of the Dog/This House is Protected by 24-hr Armed Response' signs more prominent. The suburbanites of Johannesburg have reacted like startled crabs, withdrawing to the security of their crevices. They carry panic buttons even for a spot of gardening; schools have high-voltage fences; a sideways flame-thrower contraption – the 'Blaster' – is advertised for carjack prevention at 8,000 rand per car fitting; and if you're unlucky enough not to have a garage, you can buy the Autoport, a steel cage to lock your parked vehicle in.

I know this is unfair for both white and black South Africans, but it's damn impossible for a casual viewer not to be drawn to the niggling thought that the chickens have come home to roost. There is a lost generation out there feeding the crime wave: the Soweto-strikers-cum-ANC-guerrillas who heeded the call to make the country ungovernable in their youth and, uneducated in their thirties or forties, have no place in the new South Africa they fought for – and know it. Desperation mixed with impatience in the lack of social progress and despondency combined with envy at the preservation of white privilege fuel a crime wave which has assumed the dimensions of a Pacific tsunami. In the 1980s bank hold-ups and burglaries were used to raise funds for the struggle against apartheid; now the township gangs roam the wealthy suburbs, amercing an income redistribution without mercy.

The police – demoralised, mistrusted, underpaid, overstretched and politicised by the previous regime – seem to be shrugging their shoulders with an I-told-you-so smirk. As a result, private security companies thrive, employing an estimated 150,000 bodyguards, patrollers, bouncers, heavies and ready-to-shoot gunslingers, most of them ex-policemen themselves; in fact, in certain neighbourhoods, some are even hired to protect police stations. The poorer townships, still distrustful of officialdom they see as downright inimical, rely on old-fashioned kangaroo courts and vigilante justice to counter a crime rate many times higher than what befalls the whites. A report from South Africa's own government dubbed itself the most violent country outside a war zone.

There are several factors that can explain the increase in lawlessness in South Africa, especially in the economic heart of the country, Gauteng: a greater reporting of crime, the steady migration of the poor into squatter camps – breeding grounds for gang recruitment – the ready availability of guns and the high unemployment rate. The lifting of sanctions also contributed to this rise, as it led to dozens of known criminal concerns in drug trafficking and organised crime to set up shop in South Africa. Israeli media have claimed that even terrorist organisations like Hezbollah established training camps in the bush; indeed, Islamic vigilante groups like PAGAD in Cape Town created their own small havoc. Give this to a people insecure in their status like the Afrikaners and you generate Freddy-Krueger urban myths and a mass *laager* psychosis. Whatever the statistics, it's the cumulative psychological effect that matters: something is dangerous if you think so and not because it actually is.

If we take the generally accepted measure of homicides per 100,000 of the population then the figures change over time, but their relative worldwide positions don't. At the bottom you have your Viennas, Genevas and Brussels, with London, Paris and Berlin further up the ladder. American towns figure next and cities like Rio and Mexico City vie for a place with new hubs of violence like Moscow. Then come the murder capitals of the world and South Africa is well placed with Johannesburg, Durban and Cape Town alongside Bogotá, Miami and Lagos. It is worth noting that the US, long thought of as crime-infested, has a murder rate five to ten times lower than that of South Africa.

Within those stats, however, there are some more reassuring facts for the tourist: most violent crimes are concentrated in townships, happen under the influence of alcohol on Saturday nights and weekends, and the victims – especially the rape victims – already know the perpetrators. The crime rate *does* seem to be slowing down after the stratospheric heights of the late 1990s, and many commentators have attributed the decrease to another killer, Aids. The virus has hit proportionately harder the criminal subculture carrying out shootouts and stabbings, rapes and robberies, holdouts and hijacks. HIV infection through rape is even used as punishment in jails – called, chillingly, *'a slow puncture'*. This practice, whereby unruly or disobedient inmates are ritually raped by one or several gang members, was admitted to by a spokesman for the Judicial Inspectorate of Prisons who was giving evidence to a commission of inquiry in November 2002. It may be the reason why deaths in South African jails have increased tenfold since 1995, though they are routinely ascribed to 'natural causes'.

The situation is still not reassuring enough for the foreign investor, however. January 1999 seems to have been a milestone: Kwon Yong Koo, the 50-year-old Korean president of Daewoo was shot dead in his car in Johannesburg's Morningside district and James Bartleman, the Canadian High Commissioner, was mugged in his own hotel. The incident didn't just leave him with bruises and a broken nose; it left President Mbeki's hopes of attracting foreign investment in tatters. As recently as October 2002 a fact-finding delegation of Japanese executives from the Keidanren, the employers' confederation, gave the thumbs down to South Africa because of its violent reputation. Sport is not immune: a Test match between Pakistan and South Africa in February 1998 was postponed because off-spinner Saqlain Mushtaq needed a neck-brace and fast bowler Mohammed Akram was left with a gash on his hand after they were mugged outside their hotel.

Yet, apart from all the high-profile crimes, it is the everyday ones that convey the horror: in June 2002 17-year-old Johan Jacobs was training to run in a charity cycle race in Johannesburg's Brakpan suburb. His mistake was to own a 30,000-rand pushbike. His ambushers not only robbed him of his bike, but also stripped him of his clothes and shoes, shot him and left him naked on the tarmac. He required emergency surgery on his bladder, stomach and pelvis, but thankfully survived.

Khamesh stopped at a red light.

'This is Hillbrow,' he said in an uneasy tone that made us all feel fidgety.

So this was it, the inner circle of Hell and, as you might expect from the eye of the crime cyclone, it was quiet: high-rise flats, wrecked cars which had seen better days several decades ago, steel-reinforced doors and barbed wire on the balconies, all steeped in the stillness of a cemetery. No one was walking the streets at ten in the morning. Or, rather, there was a white youth carrying a supermarket bag. Three black guys were walking towards him. I winked mischievously at the Australians.

'Hey, let's watch this guy get mugged.'

Robert took out his Nikon SLR. As he was looking through the viewfinder, the white youth and the three black guys passed each other without incident. We were disappointed.

'Very likely, he lives here,' said Khamesh. 'Or, even more likely, he's been to the South African Army, where they've taught him how to kill a man with his bare hands.'

'That's all propaganda,' I replied, annoyed. 'That's what the whites used to tell you in order for you to remain docile and quiet. It's a myth.'

'It's a good myth if it makes a white guy able to walk the streets of Hillbrow,' said Robert, and I conceded he had a point.

Khamesh stopped; we had arrived at a hostel. He got off, rang the bell of a heavily-armoured gate and waved 'It's me' to the CCTV. While he was out, a couple of well-built black men started pushing a car towards us. The Australians and I froze.

'They want to ram us!' said Wendy, her voice rising to a shriek.

The two guys accelerated and as they came closer we saw the driver in the front of the car starting a stalled engine.

They were only trying to kick-start the car by reversing downhill.

We breathed out again.

'Who the hell decides to stay in a hostel in the middle of Hillbrow?' asked Wendy, jangled nerves still present in her voice.

Elliott, that's who. He came out of the hostel smiling a wide smile, clutching his backpack and cheerfully giving us five, as he climbed aboard. Elliott was British, from Birmingham, supported West Brom, and he was black. I looked at Robert; from his expression I guessed he was thinking the same thing. Was it because of his colour that Elliott stayed in Hillbrow?

Elliott was a psychiatric nurse who had decided to pack it in and travel in South Africa for three months. He was the spitting image of Eddie Murphy in *Beverly Hills Cop*, down to the long drawn-out Axel F giggling laugh. Falco music seemed to accompany his movements.

'Man, this is a heavy place,' he said in a singing tenor, his Brummie accent mixed with hip-hop mannerisms. 'Man, I haven't seen so many guns, *ever*. I asked the guys in the hostel if I could buy a cheap Pentax and they sent me to this pawn shop on Pretoria Street. I asked how much and they said 1,000 rand, so I thought "great". I picked it up, and I looked at it, and I pointed it at a group of guys in the corner and man, they turned around and cocked their guns. Shit, man, I put the camera down carefully and said, "Cool it guys, there's no film in it, just joking."'

'Was it hot?' I asked, stating the obvious.

'Man, it was *sizzling*. In front of me there was a guy with a raincoat, and he opened it, and there were a dozen mobile phones hanging inside like keys. He was selling them for three hundred rand apiece.'

At least Elliott, because of his colour, could walk around central Johannesburg. None of the other passengers had been brave enough; we picked up Anne-Marie, a Belgian girl hauling a BMX bike she hadn't dared cycle in the streets, who started flirting with Elliott; a Danish guy called Jørgen straight out of a *Jesus Christ Superstar* dress rehearsal for His part; an Aussie tough with tight trousers called Clint; and the obligatory German couple, Ute and Herman, headstrong and sturdy like an Audi. We were chatting away, everyone in the same boat – well, *bus* – emboldened by the fact that our adventure was just beginning.

So where had people been so far?

'We visited Soweto,' said Wendy – who, even without her glasses, could pass for a trainee maths teacher. 'There were two Nigerian tourists with us and they were both terrified. We got off to take some snaps, but they wouldn't leave their seats.

Clint had stayed in the hostel smoking dope with Jørgen. 'Got out once to eat a snack. Don't think *he* ever did,' he said, pointing at Jørgen, who smiled beatifically.

We stopped at a large shopping mall to buy refreshments and victuals. Big mistake, since when backpackers disperse, it is impossible to track them: gathering backpackers is like herding cats. We left Johannesburg two hours behind schedule, but that's what the Baz Bus is about, I thought, as Elliott's Eddie Murphy laugh cut through the general buzz.

11. The mother of all storms

This was the second and hopefully the last time I was travelling the same monotonous stretch to the Kruger Park – surely there must be better fates in this lifetime. We stopped at the same petrol stations for toilet breaks, admired the same collieries and peeked at the same bland horizon until we stopped for lunch outside Nelspruit city limits. A lone, red-haired British backpacker with loose rave clothes and a freckled face was waiting for us there.

'Hi, I'm Adrian,' he said and shook hands with everyone in a somewhat stilted way. He was off to St Lucia and Umfolozi and would be spending next weekend in Durban. Although a Scouser, he was a West Brom supporter like Elliott. How odd that when a couple of Brits get together, conversation turns eventually to football. It even emerged that they drank at the same local – talk about incestuous.

I sat down with the others and ordered a hamburger with monkey gland sauce.

'Monkey gland sauce? Yuck,' said Anne-Marie.

'Haven't you heard?' said Elliott. 'It's a South African delicacy. They take the monkeys and skin alive the bitches. Then they let them run around screaming and bleeding until they die. And as they scream their glands are engorged, man, and they cut them off for the sauce.'

'Godsverdommert!' screamed Anne-Marie.

When she saw us barely able to hide our chuckles, she turned red and slapped Elliott's cheek teasingly. 'You are joking with me,' she said. We burst out laughing.

I felt someone's gaze on me. I turned around.

A family of real, life-size, breathing Boers were sitting at a table behind us and staring at us, transfixed. The father had a

Kruger-like beard of ZZ Top dimensions, the wife wore a sensible, long, blue dress and the two well-fed children's mouths were agape, letting a dribble of saliva trickle down their chins. I thought at the time that what had shocked them was our mixed-race table, but now I know better. It wasn't us – it was Elliott they were staring at: an intelligent, eloquent, humorous, self-assured black man who socialised with his white comrades as an equal. They were staring at what their books and their beliefs told them was incongruous and they were thinking 'insolence'. For this is how I know: when I eventually returned to England after my lengthy South African sojourn and saw the confident air of the black British workers at Heathrow, I caught myself staring at them with the same element of surprise I observed in my Nelspruit Boers. I am not of that metal made but, for a minute, a flash of pride gave me a shiver – this time, it felt especially good returning home.

The last passenger we picked up from Nelspruit Backpackers was Guilhermo, a bronzed Brazilian who caused a minor commotion. Anne-Marie stopped talking to Elliott and made space for Guilhermo to sit next to her, initiating a flirt triangle for the day. But I had one up on her. He was from Rondonópolis in the Mato Grosso and was mightily impressed I had visited the Pantanal – he was from the north side of this large swampland, and I had visited the south. This was the end of his trip: he was travelling to Durban to board a flight back to São Paulo. Swaziland was for him, as for most, an inconvenient but obligatory overnight stop.

We didn't follow the direct, mountainous route via Barberton to Bulembu because the weather started deteriorating and Saddleback Pass was dangerous; instead we retraced our steps to the N17 and entered Swaziland via Oshoek. I was annoyed at the time because this diversion added significantly to our journey, but I read later in the *Swazi Times* that a high-ranking Swazi judge was killed on that route that very same day, when his car didn't negotiate the curves properly in the thunderstorm and skidded off the road into a ravine. Because the storm, when it came, was the loudest, the wettest and the windiest I have experienced. Lightning transformed the landscape into a giant spider's web and made the radio crackle like a Geiger counter lying on a Nevada nuclear testing site. The thunder was so booming and visceral it interfered with our digestion. Visibility became so low everyone in the bus had assumed near-crash positions. Khamesh stopped the car, frightened.

'Anyone wearing bangles?' he asked.

Most of the jewellery was to be found on Guilhermo.

'Take them off! Now!'

Mystified, we obeyed and put our trinkets in our pockets. Khamesh said that copper and other conductors around a human body act like an induction coil and draw in lightning. I didn't dispute the wisdom, remembering Dylan's TV incident on the way back from the Kruger.

I turned to Khamesh to ask for his story, if only to ward off my skittishness, though he was a poor choice for inspiration: he lived in permafear – from the weather, from other traffic, from carjackers, from his boss. When Clint produced a spliff to Jørgen's animated delight, Khamesh nearly drove into a ditch from terror. Out of all the evils in this world, it was the police he feared the most.

Khamesh's family was from Gujarat. They still had land there, and he visited occasionally. His ancestors arrived in Natal in the late nineteenth century as 'passengers': Indians who came to trade. They were to be distinguished from the 'coolie' immigrants who arrived in Natal as indentured labourers and worked the sugar cane fields under conditions that enraged even the colonial administration in India. These 'passengers' controlled most of the corner-shop trade: sixty out of sixty-six shops in Natal by 1885. Although relatively wealthy, the Indians were still subject to the repressive colonial laws, so they complained to the British Parliament about police harassment and legal indignities, such as the 9 p.m. curfew.

It was one such merchant, Seth Dada Abdullah, who employed a British-educated, 26-year-old lawyer as legal counsel to defend a court case in 1893. The lawyer had been trying to practise in Bombay, but had failed in his endeavours and ended up unemployed. So he came to Durban and, considering himself a professional, bought himself a first class train ticket to Pretoria to research some documents. Before Pietermaritzburg, a white traveller objected to travelling with a 'coolie'. The lawyer counter-objected in the strongest terms, but was summarily ejected from the train and spent a night in the Pietermaritzburg jail. His name was Mohandas Karamchand Gandhi and his was the most significant travel upset since St-Paul-to-be was blinded by a light on the road to Damascus.

Gandhi had his work cut out. Indian shopkeepers were bloody good competition for the protective South African colonial society, so repressive laws had to be drawn upto cut down the 'merchant menace'. In 1884, the Orange Free State passed a law that classified Indians as 'Coloured'. In 1885, the South African Republic of the Transvaal passed a law for the forced removal of Indian traders from the centre of Johannesburg to five miles outside the city on 'health grounds'. Once self-government was granted to Natal by Britain in 1893, specific discriminatory measures started flooding in. The Immigration Law Amendment Bill in 1894 stipulated that Indians with normal five-year labour contracts must either return to India upon their expiration, sign a further two-year extension, or pay an annual tax if they wanted to stay. The Franchise Amendment Bill in 1896 stopped the granting of any further voting rights to Indians, because 300 had sought and obtained them by then. The Immigration Restriction Bill, whereby Indians had to possess £25 and speak and write English, effectively stopped trader-immigrants as opposed to indentured labourers who were not subject to the Bill's provisions. But it was an Act in 1907, which introduced passes for Indians in the Transvaal, that enraged the subcontinent community and spawned Gandhi's historic passive resistance movement. Maybe it's a feature of repression to produce greatness

– from the Mahatma to the Madiba – in order to bring collective sanity back to equilibrium.

This was Khamesh's heritage.

We stopped at the border with Swaziland and ran towards South African Immigration while the heavens poured mercilessly upon us.

'Any Class A's, swallow them now,' I warned Jørgen.

He smiled. 'They're underneath my seat,' he reassured me. I nearly choked. Better not tell Khamesh.

A big poster hung on the wall of the Immigration Bureau.

> **HOW TO FIGHT AIDS:**
> A. DO NOT HAVE SEX
> B. BE FAITHFUL TO YOUR PARTNER
> C. USE A CONDOM.

Do not have sex? If this was passing for sex education, that was not a useful slogan to start with. Aussie Clint went to have a close look at a big basket underneath the sign.

'Free condoms,' he said and gave some away. Jørgen turned red.

'These condoms are for *blacks*,' he said and swallowed hard. 'This could be embarrassing.'

For black or for white, we stocked up nevertheless. But not one of the Africans waiting in the queue even glanced at the basket.

There are several common African expressions for Aids: *Unamagama amane* (he's got 'the Four Words'); *Unxiba isikafu esibomvu* (he's wearing 'the Red Scarf', after the red ribbon of the Aids prevention movement); *Ubambe ilotto* (he's won the lottery). The slang epithets combine irreverence and dread in equal measures, for this is a disease that threatens the very existence of the black nations. South Africa has the fastest rate of increase in the world with infections running at ten per cent in some areas. Back in 2001 it was estimated that forty per cent of deaths of people aged 15–49 were due to Aids. It is extrapolated that between five and seven million people will die of the disease before 2010.

As sex ('wiping the axe') is an unashamedly natural pleasure in African societies, the original anti-Aids slogan of abstinence never had any chance of success – it was seen as an attempt to impose a new Puritanism. The practice of marrying many wives – a symbol of virility and status – is seen as incompatible with the safe sex message of one-partner-for-life. And as far as condoms are concerned, Africans have a contraceptive method tried and tested for centuries: *uku-hlobonga* (with the second part pronounced *shlobonga*). This is the rubbing of the penis and subsequent ejaculation against the vaginal lips without penetration and certainly without breaking the hymen. Pretty good against childbirth, but not quite foolproof against an agent such as HIV.

One result of such a lack of sex education is that cases of child rape have increased sharply, as it is believed that intercourse with a virgin wipes out the virus (a tenet also widely held in Victorian England as a cure against the then ravaging syphilis epidemic). In order to comprehend the logic behind this, you must understand the African view of infection. Illness is not brought about by unseen things like viruses, but is directly caused by people who wish the disease upon the infected, people who have been possessed by dark spirits – an extreme version of the Mediterranean 'evil eye': *so deflowered virgins won't catch Aids because the disease was not meant for them.* After all, who could wish them any harm? The disease-filled semen is expelled to those who can't get infected, or so goes the line of thinking.

Unfortunately, new South Africa's government made the problem worse. When Winnie Mandela said, 'You must not wear condoms. They do not stop disease. Anyone who tells you otherwise is a liar. They are designed to stop us from breeding,' she was latching onto a popular feeling that Aids was another big white plot. It is not just Thabo Mbeki who subscribes to the view that HIV doesn't cause Aids; this is the published view of the African National Congress. In the peculiarly named document *Castro Hlongwane, Caravans, Cats, Geese, Foot & Mouth and Statistics* issued in March 2002, the ANC intelligentsia write that: *'[This monograph] rejects as illogical the proposition that Aids is a single disease caused by a singular virus, HIV. [...] It accepts the proposition that anti-retroviral drugs can neither cure Aids nor destroy the HI virus. It therefore rejects the suggestion that the challenge of Aids in our country can be solved by resorting to anti-retroviral drugs. It rejects the assertion that, among the nations, we have the highest incidence of HIV infection and Aids deaths, caused by sexual immorality among our people. It rejects the claim that Aids is the single largest cause of death in our country.'*

Gay men can sympathise with such claims. The late eighties and early nineties saw an unlikely coalition of conservative papers, obsessive scientists and gay activists who joined forces in opposing the official theory that HIV causes Aids. They blamed a conspiracy of 'unscrupulous pharmaceutical companies, corrupt government officials, venal physicians, stupid and cowardly media people and incompetent, dishonest researchers', which sounds pretty comprehensive, if you ask me. The cabal around Peter Duesberg at Berkeley provided the scientific doubts the anti-HIV coalition required to reinforce their own prejudices. Gay activists suspected homicidal homophobia by the pharmaceutical companies. For the conservatives it was homosexual 'lifestyle' choices – such as recreational drug taking – that were responsible for a lowering of the immune system.

Duesberg's questions were valid at the start of the 1990s when the mechanism of how HIV works was ill-understood; but ten years later the viral dynamics have been explained and have led to the development of combination therapies which have proved remarkably successful. This calmed down the gay activists, and as the virus took hold in the heterosexual populations of the Third World lifestyle choice theories also went out of the window.

So what do you do if you are so obviously wrong but you can't lose face? Well, you cry, 'Our HIV is different than yours.' The ANC-drafted paper goes on to postulate that the HIV virus found in Africa is *different* from the virus in the West, because its transmission method is mostly via heterosexual intercourse. With astonishing logic or lack thereof, it then expresses the hope that the scientists working on this area might be able to prove this conjecture in the future. These are the conservatives inside the ANC speaking, aided by such figures as David Rasnick, one of that Berkeley cabal, and a member of Thabo Mbeki's Aids advisory panel. As for the ANC left-wingers, they are cast in the role of the gay activists, suspecting the usual genocide conspiracies. For them blind belief in 'white' science indicates a lack of faith in their African ancestry: *'For centuries we have carried the burden of the crimes and falsities of "scientific" Eurocentrism, its dogmas imposed upon our being as the brands of a definitive, "universal" truth.'*

In other words: a sad, mad *déjà vu*.

We ran through the downpour to the Swazi immigration post along with dozens of worried Zulus and Swazis whose contact with authority appeared to them awful and awesome. White tourists jump the queue to a fast-track counter; no one complained and no one questioned our precedence. We obtained our stamps and retired back to the bus a ten-yard soak away. And we waited. And we waited. Khamesh came back breathless. I had only seen him frantic, panicky or shaking with distress. This was a new one on me – totally berserk.

I ran back with him. The problem was Guilhermo.

'Brazilians need a visa,' explained the Swazi immigration lady. 'It is quite, quite clear.'

I consulted my guide. She was right. Brazilians needed visas for Swaziland. Furthermore, visas were only obtainable back in Pretoria by personal application. Guilhermo was in shock. Khamesh was holding his head in despair. We were a bad coachload to match the weather.

If you can't convince them, confuse them.

'This man does *not* need a proper visa,' I blurted. 'He's travelling to Durban tomorrow. He only needs a *transit* visa.'

The Swazi woman looked at me, looked at Guilhermo, who looked vulnerable and sexy, and took pity on him. 'All right. He can have a one-day visa,' she said.

Once again, laws were twisted to suit us hapless tourists. Guilhermo needed a visa for which he had to pay in Pretoria. He got one free on the border. In Khamesh's eyes I was a star. And, more importantly, in Guilhermo's. Maybe we'll get a double bunk tonight.

Any hopes I might have nursed were short-lived. When we reached Mbabane some of us jumped out and some stayed in. Guilhermo stayed in. After Mbabane, the Baz Bus stops further south at Manzini, and it's there it stays overnight before continuing to KwaZulu/Natal. Guilhermo had to spend the night in Manzini – and from what I heard later, his troubles didn't stop there. There were no free beds in the hostel, and he spent the night on Robert and Wendy's floor. It hadn't been his day and it certainly wasn't his night.

Elliott, Clint, Anne-Marie and Jørgen came with me. The hostel manager, an English girl, showed us the living room where dope clouds had been accumulating in the air, coalescing into a thick, sweet-smelling cumulonimbus just above the sofa. Jørgen plunged into an armchair and joined in for a joint, face angelically ecstatic. Apart from marijuana, on offer were undersized dorm beds and one toilet (with a glass door), but no soap, no sheets, no pillows and no covers. And, at six foot, I didn't fit in the beds.

The manager mentioned that a single room was going for 120 rand. I jumped at the opportunity. She showed me a room with a mattress on the floor that was one of those foam jobs you put underneath your sleeping bag in a tent. I lay down; no covers. I tried to close my eyes. *Maybe I can sleep this through tomorrow.*

An Indian guy entered my room without knocking. 'Oh, most sorry,' he said. 'I did not know a guest was sleeping in the corridor.'

The *corridor*? I approached the dirty, drawn curtains. They hid a set of glass doors leading to the yard where, despite the storm, a *braai* was being prepared under an awning. With a sigh, I gave up on sleep; anyway, I needed to change as I was drenched in sweat. A bath or a shower was out of the question – no towels. I groaned and turned back to check how dry my luggage was. There were three cupboards at the other end of my room – sorry, *corridor*. I opened them and a nasty smell filled the air, which should accompany *Trainspotting*, if it is ever released as a scratch-and-sniff comic. In the cupboard were items from the ghosts of backpackers past: mouldy walking shoes, torn sleeping bags, dirty towels, oily jeans and bedandruffed woolly hats. I was to sleep in a noisy corridor on a foam mattress next to a rubbish dump and pay 120 rand for the privilege! I'd had enough. I hated the place. Storm or no storm, I wanted out.

To her credit, the manager started phoning around for me – first a taxi and then various hostels in Mbabane. They were all full, but I still said my goodbyes: Anne-Marie ignored me; Elliott seemed upset at my decision. Clint waved 'See ya'. Jørgen was already too far gone to register any comprehension.

A taxi arrived. My Swazi cabbie drove me around the cheaper hotels; at every stop, he ran out, braved the relentless rain, talked to the receptionist and came back long-faced. 'Full,' he kept repeating – the storm had forced every traveller to stay in town. I was beginning to contemplate having to book into a five-star establishment, until, luckily, we reached the Hill Street

Lodge. This was a long, concrete, bungalow motel out of a Hitchcock movie, complete with lights trembling every time lightning struck. A Swazi receptionist was stretched on a sofa watching a black-and-white portable TV. Yes, he had a single room, at 80 Mlangeni (£8), shared facilities, towels and soap provided. Could I see it? The man got up drowsily and opened a door in a barely-lit corridor, smelling of *eau de toilette publique*. I scrutinised my quarters. There was a double bed in a room with cracked, knocked-about, 30-year-old furniture and a minuscule red light. As I checked in, three big Swazis entered the room next to mine, looked at me, and looked at me again with even greater surprise. This was an all-black hostel, full of stranded lorry drivers.

When I came to close my door, the lock nearly came off in my hands; it was held together with half-undone, rusty screws. I hid my passport and moneybelt under the mattress and moved on to the shower across the corridor. Hot water – bliss. As I came out, towel around my waist, I came face to face with another resident. He didn't look the kind you'd want to spend a night in a prison cell with. He grinned as if he'd been waiting for me. It was more of a hello-what-have-we-here? kind of grimace than a greeting. I can muster a disarming smile on occasion, so I forced one, and I immediately knew he knew I wasn't South African. He went back into his room without a word.

I lay on my bed exhausted and hungry. It had been a very long day. I heard a mosquito buzzing around me. This was a malarial area. I swatted the fucker against the wall. It was laden in blood. I checked myself. It wasn't mine.

Thank the Goddess for small mercies.

Chapter Five

Swazi Sleaze: Swaziland

The independence of the judiciary and the authority of the courts were seriously undermined by government officials and police in a number of cases. The security forces continued to enforce long-standing restrictions on freedom of assembly and association. Journalists were ill-treated and harassed when reporting on gatherings viewed by the authorities as political. Women were denied access to social and economic rights through discriminatory laws and practices. Asylum seekers, including children, were detained in harsh conditions.
From Amnesty International Report 2003,
AI Index POL 10/003/2003, section on Swaziland

12. A traditional African society

'Eight of our kings are buried in caves over there,' Christopher said to me, pointing at the misty mountain range beyond the Mbabane river. 'Burial takes place at night and has to finish by sunrise. The king is buried sitting on a log – and the person closest to the king, the one who knows all his secrets, gets buried with him.'

What?

'They don't exactly bury him alive. There is enough air for him to survive for a while. The cave entrance is blocked with a big stone. They leave him enough water, beer and a lot of meat to survive several days. Maybe a week.'

Oh, that's OK, then.

'How do they know which one is his confidant?'

'The witch-doctor throws the bones and finds out.'

'So what do the churches, the missionaries, have to say about that?'

'They don't like it,' said Christopher with a shrug of resignation. 'But what can they do?'

There was a poignant silence.

'When was the last time, erm... this erm... *happened*?'

'The last king, Sobhuza the Second, was buried there in 1982.'

'What! This is *horrible*.' I shuddered.

'Yes,' agreed Christopher. 'It's horrible.'

Welcome to Swaziland, a traditional African society.

The Swazis belong to South African Bantu speakers, known as Nguni, who also comprise the Tsonga, Sotho, Ndebele, Xhosa and Zulu ethnic groups. The word Bantu itself comes from the plural of the word 'person' in the Nguni languages: *umNtu* is a single person and the prefix *aba* turns it into the plural, *abaNtu*. Such plural-forming is the norm; the correct plural for the Zulu is *amaZulu*, and the 'People with the Shields', the *amaNdebele*, have been Europeanised into *Matabele*.

Christopher was a young Swazi guide who was driving me around Mbabane – I had opted for a cultural tour from an African perspective. The kings' burial rituals had frosted the atmo so I tried a more personal tack:

'Do you have to study to become a guide?' I asked, remembering Dylan. 'In South Africa they do.'

Christopher said no. He had studied environmental health.

'Surely that's an essential profession in a Third World country.'

Christopher drove on silently.

'Aren't you overqualified for a guide?' I continued. 'Your English is perfect, for a start.'

Christopher smiled bitterly: 'I cannot get a job elsewhere. I am not *connected*.'

He explained: other countries may have their secret handshakes and military-industrial complexes, but Swaziland's complex is more Oedipal, as it involves the king, his mother and his clan. Christopher's blood was on the wrong side.

'I tried to live in Johannesburg for a year,' Christopher said, 'but I hated it. I hated the commute to the townships. I hated the racial polarisation. Not all whites are our enemies. That's what they think over there.'

'Are you married, Christopher?' I asked.

'Not enough cows,' he said with another fatalistic shrug of the shoulders.

'Cows?'

'You need cows to marry. Cows are the wealth of the Swazi nation, its banking and its investment.'

'How many cows do you need for a wife?'

'About ten or twelve. If she is the daughter of a chief or the first or last child – they are important – it can rise to twenty or thirty. If the woman has a baby from you, you pay five cows for its upkeep, and the person who eventually marries the woman pays less.'

'How many cows do *you* have?'

'Only three.'

As Christopher explained, negotiations about this African dowry – or *lobola* – occur in the principal hut of a *kraal* in front of witnesses, so that there can't be any arguments about the number afterwards. This is a tradition which runs so deep in Nguni societies that even educated middle class families adhere to it; they simply swap the cattle for cash at about 1,000 rand per cow with bulls costing more. If the *lobola* is too much, the husband can pay in instalments: cohabit now, cough up later, marry upon final settlement. Like a house, the wife is only fully yours with the last mortgage payment, so woe betide the husband who doesn't pay the agreed amount: wives who have been buried next to their husbands have been dug up and reburied in their paternal plot (with the local authority's agreement) if the *lobola* had not been fully paid during their lifetime. In a well-reported case, a woman from Vaalbank, east of Pretoria, had been betrothed to her husband since 1940 and borne him seven children, but only finally married him in 1998, when her mother passed away and couldn't object: he had only paid ten of the twelve pledged cows. It's a pity that in 1998 her husband had already been dead for 25 years, but the woman duly went through the marriage ceremony with an urn containing his ashes.

Christopher expertly dodged a number of stray cattle roving on the road. Driving in Swaziland could inspire an unparalleled videogame: reach your destination manoeuvring around the bovines.

'What if one is hit by a car?' I asked, as we swerved to avoid an absent-minded specimen.

Christopher looked at me as if I was a little child.

'You worry about the car,' he said. 'It costs more than a cow.'

'So how do you find the owner to pay for any damage?'

'Ha! No one will admit to owning that cow, but everyone knows whose it was.'

In all Nguni languages, there are dozens of phrases to describe a cow's markings, the shape of its horns, its gait and demeanour in the same way that the Inuit have dozens of words for snow and the Italians hundreds of swearwords. A Swazi or Zulu shepherd can immediately tell which of his cows is missing, although he may not know how to count. And if you think that's a mean trick, the BaSotho of Lesotho do the same with *sheep*.

Cattle has been the bedrock of wealth amongst the peoples of southern Africa – as opposed to us in the West where ownership of land is paramount. From the Tsonga to the Zulu and from the Tswana to the Xhosa, life revolved around cattle: they provided milk and meat; their dung was fertiliser and fuel; their hides provided clothes and battle shields; their offspring provided the interest on capital and continued prosperity. The cattle corral, the *kraal*, became synonymous with the Nguni homestead, and cattle herding was a stepping stone to every teenage boy's ascent into manhood. More cattle meant more wives, more offspring and ultimately the creation of your own clan where you would reign like a chief. It meant more power over a larger area as other homesteads were granted cattle to look after. In European wars land changed hands: in African wars it was cattle that were appropriated to increase a chief's might. Europeans called such cattle raids 'stealing' and the perpetrators 'thieves'; yet, these very same Europeans called the plunder of the Ciskei the 'annexation' of British Kaffraria, because the land was held in common, without a solicitor's title deeds.

'What if a Swazi woman doesn't marry and doesn't have kids?'

'She becomes an 'auntie'. She looks after family children and her brothers look after her.'

'And what if a man doesn't marry or have children?' I asked.

'That *never* happens. He may not marry, but he will have children.'

'What if he doesn't like women?' I asked naively.

I might as well have shoved a red-hot poker in Christopher's butt, as he tried to visualise the unthinkable and verbalise the unmentionable.

'This is very, very rare,' he uttered after a long and uncomfortable pause.

Welcome to a traditional African society...

We reached a typical Swazi *kraal* at the same time as a party of five black IT professionals from Botswana's state telecoms company based in Gaborone. They were in Swaziland for a conference all week and this was their day off.

The village elder approached; I had been coached on what I had to say.

'*Sawubona*,' I said.

The big, tall, barefoot, semi-naked Swazi looked at me suspiciously.

'*Yebo*,' he replied, and waited.

'*Unjani*,' I said and stood my ground, a little bit worried.

The Swazi cracked up. 'You taught him that?' he asked Christopher in perfect English.

'Nah,' I remonstrated. 'This is a conventional London greeting.'

'Hahahahaha,' laughed the big Swazi holding his belly, although I didn't think it was that funny.

The village elder was called Albert. (*Albert?* How traditional was that?) He was the eldest son and was greeting us in place of his father who was absent. He showed us around the *kraal*.

'The first hut on the right next to the enclosure is the one for the unmarried girls. It's the *isigodlo*. It is the one closest to the entrance.'

Was there a reason, I wondered.

'It is so that the girls and their lovers can come in and out unnoticed early in the morning,' Albert replied, 'because if we catch the boyfriends, we have to kill them.'

Ahem, wasn't this a bit *hypocritical*?

Great peals of laughter emanated from Albert: 'Hahahahaha! You *are* funny.'

He walked towards the left where there was the boys' hut, next to the cows' enclosure. In the centre, there was the medicine man's hut with a stock of potions and herbs – the *kraal*'s pharmacy, if you like. Nguni societies still rely on such traditional medicine: the *inyanga*, the witch-doctor, throws bones on the ground to determine the causes of sickness. There is also the more personal physicianship of the *sangoma*, who goes through a trance process called *kubhula* to visualise a patient's sickness with the help of benign spirits. Such traditional healers – and Mbeki's government takes them so seriously that licensing legislation has been passed through parliament – have to spend years learning their art as apprentices and succumb to visions in the bush. (The Africans weren't at all surprised when they heard that the whites' topmost *inyanga* – Jesus Christ – had to spend forty days alone hallucinating in the desert.)

Finally, there is *umfembi*, and *Muti*, the black magic, where evil forces are invoked to cause illness and misfortune. Until late in the nineteenth century, the illness (or worse, the death) of a chief caused medicine men to seek and 'smell out' the person who was the cause. For this, communal help was at hand: everyone assembled in the allotted place and started chanting. Whenever the *inyanga* approached someone who was unpopular, the chanting became louder, so the *inyanga* knew that the victim was a safe choice. Victim? Well, yes – for the culprits were impaled with twelve-inch sticks and left to die a slow death in the bush. As a result, the Zulu, Swazi or Xhosa were generally averse to rising above others, enriching themselves or excelling in anything lest they became the object of envy and recipients of the twelve-inch stick up the backside. This was no culture to foster an entrepreneurial spirit, which goes some way to explaining the lack of will for self-improvement, so frowned upon by white settlers.

One of the Tswana guys butted in: 'These *sangoma*s – they tell you your future and how to get rich, but I ask you: why are they themselves poor? In fact so poor that they have to live off our donations?'

'Perhaps they are rich inside,' I ventured.

'Hahahahaha!' Albert was slapping his thighs. 'I like you,' he said. 'What's your name?'

Erm, John.

'So, John. This is my wife's hut,' said Albert.

Just one wife?

'My father has two wives only. I cannot do better than my father!' answered Albert, amazed at my insolence.

I see.

'And this is my girlfriend's hut,' continued Albert.

I knew it, I knew it. I knew there would be a way out!

'Hahahahaha,' laughed Albert again. 'What's your name – John? From now on you are The Funny One.'

I was touched.

Albert explained that the man has a separate hut from his wife and it is he who calls her to sleep with him; if he has more than one, they will have to await their turn.

'If I sleep with another woman, my wife asks all these questions. "Is she prettier than me?" You must always answer "Yes" to that, because otherwise she says: "So why did you go with her instead of me?" Then she asks things like: "How many times did you do it? How did you take her?"'

How did you take her?

'Yes,' answered Albert, puzzled. 'There are many ways of doing it to a woman. Hahahahaha, don't you know that in England?'

Dear, dear. Those missionaries seem to have failed in more ways than one. Didn't they teach them the only church-approved coitus position? The nodding Tswana forestalled my finger-wagging response by telling me how it was very similar in their country, until we found ourselves outside the cows' enclosure. Here men – only the men – enter to communicate with their ancestors, for only males have such powers.

How did he communicate with his ancestors, then?

'By smoking *dagga*.'

I could well imagine. And the police?

'If the policeman comes, then I tell my kids to take the policeman and give him beer, keep him busy, and say: "Mr Policeman, father is taking the cows in." By then I am finished with my smoke, and everybody is happy.'

I was impressed. No flushing of drugs down the loo. Not that there was a loo to flush anything down, of course.

'Marriages also take place here,' said Albert.

I was taken aback. In the cows' enclosure?

'*Yebo.*'

Marriages? Among these cowpats? No white bridal gowns, then.

'And this is the place where we teach the boys what to do,' said Albert, pointing at another fenced-off patch.

Did he mean the facts of life? The birds and the bees and all that?

'What birds and what bees? I teach him how to wake up every morning at four in the morning and boil hot water for his father,' Albert replied.

And how do the boys become men? Is there an initiation ceremony?

'There is, but I cannot tell you about that. The other men will kill me.' Albert said as the whole Ezulwini valley echoed his loud laugh.

This is certainly no joke. The Nguni circumcision ceremony lasts five weeks from the moment the *ingcibi,* the traditional surgeon, severs the foreskin, a few minutes after midnight, to the time when the wound is healed naturally and the boy emerges from a hut as a man. The initiate must stay in a hut with a fire permanently burning, dressed only in a red-and-white blanket.

The initiate is assigned a *khankatha*, a male nurse who looks after him and his wound, and a *nqalatha*, his boy servant. The initiate is not allowed to drink water for the first seven days to avoid urination. During that first week, he must stay in the hut and eat only samp, a maize flour concoction. He must not disgrace his family and seek Western medical attention even if the laceration turns septic. He must learn to communicate in isiSomo, the sacred initiation language which is kept secret.

On the eighth day, the men visit with a sacrificial goat and the initiate is allowed to go outdoors for the first time and drink water, though the rehydration is gradual, with *amaRhewu*, a watery pap. From then on, the initiate dresses and undresses his wound at regular intervals, and learns the correct responses to the riddles that will be asked of him by other men to determine if he has been through the proper ritual; to everyone but those who have been through the ceremony they will sound like gibberish, only deciphered by the ones in the know, like a secret handshake.

By the third week, the wound is scabby – if the *khankatha* is any good – and dries by being exposed to the wind. After about ten more days the scabs fall off and the healing is complete. Now the initiates can mix together, help a new batch of boys or return home proudly dressed as 'graduates', in a formal Western suit. They undergo the ritual questioning; if they don't answer correctly, forced inspection can take place immediately to check for hospital stitches. If any are found, the boys are punished; their shoes are swapped round and their clothes are turned inside out, their future disgrace guaranteed.

Casualties are many during botched circumcisions. Even if the wound, which is not treated with any pain-relieving drugs or antiseptics, doesn't get infected, dehydration sometimes effects permanent damage. But in a traditional African society, if you fail the test, you have been discarded by the ancestors: so your death – its real reason concealed from the authorities – was fully merited.

Albert took us to the principal assembly hut.

'It takes eight men two weeks to build a large hut like this,' said Albert. 'Constructed from natural materials, clay and thatch. Naturally air-conditioned. Cool in the summer, warm in the winter. This is where ceremonies, meetings and marriage negotiations take place.'

We sat down *à la Turque* on a floor made out of a mixture of dried cow dung and mud, men on the right, women on the left – one of the Tswana was a woman – while Albert's mum gave us some home-brewed sorghum beer called *umkombotsi*. There is an etiquette to be followed whenever a meal or a drink is taken: the males first, beginning with guests like me, women next and children last. The warm beer was nasty stuff but not nearly as foul as the soured milk, the *amasi*, we were offered from a calabash that was hanging from the rafters. Don't look around for fresh milk: it's considered only good for toddlers.

'This is like an embassy – a sanctuary,' said Albert. 'I can't beat my wife in here.'

Beat your wife?

'Yes, surely you beat your wives in England?'

I choked. Not as a rule, no.

Albert found this funny: 'Hahahahaha. You have to beat your wife to show her who is the boss. But if I beat my wife and she runs into this hut, I cannot hit her.'

Traditional African societies are *truly* no laughing matter.

Back in the car, Christopher resumed our tour of the Mbabane cultural 'sights' – for want of a better word.

'This is the Somhalo sports stadium,' said Christopher. 'One day the king woke up and he said he had a dream and that we must build a sports stadium. There it is.'

Erm, yes. Next.

'This is the statue of the last king, Sobhuza the Second.'

Right, OK, fine.

'This is the Lobamba royal village. This is where the king lives. You cannot take pictures here.'

A bunch of mean-looking guards waved us on.

The current Swazi king, the *Ngweniyama*, is Mswati III. He was in Britain, studying, when he was summoned to succeed his father in 1982. The old king, bless him, died at the age of 83, and by then he had 60 wives and 600 children. (Mswati III had already clocked twelve wives by the time I wrote this.) The successor is chosen by the royal family, and he has to be young, single and an only child to avoid sibling rivalry. If there are many such candidates (or none), the successor comes from a lineage with the fewest connections to the ruling Dlamini clan – I suppose this makes for a more eugenic mix. As a by-product of this process, along with choosing the king, the family also chooses a queen. As in other polygamous societies, such as the Ottoman, the queen is not the king's wife (far too many to choose from) but his mother. And – much like the Sultana – she wields directly and indirectly much power; for a start, she is regent until her son reaches the age of thirty. The queen is called *Ndlovukazi*, 'the Great She Elephant'. The name sounds funny in English because it's mistranslated. 'The Great Matriarch' would be closer to the intended meaning: in a group of elephants, the leader is the oldest and more experienced female, the top of the gene pool.

'This is the Parliament.'

I remained silent. In the first elections after independence, the royal Imbokodwo party won a hundred per cent of the seats. In the second election it lost two. That was bad news. King Sobhuza II suspended the constitution swiftly. Un-Swazi elements (namely opposition) had infiltrated Swazi society.

Christopher stopped the car.

'This is the museum, the *umsamo we siwe*,' he said as we got out.

I was the only person in the building, where a woman curator showed me around. I stopped in front of a large collection of cowhorns used to administer enemas. There must be something in such healing, since several cultures seem anally fixated where the causes of disease are concerned. Gandhi himself was a great believer in their efficacy, offering self-administered enemas to his guests as part of his hospitality. I would like to have been a fly on the wall when Lord and Lady Mountbatten visited him at home.

There were traditional weapons, cowhide shields, clubs to beat the enemy with and *assegais* to finish him off. On one side there were traditional men's loin cloths and lion skins made out of pelts joined at the right hip, and on the other, religiously separated, the women's clothes: skin skirts, loin aprons and hide cloaks.

Did people still wear these?

'Only for traditional ceremonies like the *Inc!wala*,' said the woman.

What was that? What did she say? How did she say that? '*Inc!wala*.'

This was my first introduction to the dental, alveolar and alveopalatal velar plosives, better known as 'Zulu clicks', which are remnants from the language of the original peoples of Africa, passed on to the Nguni tribes via the Bushmen, now more correctly termed the Khoi-San. There are three main ones: the X!- click, the C!-click and the P!-click and are impossible to describe in a European context; you have to hear them. The easiest is the C!-click, which sounds like a coachman's signal to gee up and start the horses: tongue smacking abruptly at the side of the mouth. The X!-click, which is how the word Xhosa is pronounced, is like the sound of a stutterer trying to pronounce a word like c-c-cola. As for the P!-click, this is an air-kiss, the muted parting of one's closed, slightly wetted lips.

Incwala – pronounced with a C!-click – is the first fruit ceremony when the king ritually tastes the first fruit of the harvest, in an echo of the Jewish festival of Shavuot (or Yom Habikkurim). The *Bamanti* (water people), in their ancient baboon headgear, collect foam from the Indian Ocean on a trek that lasts two weeks and return to the royal *kraal* greeted by sacred ceremonial whistles. The day after, virgin boys cut down the holy sicklebush, *lusekwane,* to make a sacred hut, the *inhlambelo,* in Ludzidzini. This is the Queen Mother's royal *kraal*, because it is she who is endowed with rainmaking qualities. (The current Queen Mother scoffed once at an insolent foreigner who was singing the praises of indoor plumbing. She is said to have boasted: 'If I need water, I issue the proper communication and the Heavens will open.')

On the third day a bull is ritually slaughtered and on the fourth the king, in full ceremonial dress, dances with his warriors and retires into the *inhlambelo* to taste the first fruit of the season and to ask for the ancestors' blessings upon the crops of the land. His bedding and other personal items are then ritually burnt to avoid them being stolen and used in black magic.

This ceremony is not to be confused with the famous *Umhlanga* reed dance, very popular with male backpackers, where maidens dance bare-breasted in front of the king displaying their wares in the hope that he will choose them and marry them. Such selection has now been made easier with the advent of the video recorder.

Yet it was face-to-face that King Mswati III met a beautiful eighteen-year-old, Zena Soraya Mahlangu, on 15 September 2002. She came from a middle-class background and was studying for her 'A' Levels. Her mother, Lindiwe Dlamini, was the communications manager of the Swazi Posts and Telecoms corporation. Zena found the king's attention flattering; unable to reach her whenever he wanted on her pay-as-you-go mobile, he bought her a brand new international roaming handset with a contract paid out of the royal coffers. But there is no such thing as a free lunch: Zena was forcibly summoned – the more accurate word is *abducted* – to service His Majesty.

Zena's family objected strongly. Her mother, Lindiwe, went to court to demand her daughter back in an act of *lèse majesté*. More diplomatically, Zena's grandmother, the Swazi minister for tourism, tried to get her back by approaching Queen Mother Ntombi: traditionally, the king could not marry twins or deformed women – and, ahem, did he know that Zena was a twin? (Ah, she was not an *identical* twin.) But the king could only marry virgins. Did he know that Zena had been going out with her boyfriend for two years? (Virginity? Who's a virgin nowadays in Swaziland?) The Queen Mother was unmoved.

And so it came to pass that three judges convened under Chief Justice Stanley Shapire who set a date for a hearing against the king's right hand man Quthuka Dlamini, named as the abductor. This was too much for the palace who assembled the Attorney General, the Chief of Security, the Police Commissioner and the Commander of the Army (if you are going to intimidate someone, do it properly) with a special mission: to visit the three judges and ask them either to resign or dismiss the case. The judges refused both and caused a constitutional stink. Amnesty International was gravely concerned at the Swaziland government's attack on High Court judges who were seeking to protect the rights of women. The Chief Justices of South Africa, Botswana, Lesotho, Namibia, Tanzania and even Zimbabwe (who relished being holier than thou) claimed that the palace action was a direct threat to the independence of the judiciary whose responsibility is to uphold the law without fear or favour.

The international furore and contempt scared the government of Swaziland; it even rattled Zena's mother, who didn't relish being cast in the role of Pandora. The result was a typical African compromise whose choreography involved several pirouettes and about-turns. Firstly, an apology was issued to the emboldened judges who had dared stand up to the king. Secondly, Queen Mother Ntombi presented Zena with ceremonial wedding attire – a beaded cloth with a portrait of the king – in a traditional engagement ceremony. Zena acquiesced and became the tenth official bride (a bride traditionally becomes a wife after she conceives a child). Zena's family stopped the proceedings. The High Court judges suspended the case indefinitely in the light of the engagement.

And everything returned to a semblance of normality.

'These are King Sobhuza's cars,' said the curator.

She turned the light switch on. I found myself in the middle of a car showroom crossed with Vienna's coach museum. Except that they were not works of art: these gas-guzzlers with four-litre engines and flat tyres were on display because they belonged to the last Swazi king. It started creeping up on me: a royal family that displays the cars of the last incumbent, a family that has suspended the democratic constitution under which Swaziland obtained its independence from Britain, a family that exercises enormous patronage, nepotism and power, is a family which may be relying upon 'traditional Swazi values' for its own convenience. Certainly this room with these old, useless Morris Ambassadors was straight out of a Bokassa scrapbook.

I got out in time to hear Christopher calling the curator 'Sissy'. Was that her name?

'My name is Lindi,' she replied.

'And I didn't know that, so I called her *sisi* – for sister,' responded Christopher.

I got it: 'And if you don't know the name of a guy you call him brother, is that correct?

'Indeed.'

How very Bronx.

'Unless he is older in which case I would call him father. Or if it's an old woman, mother.'

What would Christopher call me?

'You, I would call *sir*,' he said seriously.

As this was the end of the tour, I gave Christopher a large tip. 'That's towards your next cow,' I said. 'Get married soon.'

Christopher gave me the three-clasp black solidarity handshake: Western style, followed by a raising of the arms, a folding of the fingers around each other's thumbs and a return to Western style again.

Sala kahle.

13. Swaz song

I was sitting in my room in the Ezulwini Valley watching a Spurs game live on Sports TV; I was drinking a can of the local brew, Sibebe Special Lager, and munching unhealthily my Beeg-very-Beeg Bar-B-Q Corn Bites. The Ezulwini is a lush, green valley between Mbabane and Manzini, the two major Swazi towns; it is also the centre of the Swazi tourist industry, full of five-star hotels and luxury casinos. The Lonely Planet guide translates Ezulwini as 'A piece of Heaven', but now that I'm more familiar with the Zulu locative, I know it means '*in* Heaven'; it occurs in the first line of the Lord's prayer: 'Our Father who art in Heaven' – *Baba wethu os Ezulwini*. It is related to the word Zulu, who are the 'People of Heaven' – the Celestials, if you like.

Well, maybe I was in Heaven, but I was staying at the rather seedy Happy Valley Motel – a choice I made for many reasons. Firstly, it had a cheap weekend package. Secondly, it had Sports TV and would broadcast the Spurs game live. Finally, it was part of an isolated complex that included restaurants, cafés and Why Not?, the only club in Swaziland of any renown, where hotel clients had free entry.

Spurs predictably lost to Aston Villa; I flicked ill-temperedly through the Swazi *What's On*. What was I missing? There was a Belgian food promotion at the Royal Swazi Sun and a bingo evening at the Casino – were my Pretoria cockneys aware of such competitor penetration? There was a write-up of a 'Saturday Night Fever' disco in the Lugogo Sun Hotel – but no mention of Why Not? I wondered why, since I'd been told it was *the* place to be in Swaziland. I found out pretty quickly as I left my room, walked into the hotel foyer and saw the prostitutes.

Politically, Swaziland is a sordid, corrupt, undemocratic, repressive country, the sort which white South Africans point at, whispering, 'Should we have let ourselves become like that?' with understandable horror. Political parties are banned, and live ammunition is used to disperse political gatherings; the present king declared that 'political leaflets, like other litter, would spoil the environment'. Strikers are detained. The press is gagged and only occasionally resorts to oblique criticism of the government or the king, who is an absolute ruler.

Perhaps it is not clear why I am interested in Swaziland and its politics; it's because if one wants to examine the situation south of its border, one has to understand the fallback position of a traditional African society. This is the case of the Zulu, ostensibly 'modernised' within South Africa. Yet theirs is a society where the reed dance was revived in 1984, where oaths to King Shaka are taken, and where Inkatha 'heroes', pathetically clinging onto old traditions, run with clubs in military formation to hunt and kill political opponents.

You see, this is not just a chapter on Swaziland. This is an introduction to the mysterious, complex and frustrating politics of KwaZulu/Natal: *what would have happened if.*

The Swazi tribe was established in the region during the *mfecane* under King Sobhuza I of the Dlamini royal clan, which is still the ruling family. King Sobhuza I was followed by King Mswati II, who started conceding land to speculators for gold and diamonds in return for payment to the royal coffers. This was continued under the hapless King Ludvonga (ascended the throne at seven, poisoned at thirteen) and especially under the next king, Mbondzeni I. The Europeans asked him to sign papers he wasn't able to read and didn't quite understand. When he finally clicked, it was too late. The concessions weren't temporary as he had thought; they were permanent, the country had been sold off, and by 1907 the Swazis had nowhere to live. The problem was so big that Britain actually revoked many of these concessions so that the royal Dlamini family could have some land to reign over.

In 1921, King Sobhuza II was crowned and immediately challenged the legality of the foreign land deals. In a 1926 landmark case, *Sobhuza II v Miller and others*, the Privy Council decided that the concessions were legal and confirmed that the land does not belong to the Swazis. To his credit, the King devoted his life and resources to buying back his country. By the time of independence, in 1968, about two-thirds had been bought back. Since a large part of Swaziland still belongs to foreigners, conspiracy theorists point out that if democracy were to be brought to Swaziland, a Mugabe-style candidate might revoke those concessions; ergo, the survival of the current king and the status quo is of great benefit to Western capitalist concerns.

One of the obvious questions is how Swaziland escaped from being incorporated in South Africa. Make no mistake, the country was always being eyed by the Afrikaners. It is clear to figure out why: Swaziland is only about 50 miles from Maputo in Mozambique and tantalisingly close to the coastline of Natal. The landlocked Transvaal Republic needed access to the sea to avoid those prohibitive freight costs for the transport of its precious metals, and the Cape Colony was equally keen to block it.

In 1881, the Pretoria Convention in which Britain recognised the Transvaal Republic also guaranteed the independence of Swaziland. It was to be a buffer state between the Boer and the sea, and a buffer state it has remained since, though the temptation kept bubbling under. In 1894, another protocol was signed by both Britain and the Transvaal in which Swaziland became a Transvaal protectorate. The Boer war changed that. Britain, as the victor, claimed final authority over Swaziland which remained free of apartheid's tentacles: first a British protectorate, then a colony that was granted independence in 1968.

Yet apartheid touched upon Swaziland in a more sinister way: Dutch Reformed Church ethics did not allow for brothels, casinos or interracial sex. Enter Swaziland, the sexual and gambling playground for those South Africans who would indulge in the forbidden.

Black prostitutes, in their shiny, tight, skimpy dresses, long gazelle-like legs and protruding, impossible, 40FF busts outdo a drag queen any time. One of the girls with a dooza of a bosom, in a white leather mini skirt no longer than a wide belt, eyed me up and down, realised I was a newbie in the joint, walked up to me and ran her finger down the middle of my ribcage.

'Do you want a drink?' she asked.

'Are you buying me one?' I retorted.

She was stunned for a nanosecond which allowed me to walk away. When I looked back, she had recovered her composure and was even more interested in me – a client with a sense of humour!

Upon closer look, the prostitutes were relegated to a few areas of the Happy Valley complex: bars, corridors, disco. The eateries were thankfully free. I had what might arguably be the largest, tenderest and cheapest steak this side of Argentina at the Sir Loin restaurant and gulped down a bottle of a Chateau Libertas, a South African claret. Suitably stonkered, I left the restaurant and, like a hopping springbok, I avoided attempts by the ladies to caress *my* loin, as I made my way through. At the Why Not? disco the punters were checking in their guns at reception as if they were jackets in a coat-check.

There were few white faces inside – not that you could make out much in the low red light. The girls approached me one by one ('Do you want to talk? Do you want a drink? Do you want business?'), but they were surprisingly well behaved when rejected. White Belt was there, too, and smiled. I turned around and bumped into Clint from the Baz Bus.

'John,' he said surprised, 'What are you doing here?'

'I'm staying here,' I said. 'What are *you* doing here?'

'Oh, I… came for the disco,' Clint said unconvincingly, for he immediately went nudge-nudge on me: 'Have you been back there?'

'Back *where*?'

He pointed at a door with no handle and winked. I pushed it slowly and found myself in a strip joint where about a dozen men watched several bare-breasted female pole-dancers writhing voluptuously. A drunk, blond, British-pork-advert kind-of-guy put a wad of money into a girl's high-heel boots. She took off her panties and tossed them to him theatrically. He sniffed them, put them on his face, head poised back, and started munching. A few minutes later he spat them out and looked up puppy-like to the stripper. Feminists may bemoan the power disparity between women who work in the sex industry and their clients, and I will agree with their write-ups in theory, but there was no question who was in charge in practice. The stripper knew she could run rings around her man, as she casually took her long black leather gloves off. She baited him with one and then teasingly withdrew it. The porky guy breathed heavily, put his hand in his pocket and started grunting aloud. She waited and teased him more, but when she realised he was not going to tip her but was publicly masturbating instead, she left the stage imperiously while she was still queen.

I moved back to the main dancefloor. Someone rubbed himself against me. I looked back – a golden-ringed, rich Swazi was playing London Underground frottage with me. I shifted away instantly, as I spotted Clint nearby.

'Have you figured how it works?' Clint asked.

'How what works?'

'The girls. You know.'

'Clint, are you trying to enlighten me about sex?'

'No. The *system*.' Clint took one of my drink mats. 'You write your room number and the time on it, and you give it to her when you buy her a drink. Like "Number 4, 1.30". She will be there. The point is you walk out of the club separately – or the owners get a commission and it costs more.'

'I don't want to go to bed with one of the girls, Clint.'

'Not even with that one?' he asked.

I followed his gaze and my eyes met those of White Belt who started walking towards me.

It was my cue to flee.

By 1 a.m. the girls had found their clients and had gone. DJ Xtra Luv had started to play some deep house. Clint had disappeared. I saw White Belt move into the back of a trailer with three white men and a black Doberman that jumped on the front seat as the van roared into gear. It was then that the youth of Swaziland started crowding in, and the complexion of the club changed. On one side stood the Fellaz from the Suburbs, the *amaYos*, emulating American urban hip-hop in their phat-pharm outfits; on the other side danced the *amaTrompi* who are into South African township cool, identifying with their brothers across the border. At last, Why Not? was losing its sleaziness and was being transformed into a normal club – and a black African one at that. I danced happily in front of the stage with about a dozen white backpackers on a rafting trip and another four hundred-odd Swazis.

Now, why couldn't I do that in South Africa?

After the hubbub of Saturday night, the deserted Happy Valley complex had assumed the air of a ghost town. I jumped on a bus to the centre, but there wasn't much going on there, either: Sunday is not a great shopping day in Mbabane. I waded through benches of soapstone carvings and decorative glassware in the crafts shops that were still open. I resisted the temptation of the country's most famous export – the exquisite Swazi candles, blue and white twin spirals of thick beeswax – and bought a necklace fashioned out of painted coffee beans. I spied Danish Jørgen munching two large samosas in the pleasant and quiet Coronation Park, on a hillock opposite the expat Mbabane Club. I could imagine the ubiquitous retired colonel with the obligatory handlebar moustache sipping G&Ts and having the odd Dennis Thatcher moment with the staff. ('Waiter, did you put a lemon in my drink?' 'No, M'lud.' 'I say, I think I squeezed your canary in my gin.')

I sat down with Jørgen and smoked the joint he offered me. Out of the Sunday family strollers around us, no one seemed to mind and no one seemed to care. Certainly not the party of brown bulbuls that were twittering loudly as they pecked on the pungent-smelling, rotting fruit on our right. We sat there listening to their staccato cheedle-chaddle, which, given the state we were in, sounded Schubert-like in its tunefulness.

'I thought you were going to Maputo,' I said.

'Yeah, tomorrow. I have time. I haven't made any firm plans. Still in that dorm, I'm afraid.'

I told him that I hated that hostel.

'Yeah, it's the worst I've been to. The one in Jo'burg was like a palace. But the *dagga* is good.'

Dagga grows in Swaziland like weeds grow in English gardens. SCOSAD, the Swaziland Council On Smoking, Alcohol and Drugs, estimates that seventy per cent of farms in the area grow *dagga*. About once a month Swazi police ritually uncover an illegal shipment to Europe and then look the other way for thirty days. Europe is aflood with cheap Swazi hash, especially now that the land route through South Africa is open and sanctions have been lifted.

Jørgen and I walked around Mbabane aimlessly. We sat observing the impossibly old bangers of public buses leave the main station pursued by hawkers selling their mealies. Opposite the station there was a shopping centre, but in comparison with the ones in Pretoria it seemed not only insignificant in scale, but also lifeless; unlike Pretoria, here people lived outside the malls, not inside. But different countries, different problems: two weeks after I left town, a bomb was planted in that very same mall. It was the second bomb in a week. The first one was detonated on the route King Mswati III was expected to follow during an official function. He was, however, still far away at the time.

So is there any hope for Swaziland?

I shook my head. The Dlamini clan has got its tentacles everywhere. Following the death of King Sobhuza II, Prime Minister Sozisa Dlamini was appointed in 1982, (Foreign Minister: Richard V. Dlamini) followed by Prince Bhekimpe Dlamini in 1983 (tried for treason in 1987), followed by Mr Sotsha Dlamini in 1986, followed by Obed Dlamini in 1989 – the list goes on. His Excellency the Rt. Hon. Barnabus Sibusiso Dlamini is the PM at the time of writing along with three other Dlaminis holding ministerial positions. This is a major improvement on the previous government which contained no fewer than seven Dlaminis. Not everyone with the same surname is related directly to the royal family, but the connection is clannish and more sinister than the Oxbridge old school tie.

So I ask again: is there no hope for Swaziland? What about the big, powerful, newly democratic South African neighbour with Nelson Mandela as its beacon – and his daughter Zenani, whose full name is Zenani Mandela Dlamini. *Dlamini?* Yes, didn't you know? Zenani is married to Prince Thumbumuzi Dlamini, a brother of King Mswati III of Swaziland and the brother-in-law of Zulu King Zwelithini. Zenani and her husband have created a lobbying company, Mandela/Dlamini & Associates, whose direct access to South African business and political captains enabled them 'to build bridges between corporations and the international markets', as their website used to say. I'd advise a 'buy' in the shares of that company if it ever gets listed in the Johannesburg Stock Exchange.

Back in the hotel, there was no one in the pizzeria on a Sunday night, no one in the café, no one in the bar and no one in the disco. I supposed they were all, literally, shagged out. Bored, I took two beers to my room. I lay on my bed and read about the divorce of well-known athletic personality Sport Dlamini; I turned the radio on to relax and listened to *Killa Joe* by the young, talented and beautiful female Swazi singer Bongi – full name Bongiwe Dlamini.

Get me outta here.

Chapter Six

The Maid from Mozambique: St Lucia

Umntu ngumntu, ngabantu
('You become human through other humans')
Zulu proverb

14. Senkile

In 1864, Chancellor Otto von Bismarck started his three war campaigns which would result in a unified Prussian Germany by declaring war on Denmark over Schleswig-Holstein. The situation was so complex and confused that Schleswig-Holstein became a byword for a politically messy and incomprehensible quagmire. In the midst of it, Lord Palmerston, the prime minister at the time, gave the following answer to a parliamentary question regarding the crisis: 'There are three people in the world who could reply to this. Unfortunately one of them is dead, one of them is mad, and I have completely forgotten all about it.'

Just like that Rubik's cube of political complexity that doubles as a tinderbox, KwaZulu/Natal, I thought, as the Baz

Bus drove through a deeply green and fertile country with white acacia and sycamore trees, big torrential rivers and red, bountiful earth. From Trollope and Cecil Rhodes to the humblest backpacker, travellers have been taken in by the beauty of the Natal panorama and I was no exception. This is a beautiful place; no wonder it is full of battlefields. Boers, Brits, the Zulu: everyone has fought everybody else here.

I had better declare my hand from the beginning. Although there are innumerable scenic places in South Africa, everyone has a favourite – and I, for one, left my heart in KwaZulu/Natal, captivated by an ever-changing landscape, its edges sharpened by the long morning shadows formed by a glowing African sun. Forget Swaziland, forget the Kruger: it was in the blistering emptiness of the highway to Hluhluwe with cattle grazing unperturbed outside the Zulu *rondavels* – those circular beehive huts with conical thatched roofs dotting the countryside – that I actually *felt* I was in Africa.

As if to emphasise the point, Senkile, our Zulu driver, braked sharply and pointed at the side of the road. 'A black mamba,' he said, as the snake quickly disappeared in the bushes, head lifted about a foot from the ground.

Some useless facts about black mambas:
1. *Black mambas are not black – at best they are metallic in colour.*
2. *They will attack any person standing in their path and then deliver a large amount of poison via multiple bites. It is this that makes them so lethal.*
3. *How lethal? Will twenty minutes do you?*
4. *Dying from a mamba bite is actually quite pleasant. The poison puts you to sleep and you die relatively painlessly after having fallen unconscious.*

Senkile was twenty-eight with a proud, shiny goatee and an even prouder, shinier bicep musculature; as far as riches go, he was a man of seven cows. We hit it off from the beginning.

'Seven cows?' I asked. 'Who's looking after them?'

'Before, I have ten cows,' he said with pride. 'Last year I sell three to build a house for my parents in Gingindlovu. They are looking after my cows there.'

He paused.

'Before, we have land,' he said with no emotion. 'To grow sugar cane.'

Ah, the old staple crop: sugar cane was introduced to Natal in 1848 by British settlers from Mauritius and soon became the colony's biggest success story.

Senkile continued: 'Then I move to KwaMashu – you know KwaMashu?'

One can trace the footprints of this sugar cane past in the unlikeliest of places. One of the sugar magnates was Sir Marshall Campbell, who owned a lot of land in the north of Durban. 'Marshall's place', *kwaMarshall,* has been corrupted into KwaMashu, one of the roughest townships in South Africa with a history of gang violence since the 1980s, when it was a no-go area even for the apartheid security machine.

'It's the township north of Durban,' I replied.

'Correct.'

'So what happened to your land?' I asked.

'My parents become too old,' Senkile replied in his permanent present tense. 'They cannot work the sugar cane. It is hard work. So, we take farm hands. But they steal the fertiliser. We spend so much on the fertiliser, but they sprinkle a bit on the edges and steal the rest. No sugar cane. Cows are easy to handle. I trust them more than people.'

'Seven cows,' I ruminated. 'You're not married yet, then.'

'No, I marry when I am thirty-four.'

I giggled.

'You've got it all sussed out, Senkile,' I said.

'What do you mean "sussed out"?'

'I mean sorted out. Why exactly thirty-four?'

'Because you have to help your family. Correct?'

I shrugged my shoulders. 'If you say so.'

'Here we help our families. I have three more brothers who are alive. Before a few years, one of my brothers die. I support one to go to university. He can be a doctor now. When he finish, I am thirty-four.'

'And then you'll marry.'

'Correct. Then *he* help *me*.'

'And you're supporting your family and buying cows and helping your brother with his studies all from this job? As a Baz Bus driver?'

'Correct.'

'Do you like it, then?'

'Yes, I like it. I have freedom, the pay is good. I meet many interesting people. Nice people. Nice *white* people.'

The Zulu perceive themselves as uniquely as do the Afrikaners: a noble tribe that rises above the rest. Unlike, say, the native Indians of South America who succumbed to the Jesuits, the Zulu had their own exalted history to draw upon and feel superior. To the Zulu the various proselytising reverends were as annoying as our own millennial wacko cults. In the nineteenth century, it was the Christians who were the Moonies in Natal, and many a convert was recovered from the missions by an angry family and dragged back to the *kraal*.

In resisting Christian missionary activity, the Zulu achieved the impossible: they converted the converters. Bishop Colenso of Natal was subjected to an intelligent grilling by a Zulu, William Ngidi, who was helping him translating the Bible into siZulu in the 1850s. Ngidi could not take the Bible so literally, and made Colenso think twice. In fact, Colenso thought so many times that in 1862 he published a five-volume theological work, called *The Pentateuch and the Book of Joshua Critically Examined*, in which he proves the impossibility of many biblical claims. As Bishop Colenso explains himself in the preface to his book:

While translating the story of the Flood [into siZulu] I have had a simple-minded, but intelligent, native – one with the docility of a child, but the reasoning powers of mature age – look up and ask, 'Is all that true? Do you really believe that all this happened thus – that all the beasts, and birds, and creeping things upon the earth, large and small, from hot countries and cold, came thus in pairs, and entered into the ark with Noah? And did Noah gather food for them all, for the beasts and the birds of prey as well as the rest?' My heart answered in the words of the Prophet, 'Shall a man speak lies in the name of the Lord?' Zach. xiii. 3. I dared not do so.

According to reports of the period, the book caused more public debate than Darwin's *The Origin of Species*. The reaction of *The Times* was scathing: '*The spectacle of a bishop rushing in hot haste across 6,000 miles of ocean to proclaim his spiritual overthrow by the first barbarian he encountered in his savage diocese, has proclaimed a mixture of feelings in which gravity does not generally predominate.*' So, next time someone asks you, 'What did the Zulu ever contribute to civilisation?' you have the answer: the first chink in the armour of the Bible belters.

No mean feat.

More people got on at Kwabonambi, where we stopped by Cuckoo's Nest. This is a hostel that boasts a genuine tree house for two persons, so popular it has to be booked well in advance.

'Does the Baz Bus ever get overcrowded?' I asked Senkile.

'A few times,' he said.

'And what happens then?'

'The people with no bookings must get off.'

I thanked my lucky stars I had chosen to sit at the front with Senkile.

'Are you married?' he suddenly asked me.

'No,' I replied.

Senkile shook his head.

'Here, you marry and you marry for life. You know Winnie Mandela?'

'Of course I know Winnie Mandela.'

'When Nelson Mandela die, she is there in the funeral. She is his wife forever.'

Since the subject had turned to politics...

'Are you ANC or Inkatha?'

'ANC. Zulu who live in towns are ANC. Country Zulu are Inkatha.'

'Have you been involved in any clashes?'

He looked at me.

'That is how I lose my brother,' he said and fell silent.

The nine million Zulu are the largest ethnic group in South Africa: roughly, out of four South Africans one is a Zulu; in contrast, only one out of eight is white. As might be expected from such a numerous minority, the Zulu were at the forefront of the struggle for equal rights. In 1960, Albert Luthuli, a Zulu chief and president of the ANC, was the first South African to receive the Nobel Peace Prize. It is ironic that a country with such bloody history can claim four such honours: Albert Luthuli; Desmond Tutu; and finally Nelson Mandela who shared his with F. W. de Klerk. And yet, thirty years after the bestowing of that first Nobel Prize on a Zulu chief, an estimated 14,000 people died across South Africa in the 1990–1994 township violence involving the Zulu and the rest of the black ethnic groups. There was a danger that KwaZulu/Natal would secede from the Republic. Something had gone terribly, terribly wrong.

Explaining recent history is more challenging than playing kiss-me-quick with a black mamba, but hell, everybody will get it wrong for another hundred years, anyway, so there.

When Luthuli died suddenly, he left the Zulu nation leaderless. Slowly but surely, a split occurred within the black resistance movement. Luthuli was a man committed to negotiation, but its new leadership – Nelson Mandela, Govan Mbeki, Walter Sisulu – was Xhosa and more militant, causing the Zulu to start mumbling about the existence of a *Xhosa Nostra*. One wonders if the Zulu were ever going to be a willing partner of an institution they did not directly or indirectly control, like the Americans do today with the UN: they cooled off instead and formed their own organisation, Inkatha.

Inkatha is a charged word in Zulu. It literally means a coil woven by grass and worn on the head so that heavy objects can be carried. But in a society that still believes in the supernatural, reveres its ancestors and considers itself superior because of its triumphant warlike past, *Inkatha* is laden with historical significance. Zulu warriors prepared for battle with a religious passion the world had not seen since the samurais of the Heian period. They feasted; they danced; they sang; they went through magic rites; they drank powerful potions that made them vomit to cleanse them internally. The brave warriors communally threw up on top of a grass coil which absorbed their spewed-up fluids. This was the *Inkatha*, which to the Zulu was a cross between a West African *fetih* personifying the might of the nation and a Jewish Ark of the Covenant with its overtones of devotion, ritual and bond with the past. It must have stunk like nothing on this planet.

After the British won the Zulu war, they destroyed the *Inkatha* (plus its sacred excreta) and the name remained in abeyance until 21 March 1975, when a fresh-faced Chief Mangosutu Buthelezi – his recognition factor high after starring with Michael Caine in the film *Zulu* – started a cultural organisation, the Inkatha National Cultural Liberation Movement. The organisation tried to sever the Zulu nation from the main body of the ANC by fuelling a resurgence of petty nationalism propelled by the thrust of King Zwelithini back to the fore of Zulu consciousness and the revival of ancient customs like the reed dance. Buthelezi's main disagreement with the ANC-in-exile was the latter's policy of armed struggle. The old, non-violent legacy of Luthuli was reinterpreted as a coming to terms with Pretoria. The aims were the same with the ANC (universal suffrage), but the Inkatha strategy (*rapprochement*) different.

Buthelezi was against sanctions and was more anti-Communist than guerrilla fighter. He made tactical mistakes such as misreading the Soweto uprising and accepting Pretoria money. ANC and Inkatha tried to patch up relations in London in October 1979, but failed – terminally so. This bitter split and the ensuing unbridgeable abyss of feud and counter-feud would cost more lives than the ANC's armed struggle itself.

The apartheid government was quick to exploit Inkatha as an ally against internal insurrection, and wooed Buthelezi. At the height of ANC violence, Inkatha requested 'offensive' capacity from the apartheid government as a 'protective' objective. Two hundred Inkatha men landed at the Caprivi Strip in Namibia where they were instructed by government forces; the aim of the operation was to train Inkatha supporters so that the organisation, fired by years of hatred against the ANC, could engage in state-sponsored terrorism. Inkatha targets were approved jointly by the apartheid government's Directorate of Special Tasks with approval at the highest level. A security structure was set up to act as a cover for the Inkatha persecution of ANC undesirables: the trainees were issued with ID cards that identified them as employees of private security companies, or as members of the KwaZulu/Natal police. This was all cloak-and-dagger stuff: when one conscientious Durban police commissioner, Lt. Gen. Roy During, suspected that in one particular case his own forces under Brigadier Mzimela were involved in death squad activity, he tried to have the Brigadier transferred. Mzimela protested directly to Chief Buthelezi who summoned During to his office and asked him to explain himself.

Unsurprisingly, Inkatha were not invited in the 'talks about talks' between the ANC and F. W. de Klerk. It took Nelson

Mandela one year after his release to meet Chief Buthelezi, a rare political mistake, because it encouraged recidivist elements to set one resistance movement against the other. Policy differences were subsumed in the ethnic conflict that claimed Senkile's brother. As another Zulu proverb goes, *'a thorn in the foot is removed only by another thorn'*.

15. Rudy

We reached Bib's International Backpackers simultaneously with the Baz Bus coming north from Durban. I spotted the other driver: it was Khamesh. He was panicky as usual, but this time he had a good excuse.

'I was carjacked,' he said.

We fell quiet.

Khamesh looked at me.

'Remember the cash I collected on Friday on the bus to Swaziland from the people who paid me on the spot?'

I did.

'The banks were closed over the weekend. This morning, before we started our pick-ups, Richard, my boss, and I went to deposit the cash in a bank in Durban. At a robot, three armed men jumped in. They asked me to drive on and hand over the money. It was 5,000 rand.'

Oh, shit.

'Then they threw me out and drove off with Richard still inside.'

Oh, shit.

'I went back to HQ, called the police and picked up another bus. That's why we're late.'

As the northbound backpackers started climbing in, I wasn't sure whether it was the event itself or everyone's casual acceptance of it that was the more frightening.

And what happened to his boss?

'Just found out on my cellphone. They were driving out of town and would have killed him. He jumped off while the car was running. He's all right.'

And the carjackers?

Khamesh shrugged his shoulders. 'I don't know. But,' he said, anticipating everyone's question, 'no backpackers were affected.' He sat behind the wheel. It was time for both buses to leave in opposite directions. I shook hands with Senkile.

'I hope to meet up again,' I said.

Senkile took a pen out of his pocket and wrote down his mobile phone number.

'I am in KwaMashu in the weekend,' he said. 'If you want, call me.'

'What – you'll take me out and about in a township?'

'Correct.'

'Won't it be dangerous for me?'

'Not if you are with me and my friends.'

And with that he, too, boarded his bus and drove off. I turned to the big, bubbly redhead at the hostel's reception. Her name was Estelle.

'No more rooms, I'm afraid,' she said. 'You're too late…'

Damn that carjacking story!

'… but I have something even better. We've just finished cleaning out our other house a few blocks up. Do you mind living alone?'

I jumped at the chance. Estelle drove me those few blocks up to a six-bedroom modern bungalow with a large, sparkling kitchen, still being cleaned by a teenage maid. It had half an acre of a garden, a *braai*, several *chaises longues* to lie on, two showers, two toilets, a megaset of a television and it was all mine for 40 rand a night. That is £4 to you.

'Some of the rooms are not done yet. Choose one and ask the maid to give you the bedding and the towels,' said Estelle. 'Come to the Oasis down by the hostel at night. I'm behind the bar,' she added and left with my verbal booking for an excursion to Cape Vidal next morning.

I walked around the house not believing my luck, as the maid showed me various rooms. What was her name?

'Nomza,' she said quietly, not looking up.

Was she a Zulu?

'No. I come from Mozambique,' she replied, head still down, as if this were a crime.

Which room should I take? I couldn't make up my mind; such a wide choice – decisions, decisions.

Nomza looked up. 'Take this one,' she pleaded. 'It is done already.'

I looked at her petite, overworked figure and agreed quickly.

My luck was too good to last. An hour after I arrived in the empty hostel-cum-private-villa a Belgian couple pulled up in their car. I needn't have worried, though. You know how sometimes you share a house with strangers and you get on fine and then you go on holiday with your best friend and wreck a lifelong friendship over spilled conditioner? The Belgians and I got on like a *rondavel* on fire: no one ate each other's snacks, no one used each other's bog roll, no one drank each other's beers and no one had to wait to use the toilet. With two toilets for three people that would be difficult, I concede, but like some girls who live together and tend to menstruate in tandem, some flatmates also seem to synchronise their bowel movements. Well, *we* didn't.

We also didn't invade each other's space: they watched TV at night, while I retired to the Oasis. On my first night there, the open-air bar was empty; there was only one customer talking to Estelle. As soon as I ordered a beer, he told Estelle to put it on his tab. Now that's the way to my heart; what was his name? Rudy?

Rudy was an awesome sight. He was a big bear of a Boer with a neck the size of my thigh and a boyish face – the word 'hunk' was invented to describe him. He was a stereotypical tough-and-proud Afrikaner: ex-police force (dog trainer division) ex-army, firearm enthusiast – the type who would call a spade a *fokken shovel*. He would feel at home amongst Montana survivalists, Vietnam vets or Strangeways prison wardens. We had absolutely nothing in common, a fact that grew even more apparent as the night went on, and we became

more drunk. In theory we should have parted abruptly –
probably after a fight in which Rudy beat me to a pulp.

In theory.

'I'm twenty-five and I've done everything dangerous,'
boasted Rudy. 'I've done mountaineering, hang-gliding,
parachute jumping, deep sea fishing, big game hunting – you
name it.'

'What do you prefer?'

'Fishing. There's nothing more thrilling than holding onto a
big tuna for hours, trying to control it while it fights for its
life. Your arms must be strong. Sometimes you feel they'll
come out of their sockets – but when you win and the fish
finally lets go, you feel *invincible*.'

A whiff of soft ocean breeze punctuated that last word.

'I also used to be a guide for hunting parties in the Northern
Transvaal. Private reserves. People pay thousands of dollars
to kill one of the Big Five.'

'I didn't know that sort of thing still went on.'

'Oh, *ja*, of course, it does,' he said. 'But not with guns. I
lead parties who hunt *properly*. With bow and arrow.'

I was stunned.

'That's the latest 'in' thing. Bow and arrow. Like the Kalahari
Bushmen did 40,000 years ago. You and a big elephant and you
don't get too many tries.'

'You can kill an elephant with an *arrow*?'

'You have to hit it on the right spot. I tell my clients where
to aim at.'

I bought the next round wondering whether Rudy was taking
the piss.

'Or take a rhino. I escorted a woman once. She was a
champion medallist in archery. She shot down a charging rhino
in one.'

'Surely that's dangerous,' I said.

'*Ja*, and that's why I don't take just *anybody* hunting with
bow and arrow. They have to pass rigorous tests in a shooting
range. *And* they sign a disclaimer.'

'Has anything ever gone wrong?' I asked.

'A hippo, once. It's difficult to kill, because its skin is so thick. The guy missed and the hippo starting running towards us with its mouth open. Those teeth can cut you in half, you know.'

'So what did you do?'

'I took out my elephant gun and blasted the bastard.'

'THAT'S HARDLY FAIR!'

'Hey, I'm responsible for my clients. *They* hunt with a bow and arrow. *I* have an elephant gun.'

I wondered if he played rugby. He was built like he should be.

'I played for the Transvaal under-21s when I was sixteen,' he said. 'I broke my knee though – it got smashed to bits, and I can't play again. When it gets cold, and it gets cold there in the winter, it hurts. That's why I moved to St Lucia. It's never cold here.'

Rudy had moved to St Lucia three months ago. He'd resigned his post with the South African Police Force and became a supervisor in a St Lucia private protection firm. Two limited companies effectively manage the security in the resort. When we entered with the Baz Bus, we had to pass through a manned swing-down 'boom' gate.

'*Ja*, that was us,' Rudy said. 'There's hardly any crime here. You might have four car break-ins in a week. Compare that with Pretoria where you have seventy-five in a weekend. There would be no incidents whatsoever, because our Zulus play ball, but nearby in Dugudugu there is this large *dorp* of Mozambican refugees. Full of *fokken* thieves.'

Estelle joined in and poured us two whiskies – on the house. I was getting as soused as a maraschino cherry, and I'm proud to proclaim that Rudy had difficulty following me. In Britain, always expecting the last orders bell, we have learned to consume alcohol faster than any other nationality – except maybe the profusely sweating Australians who need to replace their liquids rapidly for purely genetic reasons.

Was Rudy married?

No, but he was going steady with Estelle's flatmate. Tonight was their designated singles night out alone. I told him that Monday doesn't count.

'You're thinking like a city man. Every day counts in St Lucia,' Rudy said, and maybe he had a point.

'You don't live together, I take it?'

'I live with my dog,' Rudy replied. 'When I left the police I took my dog with me. They want it back and they're suing me. Let them sue me. I will keep the dog.'

Was it one of those mean police dogs?

'*Ja*, he's a German Shepherd. I can take him to the bar with me and he's very docile. But if you ever come to my house for a drink, don't run towards me. He'll rip you to shreds.'

Charming.

'Do you own a gun?'

'Not just one.' Rudy droned on to describe his firearm collection, but he might as well have been talking about the National Party manifesto in the original Afrikaans, for I understood zilch.

'Have you ever used it to shoot at anyone?'

Rudy looked at me with glazed eyes: 'Forty-two times.'

Estelle walked away.

'Have you ever *killed* anyone?' I asked.

The resulting silence was the longest spell of quiet with Rudy who never answered my question. I still don't know how much was truth and how much was braggadocio, because by then Rudy was struggling to keep his poise.

'I'm so pissed,' he kept repeating. 'I'm so pissed. *Vrotdronk*. I need someone to take me home.'

He used his mobile to call the duty policeman for a ride.

'It's a company perk,' he said with a grin. 'What are you doing tomorrow?'

'I'm going to Cape Vidal,' I said.

'I'll be going there, too, with my boss,' said Rudy drunkenly. 'Hey, come with us.'

Estelle put him in his place.

'I've booked him on the tour, Rudy,' she said sharply. 'He's going with Beatrice.'

A woman safari guide. Interesting.

We heard a car arrive.

'See you there, all right?' he said, as he staggered to the door.

'Won't you get a lift with Rudy?' asked Estelle.

'I'll have a last one for the road,' I said smugly, to make a point.

As I crawled home later, I realised that I couldn't stop myself liking those Afrikaners. Maybe it's because their faults are hanging out prominently for everyone to witness, and they are easily and quickly peeled off to uncover a soft and often charming interior. Or maybe we tend to fall for the flawed characters.

Even God was a sucker for His prodigal son.

16. Beatrice

An open-top vehicle with about ten people picked me up next morning. A large, corpulent driver with a thick, black moustache stepped out.

'Hello, I'm Beatrice,' he said.

Perhaps it was too early. *'Beatrice?'* I repeated.

'Ja.'

'How do you spell that?'

'P-E-T-R-U-S,' he replied. 'Beatrice.'

I see.

St Lucia is a wetland, as big as the Okavango delta, but with a unique feature: a set of forested sand dunes facing the Indian Ocean. It has been described as 'Africa's largest coastal lagoon', spread over 135 square miles and includes a lake connected through a channel to the Indian Ocean. Four rivers flow into the lake and in the wet season the flow is outwards; but in the dry season, the sea water flows in and there are parts of the lake with a salinity three times higher than that of the ocean itself. There is a battle currently taking place on three fronts. There are the environmentalists and UNESCO backed by the tourist industry, who want to preserve the region; this was the first conservation area in South Africa's history dating from 1896. Against them stand the indigenous population who want to return to their ancestral grounds like in the Kruger Park – they can already legally fish in the St Lucia lake – who are backed by local politicians. And there is big business, backed, well, by big business, who want to mine the rare titanium and zirconium metals: St Lucia is so full of titanium that you can see the metal's grey oxides dusting the dunes of Cape Vidal. The battle is still raging, but UNESCO seems to be winning.

The Greater St Lucia Game Park contains many habitats: mangroves, open rolling grassland, casuarina trees (another Aussie export) plus marsh, reed and sedge swamps – a perfect breeding ground for crocodiles. But it's the dune forests that are unique to St Lucia: they have grown over the centuries, seeded from thicket that formed around birds' nests. Although the salt from the sea has stumped the growth of the eastern-facing trees, the ones that are sheltered more than compensate in size. There are white milkwoods, whose bark infusion is said to prevent nightmares, sweet-thorn acacias, tall water drypetes trees whose fruit is used for an alcoholic drink, fungi, moss, and *hluhluwe* thorny ropes, a kind of local liana, which gave their name to the reserve next door.

Sodwana and Kosi Bay to the north are a paradise for snorkellers and divers; here in Cape Vidal it was windy, the sea was rough and our attempts at snorkelling were a total failure, but at least the Indian Ocean was warm enough for a soak to clear my head after the previous night. I let the waves stroke my body as I watched those silliest of birds, the dikkops, wading on the beach. The dikkop looks like a chicken drawn by a toddler and it runs with its long stick-like legs along the sand like a surfer who's pissed inside his wetsuit.

Beatrice prepared a hake fish *braai* with an aromatic home-made apricot and garlic sauce, while vervet monkeys hopped and caught the flying ants around us. They mixed freely with the rare sangoma monkeys which only live in this area, every single one carefully tagged with a red label. There weren't many cars around, so I easily spotted Rudy and his boss who were lying on two portable armchairs, feet resting on their fishing rods. Rudy and I surreptitiously checked each other for signs of hangover; we were both wearing them well.

Beatrice was surprised I knew Rudy already. 'Are you also coming to that paintball battle next week?' he asked. 'Rudy's organising it.'

'No,' I said. 'I won't be here.'

'Good for you. Rudy uses automatic weapons. They throw paintballs like machine guns – and, boy, do they *hurt*. After the last game I was bruised for weeks.'

Later in the afternoon, our group hiked on the Mziki trail; Beatrice was barefoot throughout. 'Like the Zulu,' he said, 'you move quicker without shoes'. Although the trails of St Lucia are quite dangerous with crocodiles, hippos and roaming rhinos, what *really* terrified us were the giant millipedes. Red-striped and big as an adult's hand, they were hanging around us like grapes. It was the mating season and they were engaged in orgies of four upwards, twisting and writhing and gross beyond belief.

The Mziki trail was pullulating with birdlife, even if it was flapping away scared by our appearance: you could spot eagles, storks and herons, gulls, kites and terns, and the colourful hadeda ibis with its green back, blue tail and red feet. It was another ibis, though, that caught our eye: the two-tone sacred ibis. This is a bird that has been found mummified in Egyptian tombs; it represented the god Thoth because its annual arrival coincided with the flooding of the Nile. It is a species that has been worshipped by a whole civilisation, and it was easy to see why: this bird with the black-and-white plumage walks the muddy shores with a self-confident, cool poise, verging on the spiritual.

We reached the Mfazana Pan, a clearing where a pod of hippos were bathing. One was unusually hostile, baring its jaws at our direction. Its teeth were sharp like lances and curved like a bushbuck's horns, adorning a yawn to match a Great White's. We were hidden behind a reed wall, weren't we safe? They couldn't see us.

'They can smell us,' Beatrice said. 'The wind is blowing towards them.'

After about five minutes, another hippo came up to breathe from underneath our aggressive friend.

'They're mating!' cried Beatrice. My zoom lens snapped to attention, but all the action was all below water. Hippo porn must be the most boring of mating home movies.

Let's finish the trail with...

Some useless facts about hippos:

1. *Their teeth are pure ivory, considered by the experts to be of better quality than the elephant's.*
2. *More humans are killed by hippos in Africa than by any other animal. They attack primarily when the person is between them and the water, which means many African women and children fetching water from a river are attacked and killed. Disney's* Fantasia *has a lot to answer for by presenting the hippo as a large, cuddly animal dancing clumsily to Poncchieli.*
3. *A yawning hippo is trying to intimidate you. If you see one on land, quickly go climb a tree.*

Back at the hostel Nomza had washed my clothes; they were hanging out to dry. I asked her how much she wanted. She didn't answer immediately, trying to put a monetary value on her work that she could inflate without offending me.

'Thirty rand,' she said after a while.

The Belgians looked at me, their eyes saying no.

'OK,' I said and gave her the money. True, it sounded a bit too much, but I wasn't going to haggle over such small amounts. I later found this was Nomza's daily wage.

'*Fala português?*' I asked.

No, she hardly spoke Portuguese. Nomza was a refugee: her parents had emigrated when she was young to avoid the conflict in nearby Mozambique. South Africa was the country she'd been brought up in, and she spoke mostly Zulu. I invited her to stay with us for *braai*. I was naive, because she had to leave to reach her village. Only the hawkers remain in St Lucia overnight, sleeping at their coveted posts along the main street, for if they leave, they lose their business.

The Belgian guy interrupted, pointing at a black, bulbous bird flapping around the central *stoep* light, chasing the moths.

'*Intengu,*' pronounced Nomza, providing us with the Zulu name for the fork-tailed drongo, a fat swallow that thinks it's a crow. This wonderfully named bird is one of Nature's late sleepers, still agile up to ninety minutes after dusk. If the early bird catches the worm then the evening drongo catches the moth.

I turned to Nomza again. Was she happy with her life here after the 'changes'?

She chose her words carefully, maybe translating mentally into English. Every time she stalled before responding; she hesitated so long that you'd forget the question. When she finally answered this one, she said she liked the changes because tourists came.

'I like my job, but what I really want is to be a waitress.'

'A waitress?'

A pause ensued long enough for me to finish my beer.

'This is a dream job for people in Dugudugu.'

'Why?'

Nomza knew this was coming and had the answer ready: 'Tourists give big tips,' she said. 'I want to be a waitress, in the new Wimpy, to get big tips. But I have to speak good English.'

Nomza not only spoke some broken Portuguese, not only did she speak Zulu, but she was also learning English to get a better job. She was typical of many in the black population who routinely speak two or three languages. This linguistic ability was a thorn to the prevailing colonial mentality that considered the African mind inferior. Amazingly, or perhaps not so amazingly, colonists noted but discarded any fact that did not fit their prejudices.

The *braai* was good and the wine even better. I sifted through the Belgians' travel photos of palatial campings and finally of the animal that had eluded me.

'Can't understand how you've missed the rhinos,' they said. 'In Hluhluwe we had them grazing next to our car.'

Some useless facts about rhinos:

1. *Yes there are black and white rhinos, but don't try to distinguish by their colour – their colour is the colour of the mud they last wallowed in.*
2. *Powdered rhino horn is supposed to be an aphrodisiac because rhino coitus lasts for half an hour or more. They seem to be one of those animals that are perpetually in heat.*
3. *Rhinos have their own private loos. They tend to defecate in the same place but they spoil it by kicking around the dung to mark their territory. The jungle is a dangerous place in more ways than one.*

Like a drongo myself, I was reluctant to leave the Oasis, sipping the compulsory nightcap with Estelle who wouldn't let me walk home alone.

'I was told off by Rudy for not giving you a lift myself yesterday. It's dangerous to walk around here.'

'Why?' I asked. 'Because of the Zulu hawkers sleeping rough in the street? They're harmless.'

'No – because of the hippo.'

'The what?'

Estelle told me of the marauding hippo from the river who had started to enter the edge of town at night. It had been seen by quite a few residents recently without any incident, but it was getting braver by the minute, venturing further and further in. As we were in a national park, they couldn't kill it until it presented a threat. *Nah* – I was sure Rudy was lurking in some bush with his elephant gun just waiting for the hippo to attack so that he could blast the beast to smithereens.

Which meant I was safe.

17. *Nomza*

I had better describe the incident minute-by-minute.

I woke up early, hung over and not quite there (yes, those details are important) in time to go to the Tourist Information Office to check out the various excursions on offer. At the office, an elderly lady looking like a benign version of Mary Whitehouse chatted with me for half an hour about this and that before she made a suggestion.

'You can take a boat, *The Spirit of St Lucia*, and travel in the estuary for about three hours. It's a very interesting trip. There is one leaving at eleven o' clock today.'

I checked my watch. It was half past nine. I paid for the ticket in the tourist office with my last cash. *My last cash!* I needed to change some money. Were there any banks open?

'The bank is open for foreign exchange on Monday, Wednesday and Friday mornings,' replied Mary Whitehouse.

Today was Wednesday.

'You can go now,' she added, 'before you catch the boat.'

I ran back to the hostel. The Belgians were still in bed. I barged into my room, took out five twenty-pound notes out of my moneybelt and sped out of the house without acknowledging Nomza, who was washing the dishes in the kitchen. Halfway through I realised I didn't have my binoculars with me; no point starting a nature trip without them. I had to dash back. Damn, it was already quarter past ten.

I searched frantically for my key outside the bungalow door. Where was it? So many pockets in my combats. There it was, right at the bottom. I pulled it out and some hankies fell on the ground – no time to pick them up. I unlocked the door. Nomza greeted me, reticent as ever. She had been in all along – I could have rung the bell! I ran to my room and looked around for my binoculars. There they were! I picked them up and dashed out. I arrived at the bank ten minutes later.

Except that the five twenty-pound notes had vanished from my pocket.

I thought in a flash: could I have been pickpocketed? But no one had come near me.

The hankies! The money must have fallen out when I was looking for my key.

I returned home for the third time and looked around the courtyard. Nothing. Maybe in my room? Nothing. The kitchen? Nothing.

Nomza came out of one room.

'Is this what you're looking for?' she asked.

She handed me five twenty-pound notes. 'I found them outside,' she said timidly.

I jumped and nearly kissed her. I grabbed the money and ran out with a quick 'Thank you, Nomza, you're fab!' It was half past ten.

There were no clients in the bank so I changed the money quickly and ran to the moor where I reached the boat with only five minutes to spare. I sat down breathless and then I realised that Nomza had just returned to me the equivalent of three months' wages in cash she had found lying on the ground.

I had just made myself comfortable on the deck next to a party I recognised from Beatrice's expedition the other day, when the captain introduced himself over the Tannoy and started his commentary: 'Welcome on board, everybody,' he said.

'Welcome to the Greater St Lucia Wetland Park, South Africa's first ever heritage site. You will observe a wide variety of animal life during our trip. This is an area of high biodiversity due to a combination of several, distinct habitats.'

As the St Lucia estuary lies between the lake and the Indian Ocean, the salt concentration creates many diverse ecosystems depending on salinity. The most prominent and pristine are the mudflats that are populated by tall, white mangrove trees, roots extending upwards, and by short, black mangrove bushes sprouting in between the flowering swamp hibiscus. These are the oxygen generators of the planet; its lungs, if you like. It is a common misconception that rainforests are responsible for the oxygen, but no, they consume almost as much oxygen during the day as they produce at night.

The crew gave us each a white mangrove leaf. On top it was green; below it was silver.

'Now lick the bottom side,' said the captain.

Everyone licked their leaves and looked at each other. *Salt!* The bottom of my leaf had turned green again.

'The white mangrove can filter out the salt from the water in the estuary and they have 'glands' to remove the salt through their leaves,' the captain explained.

We passed below a bridge full of birds' nests that looked familiar. 'This is the European swallow,' said the captain. 'It has migrated from the Mediterranean and has found its way to the same nest it left last summer.' Above the bridge, an avian version of the Battle of Britain was raging. A fish eagle was being chased away by a crow; the crow then left to attack a swift tern who, for its part, chased the eagle again. The food chain got a bit confused up there, methinks.

We stopped by the kingfisher nests on a rocky outcrop. A pied kingfisher fed its young, and a brown-headed kingfisher picked up worms unselfconsciously in front of us. Nearby, unidentified chicks were crying, open beaks expecting to be fed. Yellow weavers were involved in an orgy of nest building as usual. Three large crocodiles were inching their way among the mangrove roots. They are sometimes presumed to be salt-water crocs, but no, they still need fresh water to drink. One interesting factoid is that St Lucia's crocodiles are mostly female, because of a strange pollution side-effect. An extraneous species of triffid, brought in casually through shipping, has infested the wilderness of St Lucia, cooling the few sand sites through intense shading. Sand temperature determines not only the hatching of crocodile eggs, but also the sex of the young. Cooler, shady sand either arrests development completely or turns the hatchlings into females. Such an abundance of female crocodiles must delight the males, but the stark reality is that it threatens to wreck the whole estuary eco-balance.

Herons and yellow-billed storks waded at the reed fringes of the mudflats – a dangerous life, as a large, submerged crocodile was lurking not far from the birds' picnic spot. White herons are the queens of the swamp in terms of sheer elegance, but it's the yellow-billed storks I was watching: their pinkish-grey bodies were long and slender, their conical beaks long and versatile, and their eyes, masked by an orange-red band, were staring curiously at the boat. They are intelligent birds and canny hunters: they stand on one leg and stir the mud of the swamp with the other to disorient their prey and catch it unawares.

We came right up close to the edge of the mudflats, which are created by the mangrove trees; they are silt held by the tree's roots. This is a fractal environment; the closer you look the more lifeforms you observe: a red mangrove crab, a fiddler crab with one claw larger than the other, a mudskipper – a strange fish with gills that lives on land, and moves by jumping up and down like a frog – and an amazing mangrove whelk that, just before the time of a tide, climbs up a tree high enough to be exactly above the watermark.

Despite all this, the most interesting lifeform in St Lucia was a fearless hamerkop which was walking awkwardly, bobbing this and the other way amongst the crocodiles, like a pterodactyl model at Spielberg's studios during the filming of *Jurassic Park III*. These hammerhead birds are a unique breed with their family branch lost somewhere between storks and flamingos. Hamerkops are called *uthekwane* in siZulu, the 'lightning bird', and Zulu kids learn to desist from killing them because if they do, they will be struck by lightning. This respect for the birds is probably rooted on their usefulness: hamerkops feed almost exclusively on frogs. Poisonous snakes also eat frogs and if there are no frogs, there are no snakes around waterholes: bush wisdom in a nutshell.

Some useless facts about hamerkops:

1. *They exhibit homosexual tendencies, or what researchers call 'false mounting', where a bird mounts another and pretends to mate, shrieking in fake orgasm. Fake? How can they tell, I wonder.*
2. *Their nests are big, strong, inaccessible and made out of whatever they can find. Researchers have reported building materials ranging from 'sticks and cattle manure, to wash-rags, dusters, a bathing costume, a ball of string and handkerchiefs pilfered from a clothes line'.*

18. Estelle

Back from the trip, I found my Belgians in front of the TV as usual. I told them of the day's events, focusing on Nomza.

'Perhaps it was the money you paid yesterday without arguing,' said the girl.

'What do you mean?'

'If you had tried to – what's the word – *haggle* over the thirty rand, perhaps she would have kept the money.'

'Or maybe,' said the guy, 'it's because you asked her to stay for the *braai*. She likes you.'

I shrugged my shoulders and strolled down to the Oasis when Rudy was just leaving.

'You're off home early,' I said. 'It's only ten o'clock.'

'I'm going away. I have to travel to a court in Mpumalanga tomorrow and I can't drink tonight.'

'About your dog?'

'No. I'm a witness in a crime from my last post as policeman. I must be one hundred per cent alert or else the bastards will walk away.'

'What happened?'

'I was in civil gear and these two guys tried to mug me with a knife. Me! A *knife*? I was carrying a gun with me at the time, so tough luck – they picked on the wrong victim.'

'Did you shoot them?'

'Should have done! No, just arrested them.'

I bid him farewell.

'You're not staying here for the weekend? It gets very lively over the weekend,' he said. 'On Monday we have a paintball game. I'm organising it.'

I politely declined.

Once more, I found myself sipping my last whisky alone with Estelle. Where is it she came from?

'From the Transvaal. Nelspruit.'

I teased her: Transvaal? She meant Mpumalanga.

'It was called Transvaal when I was born, and that's where I come from,' she said defiantly. 'Not Mpumalanga.'

She must have been to the Kruger a lot, then.

She nodded *ja*. 'That's why I like it here. St Lucia is the same as the Kruger but near the sea. I only arrived four months ago.'

Rudy had arrived three months ago.

'It's the summer season,' she said. 'Young people are migrating down to the beach.' she said. 'Like the swallows. Did you see your European swallows?'

There was something I wanted to tell Estelle, but I forgot what it was.

'We do employ reliable staff, don't we?' she said out of the blue.

Ah yes. That.

'Nomza told me. How much did she find? She didn't recognise the money. She thought she'd found a fortune.'

'About a thousand rand,' I replied.

'She thought it was ten thousand,' Estelle laughed.

Next day I woke up late. The Belgians had already left. I met Nomza in the kitchen, said 'Hello' to her gruffly and went into the bathroom. When I got out, she was waiting for me in the corridor.

'How much money did you lose?' she asked me immediately.

I toned it down to make her feel more comfortable. 'Five hundred rand,' I said. 'Nomza, thanks again.'

She turned away silently, an inscrutable expression on her face. I packed my things and put a big tip in an ashtray. I waved at Nomza and pointed discreetly at the money. I hoped it was enough.

The morning's heat was humid and uncomfortable. I walked down to the Oasis to wait for the Baz Bus in the fan-cooled atmosphere of Estelle's office. When I entered, she was sorting out my bill and booking me a place in Durban.

'By the way, you were right about Nomza,' I said. 'She asked me this morning how much I'd lost. It's preying on her mind. Give her a raise, will you?'

Estelle laughed. 'Our employees are honest, nice Zulu girls. Unlike those thieves from Mozambique who live in Dugudugu.'

I cleared my throat.

'Estelle,' I said. 'Nomza *is* from Mozambique. She *lives* in Dugudugu.'

She stared at me, surprised.

'Is she? Huh! How do *you* know?'

'I asked her.'

Estelle looked at me sideways and continued with her paperwork.

'Hmmm,' she mumbled. 'Unfortunately I don't have time to talk to them individually.'

I looked up and let my head roll back slowly, until it banged against the wall.

Chapter Seven

Mad Max IV – Tamin' Durban: Durban

The Kid is cuffed to a car that's about to explode.
MAX: These cuffs are made of tensilled steel. It would take you ten minutes to hack through them.' He hands Kid the hacksaw. 'If you're quick, and if you're lucky, you can hack through your ankle in five.
Mad Max

WEZ: They kill us, we kill them! Kill them! Kill them! Kill! Kill!
Mad Max II

THE PIGKILLER: No matter where you go, there you are.
Mad Max: Beyond Thunderdome

THE INDIAN: It happened last week. I was walking behind the Holiday Inn in Central Beachfront and suddenly two guys pinned me against the wall and tried to take off my watch. It was not an expensive watch. But it had a leather strap which would not get loose. So they broke my wrist.
Later on in this chapter

19. Size fixation – black

'So what happened with Monday's carjack?' I asked Rodney, another of the endless sequence of sociable Baz Bus drivers.

Rodney turned to me, surprised. 'You know about it?'

I kept my silence and nodded in the affirmative. Rodney looked at the rest of the bus and spoke in a hushed voice: 'The three men,' he said to me in that laconic, Zulu monotone, 'they try to drive through the border to Mozambique. The police wait for them.'

He paused as if he wanted my confirmation to continue. 'And?' I obliged.

'One dead, one wounded and one they catch him. They also get the bus and the money back.'

'Dangerous job you've chosen.'

Rodney waved 'no matter' with a regal nod. 'You meet many nice people,' he said, echoing his cousin, Senkile, who had introduced him to the Baz Bus. This had happened only recently, which is why there were no cows yet grazing in KwaZulu Rodney could call his own.

'Your cousin has bought seven cows from this job.'

'Before, Senkile has more cows.'

'He built his parents a house,' I said. 'A good son.'

Rodney turned to me and for the first time since I started conversing with the Zulu, I noticed a break in the lofty, impenetrable mask they all put on.

'You hear them talk about Senkile,' he said softly. 'They cry when they talk about him. He is buying them a house, he is paying for his brother to go to university. The neighbours say they are blessed.'

I switched off, for we were crossing the black Umfolozi, the first of the great Zululand rivers that originate from the Drakensberg and turn this hilly land into a fertile Eden; even rice has been cultivated in Natal, by none other than Cecil Rhodes. But it was plantations of the region's primary commodity that dominated the horizon: after we had traversed the river, we saw the fires and the smoke from the burning of sugar cane, a spectacle that rendered the landscape quasi-apocalyptic, as silhouettes of silhouettes were barely visible amidst the flames.

This was Shaka territory.

Even the most unrepentant white supremacist can't contest the fact that the greatest figures in the South African pantheon have been black. King Shaka is by far the most notorious. He is the biggest African personality in history and his name has become an oath and a symbol that rises above the confines of the Zulu nation. He even inspired a ten-part TV mini-series that was broadcast worldwide in the mid-eighties, riding the wave of the 'Roots' movement of black consciousness. That series was my first encounter with the saga of the black Napoleon, and I was hooked by the cruelty and the gore.

A combination of Bismarck, Genghis Khan, Conan the Barbarian and Pol Pot, Shaka was born – probably in 1787 – to King Senzangakoma, by Nandi, the Sweet One, a beauty the king had not yet married. Theirs was an *uku-hlobonga* gone wrong: during what was supposed to be loveplay, Nandi conceived and became an *izirobo*, an unmarried mother. For this, she was relentlessly ridiculed by everyone: they asked her mockingly whether an intestinal beetle – *shaka* – had caused her belly to swell.

It was the real thing, all right.

Although Senzangakoma married her and she was accepted into the royal *kraal*, Nandi and her son were later exiled to live with the Langeni tribe, because apparently she was a bit of a bitch with a terrible temper. (Zulu oral tradition grants her a great epithet: 'She Whose Thighs Do Not Meet Except When Seeing Her Husband'.) Among the Langeni, Shaka was taunted not only about being a bastard, but also because of the size of his small male member – he was a late developer. His was the worst case of size fixation ever documented in history and turned him – I suppose, literally – into the meanest son of a bitch Africa has ever seen, and Africa has had its fair share.

Rodney's voice interrupted my thoughts: 'That is where Senkile's parents live,' he said and pointed at a village by the side of the highway.

I looked at the sign: *Gingindlovu*, the Fallen Elephant.

'Does it refer to Shaka?' I asked. 'Was Shaka killed here?'

Rodney looked at me enquiringly. '*King* Shaka,' he corrected me, 'die near Stanger.'

Shaka is the reason the Zulu name is famed and feared. He externalised his aggression in war and he revolutionised it. Before Shaka, war in tribal Africa was an elaborate version of football hooliganism: posturing, looting, swearing and taunting with the odd scuffle here and there, perchance a death. A warrior had three long *assegais*; he threw them at his enemy who was standing many yards away and could avoid them with his shield. They each had three goes before they threw their *assegais* back and so on. Laughable, huh? Shaka thought so, too: according to tradition, he devised the *iXhwa,* a short, thrustful, sharp spear, which was not thrown and wasted, but used as a bayonet to slaughter. No more games for the boy – he was in for the kill, and he was rather good at it.

Shaka was his father's first male child, but because he was conceived out of wedlock, Senzangakoma would not sanction his succession. Shaka lived with his mother in exile and did not meet his father until 25 years later, when father and son were partly reconciled. Shortly afterwards, in 1816, Senzangakoma died and Shaka – popular with the army regiments – declared himself king by impaling the legal heir to the Zulu throne. He immediately proceeded to take revenge on the Langeni who had derided his small willy when he was young. Oral tradition has it that he assembled the whole clan before him and asked publicly who could remember an act of kindness to him or his mother. Twelve people came forward. He had them culled with clubs out of mercy. The rest he had impaled in the place of killing, or *Bulawayo*, we were just passing. Don't confuse it with Bulawayo in Zimbabwe: there are plenty of places of killing in Africa.

This coast was built with a T-square, I ruminated, as the N2 followed a bayless, featureless seashore beyond the Tugela river, which marks the boundary between traditional KwaZulu and British Natal.

'There,' said Rodney and pointed at a sign saying 'Shaka's memorial', just after the town of Stanger. 'King Shaka die there. By –' he stopped and almost spat the name, '*Dingaan*.'

Although Shaka was a Gothic monster for the Victorians, he is revered by the Zulu to this day, whereas Dingaan, his assassin brother, is reviled by everyone. He did, after all, murder Shaka, kill Piet Retief, wage an unsuccessful war against the Boers and was roundly defeated at Blood River.

In contrast to Dingaan, Shaka is commemorated everywhere, and his shadow still looms upon the land he united in blood. Soon after we happened upon a place called Shaka's Rock. This particular rock was the subject of an investigation by a magistrate in 1949 who was asked to rule on the authenticity of an assertion that it was a rock Shaka used to sit on. The magistrate noted dismissively that '*many rocks have been pointed out all over the country as having been sat upon by the king at one time or another*'. Indeed, on the southern side of Durban Bay there was a rock, dynamited in the Second World War, called Cave Rock. It is said that when Shaka was staying at his Congella military camp, very near the present King Edward VIII hospital in Durban, he marched his soldiers across the bay, sat on Cave Rock and watched them trying to tame the waves as the tide came fiercely in, a thousand years after King Canute. A sign of a good military disciplinarian? A sign of madness? A sign of sadism? Perhaps all three?

It's difficult to know where legend and exaggeration ends and history or slander commences. Zulu tradition is oral and written histories have been compiled mostly by hostile opportunist white settlers who wanted to make a quick buck by selling their memoirs in Victorian London and promote British occupation of Natal. Nathaniel Isaacs who first published a harsh account of Shaka in 1836 was the prime instigator: '*The world has heard of monsters – Rome had her Nero, the Huns their Attila and Syracuse her Dionysius; the East has likewise produced her tyrants; but for ferocity Shaka has exceeded them all.*' One advisory letter by Isaacs to Henry Fynn, who published his own diary later, was discovered in 1941, vitiating the credibility of those early accounts: '*Make them as blood-thirsty as you can […] and also describe the frivolous crimes people lose their lives for. It all tends to swell up the work and make it interesting.*'

Did Shaka really ask a father to kill his young daughter in front of him to show his loyalty? Did he really slice open the bellies of pregnant women in order to observe the foetuses in various stages of development? Was he trying to breed a master race when he carefully matched husbands and wives from his regiments? Did he adopt vultures as royal birds and have his subjects slain to feed them? Did he lock Queen Ntombazi – the mother of Chief Zwide of the Ndwandwe – in a hut with a hyena long enough for the hungry animal to overcome its natural timidity and start slowly snapping off the woman's extremities when, after torturous days of demented fear, she fell asleep? Did he ask, after his mother died, that the soldiers of a regiment stand naked and maidens dance voluptuously in front of them so that the men who involuntarily got erections were executed? We'll never know. What we do know is that Shaka 'was using indiscriminate killing, fear and violence to bolster authority and enforce consent', as scholars agree. What we also know is that he considered the British punishment of incarceration as inhuman as we consider his lackadaisical dishing out of the death penalty.

We were entering a large built-up area. I guessed we were reaching Durban's northern suburbs. Rodney pointed to my right. 'That is where we live', he said. 'Senkile and I. KwaMashu.'

'I'll be calling Senkile tomorrow,' I said. 'He'll take me to a shebeen.'

Rodney couldn't hide his incredulity very well. 'Tomorrow you come to KwaMashu?' he asked.

'Yes, why not?'

'It is very dangerous. Senkile is wrong to invite you.'

'Why? I won't take much money with me.'

'I am not talking about money,' said Rodney and let the matter hang.

20. Disturbin' Durban

Although the Baz Bus only made stops at designated hostels, Rodney helpfully drove me all the way to the large Induna Holiday Flats on Gillespie Street where Estelle had made me a booking. Odd – I was the only white face for as far as the eye could see. Wasn't this a street parallel to the Beachfront, where the big and expensive hotels were? I should have known by now that glancing at a map does not convey the realities on the ground as many a sergeant major has discovered at war.

I entered the Induna Holiday Flats. A short Indian guy with a pointy Lucifer beard at the end of a face straight out of an Evil Dead video, was sitting behind bullet-proof glass. He was unsmiling and curt. I mentioned Estelle's reservation.

'For you, I have an apartment on the eighteenth floor. Only 160 rand.'

'I thought I had one booked for 120.'

'I have another for 120 rand, but you won't like it.'

'I would still like to see it,' I insisted.

He gave me a key. 'Second floor,' he said.

When the slow-moving lift reached the second floor, I walked into what looked uncannily like a corridor in a poorly maintained Hackney high rise. There was graffiti on the walls, broken bottles by the staircase and peeling paint on the metal railings. The lights were out of order; I would need a torch at night.

My 'apartment' hardly needed a key; I could have just blown the lock away with my breath, like the Big Bad Wolf. Inside, the grime in the windows was so thick it acted as a natural solar barrier. The kitchen – equipped with dangling bare wires and loose pipes – was not only highly explodable, but also highly burglarable, overlooking as it did the outside walkway with a window that wouldn't close properly. This was not an apartment costing 120 rand: this was a decoy to make me rent the more expensive one.

It worked, for when I walked back the two floors to reception, I asked: 'Could I see the apartment on the eighteenth floor, please?'

The Indian was aggravated. 'I told you you wouldn't like it,' he said. 'Why didn't you listen to me?'

The lift took a good number of minutes to reach the eighteenth floor – maybe three, or maybe five. I didn't pay much attention, until the twelfth when I realised I was progressively slowing down and might never reach the top. When I did, it took a prayer and a half for the door to open.

Yes, the 160-rand apartment contained all mod cons behind a proper lock and a one-foot-thick steel door. This wasn't just burglar-proof – this was nuclear-attack-proof (well, as close as you can get in a tower block). I walked down the eighteen floors in two minds. By the tenth I had decided to escape.

'Well?' said the Indian who had been joined by a tall Zulu with a pocked face.

My luggage was locked on the other side of the glass. *Damn*!

'OK,' I said.

'Cash,' said the Indian. 'In advance.'

'Oh, no,' I lied. 'I don't have that much cash. Credit card. Can I get my luggage back?'

The Indian ignored me and insisted on cash. The tall Zulu said something to him. The Indian smiled – or rather snarled – for the first time.

'All right,' he said. 'Give us the card.'

'It's in my luggage,' I lied.

Now the Indian had to give me my stuff back. I pretended I was searching.

'One night,' I said, trying to break the contract.

The Indian turned surly. 'The booking was for four.'

'But at 160 rand the room is more expensive,' I countered.

'If it's only one night, it's more expensive,' the Indian hissed. 'It's 220 rand per night.'

That was my chance. 'Sorry, no deal,' I said and walked out before they could muster back their composure.

I started walking down Gillespie. By now it was dark. There were hustlers hanging around aimlessly in shop doorways and down-and-outs squatting on the pavement aggressively demanding spare change. 'Excuse me,' said one who bumped into me. I ignored him. He followed me: 'EXCUSE ME! COME HERE! EXCUUUUUSE ME!' There were familiar signs about how firearms were not allowed in the establishment, but this time they were hanging above the doorways of fast food joints that sported bars in their windows; in the streets were mirrorless cars, tyreless cars, windowless cars, burnt cars; domineering prostitutes were plying their wares, commencing a night's work by fighting with their pimps. Rio de Janeiro would feel like the courtyard of a convent after this.

In the middle of it all, there I was, looking *so* like a tourist with my backpack and a map of Durban, like a little lost impala in a lion's den. I passed a doorway where four youths fixed their eyes on me with a glassy, wall-eyed stare. I heard them move – slight twist of the head: yes, they were following me, covering the breadth of the road. For the first time in South Africa, I panicked. I took a left to reach the Beachfront: the walk down the small, narrow side street seemed eternal. I saw a door with an armed guard and walked inside. It was the Durban swimming pool.

'*Help,*' I said, in a cold sweat. 'I'm being followed.'

I must have been in quite a state because the girl at the entrance desk offered to find me a place there and then. She made a few phone calls and announced: 'The Tropicana has a single room for 250 rand a night. It's only a few blocks up.' The armed guard offered to accompany me to the hotel: I was frightened, he said, and it was his duty to protect me. The concern South Africans show for their guests is sometimes overwhelming.

When I arrived in the Tropicana, I was astounded. This was a four-star hotel. My room had TV, a minibar, aircon, and a view of the ocean. Breakfast was included and it was an eat-as-much-as-you-can-lift occasion in a superbly decorated dining room.

In Durban I started tasting luxury, and it became addictive.

I left the Tropicana at around ten in the evening and had a walk along the Beachfront, which was gradually becoming deserted. The Late Night Galleon at Point and West was as rough as the rest of the town. The bar staff were three young surfers with their tops off, their backs tattooed, and their bodies gleaming with pecs and abs. They were high on an upper – coke? Speed? The clientele was composed of young men in the company of older gentlemen and guys with makeshift ink tattoos on the knuckles and dirt (*real* dirt) under their fingernails. The pretty things were very pretty and the ugly buggers very ugly indeed. As the toilet graffiti says, *beauty may be skin deep, but ugliness goes right to the bone*. It could have been the motto of the house.

'Hi,' I said to the barman and ordered a beer. I asked him his name. It was Zack.

'I'm John.'

'*Good*,' he said and walked away.

I sipped my beer quietly and worriedly until I noticed a poster behind the bar: it was a Trade calendar – breakthrough! I smiled at Zack, pointed at the poster and said: 'That's my club. Trade in London. I'm a member.'

He looked at me in that dizzy, indirect way surfers do, avoided an imaginary fly, whistled and said: '*Good*.'

This was very unnerving. I had to talk to someone, if only to contain my apprehension. I turned to the bald, plump guy next to me.

'Overwhelming, isn't it?' I asked and pointed at the crowded bar.

'It is, if you are new,' he replied.

We introduced ourselves to each other. His name was Alwyn.

'What do you do?' I asked him, relieved to talk to a friendly face.

'I'm a prostitute,' he said, drawing unbelieving looks from me. If this was true, there was serious money to be made in this town. 'I mean a lawyer,' he added.

Oh, a *joke*. How welcome after this stressful day.

Alwyn had been on the razzle since four o'clock in the afternoon, like a proper solicitor. He was considering emigrating. 'But I can't, you see. Lawyers are trapped in South Africa. Here we follow something called the Roman-Dutch law which is different from other English-speaking countries. The only other place where we can practise is Sri Lanka.'

'Not even in the right hemisphere,' I sympathised.

He droned on well-meaningly until a commotion stopped his rambling.

'What's that?' I asked.

'There's a stripper on Thursdays. Tonight it's André.'

A young guy with a body straight out of a muscle magazine jumped on a table and started gyrating to the techno beat. The show was a bit amateurish and, as with everything in Durban, a bit dangerous. André liked to dance with his arms held high, and he nearly lost his fingers when they reached perilously close to the rotating blades of a ceiling fan.

I tried to gather information about the scene. Back in London I'd heard about Club 330; was it any good? Zack behind the bar focused on me and, with a few hours' delay, picked up on my very first comment: 'You are a Trade member?'

'Yes.'

'You know Tony De Vit?'

'Not personally,' I said. 'I heard him DJ, though, when he was alive.'

I had passed some test or other. I knew he had died. The barman took a big breath as if concentrating on talking was an effort.

'Tony De Vit used to DJ at Club 330. It's best on Saturdays. Tomorrow go to Club Axis –' he started.

'Tomorrow I'm going to KwaMashu,' I interrupted him.

The whole place went quiet as if I'd said I was planning to castrate Chief Buthelezi with a pair of garden pliers. Alwyn broke the silence: 'You know KwaMashu is a *black township*?' he said.

'Yes, I do. I know two guys who live there. They promised to take me to a shebeen.'

Zack looked at me in awe: 'They'll kill you, dude,' he said, eyes involuntarily twitching.

Alwyn joined forces. Yes, I was going with a friend, but how would I get there? No taxis would take me there. Minibuses? A white face in a township-bound minibus?

'I'll ask him to meet me here, in town,' I said.

They changed their tack. I might be safe with Senkile and Rodney, but it only takes a *domkop* with a gun and a grudge to spoil the evening. Did *I* have a gun? Did Senkile? Was I aware of the random nature of violence? That innocent passers-by have been caught in crossfire and killed? Did I know there was no electricity at night and that everywhere was dark? That this was no Soweto awash with tourists, but rude, raw, raucous KwaMashu, a Zulu township, not a harmless, docile *dorp*?

I shrugged my shoulders noncommittally. 'OK, I'll think about it,' I said. 'I'm off back to my hotel.'

'I'll walk you there,' said Alwyn.

'Is it dangerous?'

'My worst experience was when I left here last night. Someone stopped me, pushed me against a wall and spread my arms before I could react. He was after my watch, but when I recovered and made a threatening move, he disappeared.'

I strolled with Alwyn to the Beachfront where I walked the last couple of hundred yards alone. It was long after midnight and the silence was thick, interrupted occasionally by ghostly stirrings emanating from the bushes. Were the hawkers sleeping roughly or was there a gang stalking the pavement? If thoughts could quiver like voices, mine would be as tremulous as a snowy TV set with a shaky indoor aerial.

21. Dreadin' Durban

The Durban Beachfront lends new meaning to the word 'garish'. Not only is it painted in the brightest and gaudiest of colours that would make Gaudí himself salivate, but it is also populated by Zulu rickshaw drivers, each one resembling a small carnival float, dressed in a plethora of animal tails, bird feathers and orchidaceous headgear no respectable drag queen would ever dare to don. The place is so over the top, its style transcends mere bad taste and levitates into heavy-duty kitsch. I loved it.

Every inch of pavement on the Beachfront had been claimed by Zulu hawkers peddling their wares under vast umbrellas to escape the blistering sun: weaved baskets, woodcarvings, beadwork. They were mostly women who spent their time conversing animatedly with each other. I wondered whether they had come to sell their goods or socialise with their friends.

Women talk differently in Zulu societies, and everyone who delves in their language is fascinated by the practice of *uku-hlonipa*. This is the most outlandish linguistic contrivance I have come across: out of respect, women members of a *kraal* avoid using the name of an object if it resembles the name of a male relative and resort to mispronouncing syllables or referring to concepts indirectly; imagine Cockney rhyming slang with every family using its own version. In the case of a chief, the whole tribe uses another name. E. A. Ritter, the chief Shaka hagiographer, mentions the Ngwane chief Tshani, whose name used to mean 'grass'; his tribe invented the new word *ince* which is still used for grass to this day. Catherine Barter, a nineteenth century Anglican Church volunteer, observed that the Zulu King Mpande had a name which meant 'root' and was related to the word 'cave' and the verb 'dig'. Throughout the Zulu dominions, the people invented new words for those. Even now some traditional Zulu avoid the word for 'stick' which is '*Buthelezi*'. Urbanisation has worked against the practice of *uku-hlonipa,* which may be manageable in the confines of the *kraal*, but is not suited to wider township life: it would make everyday city-living seem like a scene from an Ionesco play. Imagine poor Mrs Pongolo who wants to buy a six-pack of beer and ends up with a litre of colon cleanser.

The Beachfront hawkers were barefoot; the rickshaw drivers were barefoot; the town was full of barefoot people. It was Shaka who discarded his sandals and forced his soldiers to march on thorns for hours until their feet first became torn and bloody but ultimately hard and crusty. In Durban, however, it was not just the Zulu I saw shoeless. Like Beatrice in St Lucia, it was the whites, too – and not only the surfers and the swimmers, but also the car drivers and the shoppers in the malls.

It was also Shaka who put Durban on the map. The explorers-cum-adventurers Henry Fynn and Francis Farewell had arrived in his court and Shaka was impressed by their stiff upper lip. He liked the British and granted them land in Port Natal (later renamed by the settlers after the Cape Governor Sir Benjamin d'Urban in the hope that he'd annex the land for the Crown). Shaka made Port Natal *the* trade port of preference for ivory in the east coast of South Africa, eventually to eclipse its main competitor, the earlier Portuguese base at Delagoa Bay.

I hurriedly took my seat at the Reptile House auditorium as a snake-keeper with a small, blond goatee jumped into a walled snake pit with trees and shrubs for his lecture-cum-demonstration. Young and skinny, he looked more like a meal than a master.

'Some of the most venomous snakes in South Africa are in this pit,' he said. He fished out a puff adder from below a bush and picked it up with a stick. We stared in horror.

'Puff adders have moving front fangs and their poison is *cytotoxic*. It kills the cells and a bite on the leg makes it swell to two, three times its normal size. The skin bursts and gangrene sets in, so it's only indirectly fatal if you don't get treatment quickly enough. Adder bites account for seventy to eighty per cent of snake bites in South Africa. What snakes want is to get out of your way. But the puff adder is a slow mover, so you step on it, you break a few of its ribs, and it bites you.'

He let the adder climb down from his stick, and, as predicted, it moved away painfully slowly. We clapped and exhaled. Next he picked up a Mozambican spitting cobra. 'The teeth of this snake are fixed at the front,' he said, letting the snake slide away. 'Such a snake has a *neurotoxic*, nerve-attacking poison. If it spits on your skin, there is no damage; if it spits in your eye, though, the poison makes them burn and you must wash them with water or milk immediately.' We gulped and held our breath once more: the keeper wasn't wearing any goggles.

'And here's another snake with fixed front teeth: the green mamba.'

A big Zulu mama next to me shrieked as the keeper searched among the branches and pulled out a long, agile snake with his bare hands.

'Reports of mamba poison are exaggerated. Death is not instantaneous – it takes from twenty minutes to six hours for the poison to have an effect. It's not necessary to kill the snake; from the type of wound and the symptoms the doctors can tell what type of antivenin to provide. Except for this one.'

To our astonishment, he probed some branches with his stick and picked up a *boomslang,* an African tree-snake, the most feared bastard of them all. He nonchalantly continued as the snake tried to bite him several times, avoiding every attack by shaking his arms like a conductor in front of an orchestra. And when the snake, worn out and stressed, tried to move away, he expertly picked it up with the stick in no time and only let it go when he'd finished. The Zulu mama was agog, and so was I.

'This is a back-fanged snake. It has to open its mouth 170 degrees to bite. Its venom is *haemotoxic*, attacks the blood, that is, and is so concentrated that a drop can kill fifty adult humans. But don't worry. It takes many days to a few weeks for a human to die. Although antivenin exists, it alone may not be sufficient, and we have to treat the individual toxic effects such as internal bleeding and liver or kidney failure. So, if you go to hospital, you will have several very painful weeks, but you will very probably not die.'

The demo over, we started clapping, relief evident in our ardour. Now it was feeding time. I'd always been curious as to how snakes swallow their victims whole, so I waited patiently by the baby pythons. I was disappointed to see a dead rat thrown in the cage.

'I thought snakes eat *live* prey,' I complained.

'In the zoos only when it is absolutely essential,' answered the snake keeper. 'Cruelty to animals, see?'

He wiggled the bait with a stick. The python attacked and coiled itself around the rodent. 'The rats are freshly killed by us. If they move, then the snakes think they're alive,' he explained. I watched as the python started licking its prey to lubricate it for a long, long swallow.

'You may like this,' the keeper said. He pointed at a glass cage, where a live, white lab mouse was trembling with fear in the opposite corner from a snake that was lying indifferent – or asleep, you never can tell – inside its den. The mouse did not dare move; it knew it was a goner, a spectacle appalling yet oddly captivating.

The keeper waved me over to the other side.

A massive tree python was due a big chicken and one was fed to him in front of my eyes. The large snake pierced its throat with fangs the size of my fingers and started strangling the dead bird as the blood ran down its scales. The tree python then began licking the chicken; it would take hours to complete the deglutition. I walked back to the baby python whose mouth had by now been completely dislocated; after twenty minutes the rat was in up to its front legs. In the glass cage, the mouse was still alive, sobbing tearlessly. I had seen enough.

Should I call Senkile?

I hesitated.

Later.

'Talk to me,' Stuart commanded me giddily.

Stuart was a thirty-something in an expensive designer suit who'd offered me one of the shots he was buying in the Galleon. He meant that this was the least I could do to repay my free schnapps. Everyone seemed to be impressed that I was European, including Stuart who had been to Italy.

'I spent 4,000 rand during one night in Venice,' he said drunkenly. 'Gondola hire, nice dinner, the works.'

'With your boyfriend?' I asked pointing at the hunk who was holding Stuart by the waist.

Stuart looked at me, shocked.

'Boyfriend?' he asked indignantly. 'I wouldn't splash 4,000 rand on a *boyfriend*! No, I was there with my *mother*.'

Sorry.

'We saw Pavarotti. And Celine Dion,' Stuart said and turned to Zack who was once again behind the bar. 'The teddy, please,' he added.

Zack gave him a worn cuddly toy and Stuart left the bar.

A tall, gangly guy with long hair and glasses approached me, reeking of whisky. His BO preceded him and in the fetid atmosphere of the bar I passively inhaled some smoke from a lit cigarette stuck on an ashtray to drown the smell and allay the queasiness. Maybe he was one of those marine biologists in the Natal Shark Board who were publicly dissecting sharks and couldn't get rid of the smell in time for the weekend. I had been hoping to witness the spectacle of opening one of the beasts' bellies and finding a car registration number, a chainsaw and a small sofabed, as one does in films, but sadly there were no dissections on Fridays. Luckily, with the gangly guy next to me, I could at least imagine the smell of the occasion.

'Where is Stuart going with that teddy bear?' I asked Zack.

'Oh, he's only going to the toilets,' replied the shark dissector instead and, seeing that he drew a blank from me, he explained further: 'The toilets are *outside*. You have to open an iron door with the key that's hanging from the teddy bear. You must also lock the door behind you, because someone might slip in and mug you.'

Outside sounded a very hazardous place. I must remember not to venture there.

'But why a teddy bear?'

He made a 'why not?' gesture. 'It's a heavy key.'

Impeccable logic.

Stuart returned. 'We're going to Axis,' he announced throwing the teddy in the barman's face.

Should I call Senkile? Too late now.

We got into Stuart's sports BMW, and he sped off. I was doubly concerned: firstly for our lives, as Stuart was driving drunk and one-handed, and secondly because the shark dissector was sitting next to me, and I was afraid the stench might be infectious. Thankfully Axis was only a short distance away and the waft didn't have time to settle. Once inside, Stuart kept buying me grapefruit schnapps shots, and the only thing I had to do was let him diss the Brits.

'I've been to London,' he said. 'I found it frightening. They say that South Africa is dangerous. Huh! London is much worse.'

'I'm not so sure, ' I replied. 'I've met several people in London glad to have left South Africa.'

'It's the Joeys who fly away scared. Let them,' he said. 'Us here in Natal will stay. We know our Zulus and the Zulus know us. Now shush, I like this video.'

Stuart pointed at the big MTV screen that was showing Stardust's 'Music Sounds Better with You'. Then the door behind him opened and Kahle walked in.

Kahle was quite conspicuous, for he was a Zulu. He was beautiful, with deep-set, puckish eyes, smooth complexion and sensuous lips. I felt my heart flutter, as he moved towards us and his glance lingered on me for a few seconds. One eye on him, one eye on Stuart, I started bullshitting about the video ('It has an Alan Parker feel to it with its theme of the boy and the glider, camera work straight out of *Birdie*') and then I asked Kahle casually if he liked this kind of music, to make conversation.

'Most of my friends listen to *kwaito*,' said Kahle in very passable English, 'but I like house music. I cannot listen to *kwaito* and be gay.'

I smiled when I heard the emphasised last sentence. The Zulu love vowels, using 'I cannot', 'I will not' and 'I do not' rather than can't, won't, don't. There is something deeply combative in this manner of speech.

'Why?'

'Because they do not play *kwaito* in gay bars.'

More impeccable logic.

'Do your parents know you're gay?'

'I told my mother.'

'And?'

'My father threw me out of the house.'

'She shouldn't have told him.'

Kahle looked at me.

'You do not understand,' he said in that assertive Zulu manner: *yuduno tande stand*. 'I never talk to my father about anything. I talk to my mother and *she* talks to *him*.'

'Why?'

'Because if I talk to my father, it is too rude. I do not even look him in the eye.'

I sighed. Deference before authority: that's why *baaskap* lasted so long.

'Sorry for asking such questions,' I excused myself. 'I'm a foreigner. The others here,' I pointed at the Durbanites around us, 'know more about it.'

'The others here,' Kahle said, 'do not even ask.' He smiled coyly. 'It is good to ask,' he added.

'And what do you do for a living?'

'I am a hairdresser,' he said. 'Very gay, I know.'

I stood up as the schnapps burst through my veins and flooded my brain cells.

'I'll teach you how to dance,' I said to Kahle.

'You will teach *me*?' he laughed.

I ignored him. 'There are a discrete number of dance moves,' I said. 'First off, Hammer the Nails.'

I hammered an imaginary nail on the wall.

'Feed the Chickens.'

I jigged my forearm back and forth and tossed my wrist liberally, as if dispensing feed to fowl.

'How Big's Your Fridge.'

My hands went to various positions horizontally and vertically as if estimating the size of a box.

'Big Fish, Little Fish.'

I swayed my arms psychedelically in front of me, the left one following the right after an interval of a second – and vice versa.

'Washing Machine.'

I shook my hips and torso as if trying to balance on a Zanussi at its highest spin cycle. I must have done well, because a laughing Kahle followed me to the dancefloor. Not long after, he was holding me, and we were kissing.

'Let's go!'

Go where?

Reality got a grip on me. I couldn't take Kahle with me to the Tropicana. The hotel was under armed guard. He wouldn't get past security.

'You can come with me,' he said.

'You don't live in a township? You live in Durban?' I said.

'I live in the south suburbs,' he said. 'But my friend has a flat, not too far from here.'

He flashed me one of those sparkling African smiles.

'OK,' I said. 'I'll just be off for a sec.'

Like a character out of a nightmare, my shark dissector appeared and followed me to the toilet.

'Are you going home with that Zulu?' he asked, choosing the urinal next to me.

'Yes, I am,' I said, averting my gaze.

'Then be careful.'

'What do you mean?'

'Has he asked you for money?'

I turned to face him. 'Actually, no, he hasn't. He's got a job. He's a hairdresser.'

The shark dissector laughed.

'Hairdresser? You fell for it? I've seen him around a lot with other guys. He's no good.'

His words had a sudden sobering effect; I could feel the poison spreading in my innards like a *boomslang* bite. South African segregated mentality clouded my thoughts. Was I making a fatal mistake? What if I woke up three days later drugged, with my possessions gone? Or worse: without my right kidney, like in those urban legends?

I returned back to the bar.

'Shall we go?' Kahle asked.

I snapped out of it. 'Yep.'

We walked out of the club and turned left into the darkness. At night, the *outside* felt even more forbidding. Were these shadows in the doorways?

'You know, my friend has a friend, also from London,' Kahle started saying.

Was this one coincidence too many?

With the corner of my eye I saw a man's silhouette detach itself from a wall. He started walking towards us. Was I being lured into a trap?

Was that a big stick he was holding?

I left Kahle behind and ran back to the club shaking and trembling. A guy and his girlfriend were leaving. I didn't know them, but I asked them whether they had a car. They did. Could they give me a lift to the Tropicana? It wasn't far. *Please?* The couple took pity on me and waved me to follow them. We turned left into the same darkness I had walked in earlier; there was no sign of Kahle. As we got into the car, the same shadow with the stick moved towards us. I could make out a big Zulu who leaned over the window with his palm open. The guy gave him a few rand.

'Who is he?' I asked.

'Him? Oh, he's employed by the club to look after our cars so that they don't get broken into. But we also tip him normally.'

I woke up with a mixture of emotions: disappointment, resentment, anger at myself. I hadn't called Senkile. I hadn't been to KwaMashu. I had rejected Kahle. People in the new South Africa seemed to follow the Hawkin's Theory of Progress: *Progress does not consist of replacing a theory that is wrong with one that is right, but of replacing one that is wrong with one that is more subtly wrong.*

And I was as wrong as they were.

22. Ravin' Durban

On the spur of the moment – maybe to escape those mixed emotions – I took a tour to the PheZulu cultural village with a lively, septuagenarian Irish widower whom I had met in my hotel.

'I was here during the war,' he said. 'The town was only a single street then.'

Well, it's many streets now. We paced apprehensively around the central district ('dangerous even at daytime', according to our driver), which was a giant hawker stall, before we drove to Kloof; this was the posh villa neighbourhood, full of the now familiar barbed wire fences. An Englishman's home is his castle, but an Afrikaner's home is a veritable laager.

The cultural village was situated in the wondrously named Valley of One Thousand Hills amid an intensely green landscape, undulating gently as far as the eye could see in the afternoon haze. At the entrance, we passed by a crocodile farm. I had seen enough of these reptiles in St Lucia to anticipate being bored, but we had arrived in time for their feeding which, as snouts snapped and teeth ripped flesh from carcass, turned out to be quite a spectacle.

About time for...

Some useless facts about crocodiles:
1. *They eat less and less as they grow older. A large crocodile of twelve feet will have a meal every two to three weeks. Babies eat every day. The 80-year-old twenty-footer at PheZulu eats only once or twice a year and lives off its fat the rest of the time.*
2. *They can't swallow under water.*
3. *Once they do manage to swallow – a complicated process, especially if your food still wants to escape – they digest the meat, the bones, the hairs; even the horns and hooves. Some stomach juices, eh?*
4. *Although books say that crocodiles can run as fast as a man, they can only achieve this speed for short distances.*

I was so mesmerised by the feasting performance in the crocodile pit, I had to be coaxed to move on. The Zulu dances were about to begin.

The spectators sat in a makeshift open-air amphitheatre, overlooking the Valley of One Thousand Hills. I started counting – only thirty! I was going to shout 'Fraud!' when a female *sangoma* presented us with a smoking pot and asked us to breathe deeply over it. Before the pot came to me I could smell what it was: pot-in-a-pot. I took a deep breath, and another one and another one – the *sangoma* had to pull back forcefully to separate me from the *dagga* fumes. It was then I counted the hills again, and yes, they had multiplied to one thousand.

The male dancers wore lengthy *amaShoba* – tufts of cows' tails – on their knees and upper arms, *iBeshu* aprons over their front and back, and diverse *iNjobo* animal skins joined at the hip. The leader wore a small piece of a leopard skin. The leopard is a royal animal: only the ruling dynasty is allowed use of their hides, and the quantity of leopard a chief has been granted to wear determines his social status in the Zulu equivalent of Debrett's. Great idea – I can never figure out whether a marquess ranks higher than a baronet, but it would be so much simpler if you could work out a peer's station in life by counting the tufts of ermine they sported.

It's easy to figure why so many Westerners have fallen under the Zulu spell. There is something intrinsically majestic about the Zulu male demeanour. This is a society of alpha-males: they exude that imperceptible quality, part charismatic reassurance, part potential aggression, that constitutes the thin line between an inspirational sports captain and a school bully. It's also an exhibitionistic culture: like their bare-breasted women, the males want to flaunt their virility. The dancers' whole attire and their studied moves appeared attuned to show off their flat hairless stomachs and tight biceps, triceps, quadriceps, flexors, extensors – you name the muscle, they had got it trained.

Just like those surfers on the Beachfront.

Single women displayed their breasts boldly and wore beads around the neck and waist, exposing more flesh than

Westminster Council allows in Soho strip joints. Engaged women, like our *sangoma* with the pot, cover their breasts and married ones cover themselves outright with cow hides; a large grass hat is sewn in with their hair; when it rots away, the woman washes her hair and another is sewn back on – think of it as a wedding ring that can't be discarded when the husband's away.

Our female dancers were all single; but, alas, they looked as if they had stepped out of a Rubens painting. Zulu men like their own bodies lithe, but they want their women with buffalo-bearing hips. In fact, some of the hips I saw in KwaZulu/Natal – even amongst those dancers – I thought humanly impossible. I suppose that evolutionarily they facilitate pregnancy, since only in this way can the women balance properly.

Zulu traditional dancing accompanied by drumming and singing is an extremely athletic exercise. The most spectacular is the bull dance: it involves the leg being extended up high and encircled by the arms snappily; to my astonishment it was not just the men who managed the contortions, but those big-bottomed females, as well. This is a dance invented in the Johannesburg miners' hostels where the men hardly had any space to move within the bunk beds.

My interest waned at this point. The pot-in-the-pot was being passed around again and this time I felt very possessive.

[The songs] are, as a rule, monotonous and uninteresting; but the people sing in tune, and have a notion of harmony. It is a reproach to a man to say that he cannot sing a second. They keep time in the most correct and precise manner. Their howlings are often uncouth in the extreme, and the stamping of their feet and the motions of their bodies form no inappropriate accompaniment. The whole is simply disgusting.

Yet on one occasion when I was present at a native dance, given in my honour by a friend in Natal, I was much struck by the graceful movements of the men. They were about eighty in number, and they waved their shields to and fro, as by one consent, in perfect time to a low chant or song. It was a pleasing sight to see until the women joined in with their awkward gestures and screaming voices which entirely spoiled the effect.

That Catherine Barter, mentioned earlier, unable to admit she enjoyed herself in her 1866 book *Alone Among the Zulus.*

In Joe Kool's, a round two-storey bar in the middle of the Beachfront, the crowd could have descended from Malibu or Bondi. Surfers and their 'gals' the world over have developed an international culture and manner of speech. Their arms keep balancing the surfboard even on land. Their limbs seem to shake independently of each other and are only called to a common direction by sheer chance. During conversation, a surfer moves his body backwards, his arms upwards or sideways and his fingers strike 1-2-3-4 against his thumbs. In Britain, some silly old judge might have them certified and detained at Her Majesty's pleasure under the Lunacy Act, 1865.

At Joe Kool's a conversation goes like this:

SURFER A [*whistling*]: Anyone for more – [*shoulders up, body tense*] – beer?' [*Whistle, handclap.*]
SURFER B [*drumming on table*]: One Castle, Rox. [*Surfers are not called Michael, David or Robert. They are called Rox, Buck or Skip.*]
SURFER C [*scratching armpit, count to two*]: Geddabucket, dude. [*In Joe Kool's a six-pack and assorted ice is sold in a large 'bucket' which resembles a small wheelbarrow.*]
SURFER D: Yeah, [*Handclap.*] Sure! [*Fights off virtual killer bees.*] A bucket of Castle, dude. [*Body twitch.*]

One thing about the surfers though, resplendent in their tight Rip Curl, Icuba or Billabong tops and Reef sandals (if worn at all), is their cliquishness. You're either a surfer or you're not.

You either wake up at the crack of dawn to surf those mothers or you don't. Afterwards you either have an enormous breakfast at Joe Kool's at 8.30 a.m. or you don't. And if your face hasn't been seen for breakfast – which in my book is the most expendable meal of the day – you have no social life in Joe Kool's.

As yours truly realised after a few hours.

I didn't care that much, since it was Saturday night and I was going to Club 330. This is one of the most famous clubs in South Africa: a converted large, labyrinthine villa in the south of Durban with the loudest dancefloor *anywhere*. I arrived with my fingers crossed – a clubbing mate in London knew the manager and should have e-mailed him that I'd be there that weekend.

'I'm on the guest list,' I told the girl at the door. 'John from London.'

The girl looked down the list.

'Is your name John Mala... Malth... Malanth...' she said trying to pronounce my surname.

'That's me!' I cried. *'Malathronas!'*

She gave me a free VIP pass, and I loved Durban there and then.

As this had been such an intense moment, I needed to relieve myself. Now toilets are very sociable places in clubs, and it was there I met...

'Adrian!' I exclaimed.

'John!'

It was Adrian the raver and West Brom supporter from the Baz Bus to Mbabane.

'Fancy meeting you here, mate,' he said.

'Well, I needed a pee,' I replied.

'No, in Durban!'

We were both buzzing. Adrian introduced me to his cousin, Sandra, whom he hadn't seen since she was five – distant relatives' addresses are taken out and dusted when we travel to foreign places. We chatted for a long time. We chatted very, very fast.

'You won't believe this, mate,' he said. 'Last night we were drinking vodka and doing coke. We'd been drinking non-stop for twenty-four hours. My other cousin, Sandra's sis, got ill 'cos she'd eaten nowt and got some serious stomach cramps. So we called the hospital. We also told her boyfriend. Now *he's* against drugs and came in with a fucking gun. He was fucking pointing it at us, accusing us of fucking poisoning his girlfriend! I thought he was going to shoot us.'

'Sounds like a Hunter Thompson story,' I said.

'Sorry, mate?' Adrian didn't get it.

'So what happened?'

'We took Sandra's sis to the hospital and they pumped her stomach. She's cool now but her boyf doesn't want me near her. I haven't slept for two days. But this place is great. It reminds me of Cream in Liverpool.'

My pink champagne was kicking in, so I went downstairs to dance with Adrian and his cousin. Now, if the DJ wasn't Tony De Vit himself, then it was surely his ghost: the bass line was surrounded by a meander of rhythms, looping, yet coalescing around the main riff straight out of one of those Tinrib compilations. It was bliss.

Now, I know that bliss and heaven and such have had bad press. Christians keep describing heaven as the sun shining on green pastures accompanied by angels playing harps and the rest of us have easily assumed that it's boring – who likes harps anyway? I much prefer the Islamic version of heaven with its emphasis on corporeal hedonism: rivers of honey, mountains of pillau rice, beautiful boys and loads of *houris*, those snow-white nymphets. I believe that heaven is a place highly personal: for couch potatoes it's non-stop quiz shows and take-away pizzas; for sports fans it's an eternity of World Cup matches; for trainspotters it's a spaghetti network of Clapham Junctions. My own private heaven is an all-night non-stop rave with the added bonus of bumping into famous dead people.

The only dead South African personality I would like to meet would be King Shaka.

Shaka was not as beautiful as some sycophantic paintings show him and had buck teeth through which he lisped. He was an exhibitionist: in order to display the length of his adult genitalia, he took a public bath every day, an activity the inhabitants of the royal *kraal* were compelled to watch. It is here we enter the unorthodox sexual domain occupied by the Zulu nation-builder. Shaka enjoyed impaling his adversaries. He was very, very attached to his mother. He never married. He assembled a harem to show his virility, but never called any of the women his 'wife': they were either his 'sisters' or his 'daughters'. He never fathered a child, and any royal 'sisters' who got pregnant were killed for adultery, since he claimed the child could never be his.

Latent homosexual, you cry. Why latent? I ask.

Most historians agree that Shaka did not like sex and by that everyone implies sex with women. They are divided between the ones who consider him homosexual and the ones who consider him asexual. *Asexual?* Shaka as a Zulu Sir Cliff Richard? Pull the other one, mate.

If you aren't convinced yet, how about this: at the age of forty, Shaka started greying and, like any self-obsessed queen, he got quite, quite upset. Francis Farewell, who was a guest of honour in his royal *kraal*, tried to form an embassy to travel to Cape Town and forge an alliance with Britain. The way he got it off the ground was to promise Shaka that he would bring back some hair colouring (macassar oil, which is the origin of 'mascara') so that Shaka would look youthful again. Asexual? What with the lisp and all, he must have been *screaming*.

'What is Shaka?' asked Adrian.

'Hey?'

'You've been mumbling about something called Shaka,' he said. 'Do you often talk to yourself?'

Erm, not as a rule, no. But who was I to judge? I had just realised that Adrian and I were sitting at the bar in the VIP room and I couldn't remember walking there. As I looked around, one member of Adrian's posse collapsed in a heap. This was highly uncool.

'His wife is expecting in two weeks' time,' explained Adrian, 'and he is giving it all tonight. He's thirty-two and must now become responsible.'

Responsible?

'You know, support wife and kid.'

'And tonight is his final blow-out?'

'Indeed.'

Adrian picked up his friend who was tripping heavily, as I comradely offered my seat and went to the loo; this last conversation had exhausted me. It's hell trying to urinate when you are high, especially with people coming and going around you. Perhaps in heaven one permanently has that feeling of relief that comes when peeing after watching a production of Wagner's *Siegfried* – with no intervals – having drunk six pints of lager.

Now where was that VIP room?

I took a wrong turn in the maze that is Club 330 and found myself in a narrow corridor which zigged and zagged onto a staircase. I climbed up and accidentally discovered the chill-out terrace. Below me was Point Street, deserted, except for the odd open truck carrying black workers to the centre. In the east, the sun was rising in a brilliant salmon pink over the Indian Ocean. And north was the strange, variegated skyline of a city which is slow in drawing you in, but very skilful in keeping you hooked once you dare to make the plunge.

23. Size fixation – white

I arrived in my hotel unkempt and sweaty straight from the club; I caused a minor kerfuffle by walking into the dining room, making a beeline for the laid-out buffet and gulping a gallon of orange juice in one, straight from the carafe. This was a *four-star hotel* with a *fax* room and a *business centre*, I vaguely remember someone telling me – or rather telling me off, despite my protestations that I was very thirsty.

The continuous clubbing in Durban had turned me into a vespertine creature; true to form, I slept during the day and only woke up in time for the late afternoon performance at the Beachfront Aquarium. Now, I've never been impressed with dolphins, which have persuaded biologists they're not fish. Who are they kidding? Dolphins have fins, they have tails and if they wanted to be mammals they'd be seals. I mean, don't they die out of water? QED. And if you want a good piece of advice, don't sit too close for their act. By the time the 45-minute show was over I might as well have swam with them.

There were, however, some great sharks in the big tank. Sharks just *love* South African beaches. In Durban, the jaws of many a short-sighted shark that thinks it's spotted a sea lion have snapped an unlucky surfer. The coast is now protected with a set of nets that goes on for miles and miles. In the Aquarium's main tank, the ragged-tooth shark must be one of the meanest-looking creatures ever and the Zambezi variety, gliding nearby, is its match. They are both used to confined spaces and can happily live in a large aquarium: the ragged-tooths dwell in underwater caves and the Zambezis swim in the mouth of the eponymous river. One of the most hair-raising titbits of ragged-tooth biology is what happens to the unborn: there is only room for one baby shark, so if more are fertilised, the top kid devours its brothers and sisters in their mother's belly in a Hammer Horror variation of Darwinian selection.

This was my last night in Durban, so I chose the familiar ambience of the Galleon again. Zack was behind the bar. Stuart was there, drunk as usual. André, Thursday's stripper, was there, wearing only a loose pair of sports trousers and frolicking with an older, silver-haired guy. They were joined by Slade, a peroxide blond surfer, cute as they come, thankfully free of those Turettesian mannerisms. He was wearing one of those T-shirts where the sole design consists of a double integer ('Hey mate, you should buy that 33.' 'No way, number 16 suits me better.') The final Sunday night barfly was a middle-aged frail Indian, with his arm in a sling. He exuded an aura of PLUR (ravespeak for Peace, Love, Unity and Respect), smiling blissfully like the Mahatma after a juicy enema.

I had never seen Stuart sober but never that drunk. Every now and again he stopped and forgot how he had begun a sentence. Zack told him politely it was time to go. Stuart traipsed off unsteadily. André and Slade accompanied him.

'Are they going to drive him home?' I asked. 'He looks very drunk.'

'Oh, no,' said Zack. 'They're only going to walk him to his car, in case he gets mugged.'

'I would have thought he'd be in greater danger *behind* the wheel,' I said.

'You don't know Durban, dude,' countered Zack.

I gave up. My attention turned to the Indian.

'What happened to your arm?' I asked him.

The Indian kept smiling. 'It happened last week. I was walking behind the Holiday Inn in Central Beachfront and suddenly two guys pinned me against the wall and tried to take off my watch. It was not an expensive watch. But it had a leather strap which would not get loose. So they broke my wrist.'

I didn't know what to say but, somehow, I wasn't shocked.

'That's Durban,' he said. 'I would not mind it so much, but I am in pain. Even in a sling, it is hurting. I have been in agony for ten days.'

He smiled that karmic smile again.

I noticed some parallel straight lines carved on the bar. Each one had a name: Albert, Simon, Paul.

'What are these?' I asked.

Before Zack could answer, Slade and André returned.

'It's a good thing we went with him,' Slade said. 'He was so drunk he couldn't unlock the car.'

Thank goodness he's safe now…

'What are these straight lines on the bar?' I asked again.

Everyone looked meaningfully at each other.

'André will show you,' Zack said. 'Remember André, the other night you said you'd do it.'

André grinned and lowered his slacks. He was wearing no underwear and was highly tumescent.

'That's it,' Zack said. '*Now* André.'

André laid his erect penis against the bar. Zack marked the tip and took a ruler. I looked down.

'I see you're not from the Transvaal,' I remarked.

'How did you guess?' André replied.

I didn't answer. My eyes focused on a line longer than the rest by a good two inches. It must have been the biggest *Schwanzstucker* this side of the Limpopo.

Slade followed my gaze.

'This was John,' he said. 'He was six-foot-five.'

'I'm also called John,' I mused.

My companions fixed their gaze on me. Even Blind Freddie could see what they were thinking. I jumped. '*No way.*'

André winked at me.

'No, no, no,' I repeated. 'I'm on my comedown.'

Slade gave me one of *those* stares.

'No,' I said. 'I'm off tomorrow. I'm flying to Port Elizabeth.'

They gave up. 'Are you coming with us to Joe Kool's?' Slade asked. 'Sunday is great after midnight.'

'I'd love to,' I said and moved away, 'but I'll pass. I really am dead.'

Well, I might have been dead, but, as I walked the short distance to my hotel, I wasn't afraid any more.

24. Tamin' Durban

My flight to Port Elizabeth was in the afternoon, so I had a long promenade on Marine Parade. I bought the local paper and lay down on North Beach. So what had happened over the weekend?

A 74-year-old woman was raped and murdered in Sydenham. Minibus wars in Umbumbulu; two killed, two injured. A woman was bludgeoned with a lead pipe after an argument with her boyfriend on Brighton Beach. A man was stabbed to death by his girlfriend. An unidentified corpse was found on Chatsworth Road stoned to death; neighbourhood vigilante justice? A man was discovered shot in Camerdown – two 7.65mm cartridges were found by the scene. Six policemen appeared in court for stealing the money from a gang of robbers after they arrested them for holding up a bank. An unnamed but prominent businessman from Pietermaritzburg turned up drowned, floating in the Msunduzi river. An armed robbery in a shopfitter's left the wife of the owner dead; the perpetrators left boarding a bus.

I strolled along the pavements where back-to-back hawkers were less busy on a Monday and took more interest in me. I was drawn to the spreads of distinctive Zulu beadwork and bought myself a black-on-gold *incwadi*. This is a wrist-bracelet woven in intricate geometrical patterns with beads, given to lovers, bearing a message of love and affection. Zulu written communication was based on coloured beads, not a million miles from the Incas' knotted *quipu*. According to the accompanying brochure, my *incwadi* meant: '*I am jealous and have turned pitch black as the rafters of the hut as I hear you have taken another maiden.*' Silly purchase, but more sensible than the Smith and Wesson range next hawker along.

I found myself accidentally outside the swimming pool I had entered so scared on my first day. For good measure, I walked up all the way to the Induna Holiday Flats and hung out in a doorway, bored and weary, like the rest of the Zulu around me; this time I blended in, invisible. Walking towards the port, I noticed that police cars had surrounded a man who lay on the tarmac by the Vasco da Gama clock. I couldn't tell whether he was dead or not. Motorists sped by, uninterested.

It's the tough towns that are tops.

We were on the tarmac waiting to take off. I thought of last night's imbroglio in the Galleon. Measured publicly for your hard-on! Imagine!

I did.

I saw a group of Zulu teenagers in the forest, naked, their still uncircumcised members stretched on a tree log, an elder boy walking around with a dagger marking the tips, laughing at one boy's small signature; 'What is this, Shaka? I have seen better cashew nuts,' little knowing that these words had already marked him for the stake. The Zulu bodies were strong, athletic, lean and hairless, and they were sitting side by side at Joe Kool's with twitching and whistling surfers – strong, athletic, lean and hairless – worshipping the body beautiful. They were barefoot as Shaka had decreed, for who wants to be encumbered with shoes when running in the woods or surfing those swells?

As the plane took off and the trees merged into woods, I only wished the inhabitants of KwaZulu/Natal could see it all from where I was sitting, for they seemed so alike, so cross-pollinated with similar ideas, so proud and fearless, so absorbed in their frenetic dances and physical narcissism and so devoted in their common love for this stunning country of theirs: the black Zulu and the white Zulu who mistrust each other, but sadly refuse to acknowledge that their values, shaped by their close proximity and mutual admiration, are ultimately based on the same passions and obsessions, and that if their culture is not yet homogeneous, then hey, they've only just begun.

Chapter Eight

Garden Rout(e): Port Elizabeth to Knysna

One touch of Nature makes the whole world kin.
Shakespeare, *Troilus and Cressida*

25. Those Donut moments

Rain clouds shrouded the shores of the Eastern Cape and only shortly before we were about to land did I set my eyes on the province. It was worth it: the best part of my trip was that last approach from the sky, gazing at the perfect hyperbola of bottle-green Algoa Bay, its sandy shore unsullied by harbours or motorways.

The internal flight with SAA was adventuresome. For a start, they lost my luggage *before* I checked in. I was queuing behind one of those *backveld* Boer families of thirteen-plus. As soon as their bags had been tagged, I placed mine on the scales. The check-in girl pressed the buttons liberally and my luggage disappeared with the others without a check-in slip. By the time I shouted 'Stop!' it was too late. She had to go downstairs and search manually before reappearing twenty minutes later, by which time the unfortunates in the queue behind me were probably devising an assassination attempt. This being South Africa, it would be a trifle; in all probability they all carried handguns.

Guns at an airport? But of course. This being South Africa, there was a 'Gun Check-In'. Apparently they wrap your gun, seal it and take it on board; you pick it up and unseal it at your destination (counting back the bullets as you disembark, I presume). This being South Africa, there were also abrupt messages spat abrasively over the Tannoy: 'Will the passenger who is successfully delaying South African Airlines flight number 607 to Cape Town please board now?' Or 'If the two passengers on flight number SA 8230 to Bloemfontein do not show up within five minutes, THEY WILL BE REMOVED FROM THE FLIGHT!'

But that was KwaZulu/Natal. This was the Eastern Cape, and I could hardly disguise my excitement. Here I was in the anglicised ex-Cape Colony, the self-professed liberal beacon in the racial hurricane that was South Africa. And where better to start than Port Elizabeth? The town was established in 1820 with an infusion of settlers of good British stock. Missionary associations were at the forefront of the venture, aching to save souls and spread the word of the Lord. One of the ways they were to accomplish this was by translating the Bible and teaching the locals how to read it. It is no coincidence that the Eastern Cape urban centres with their educated black leadership were primary focal points of the resistance against apartheid.

Of course, high expectations lead to greater disappointments: maybe it was the incessant drizzle that welcomed me, but as soon I saw the industrial, nondescript centre of Port Elizabeth, all bypasses and featureless streets, I wanted to leave immediately. In this Rainbow Nation it is the only town that looks grey. My heart sank in sync with Adulphe Delegorgue's, who arrived in May 1839 after a four-day sea trip from Cape Town: *'The establishment of Graham's Town situated 60 miles away has brought Port Elizabeth into being. These two towns, which are already of some importance, date back only twenty-five years. All Graham's Town trade must pass through Port Elizabeth. This place, however, offers nothing of interest.'* Nuff said, Adulphe.

Then maybe it was the wind – the Shipwreck Coast beyond Algoa Bay has not gained this morbid nickname by coincidence. There are 46 wrecks just in Plettenberg Bay. Any winds reaching these shores have swept in from Antarctica, gaining speed over an ocean the size of Europe, unhindered by mountains or cliffs. The southern Cape winds have been the source of trepidation for generations of seamen and, after a few hours' walk in Port Elizabeth, I could well sympathise with them: the occasional blast, when it came, put me several times off-balance.

'What is there to do in Port Elizabeth?' I asked, fresh-faced, in the local tourist office.

South African tourist organisations seem to hire frail elderly ladies who are totally uninterested in their work, in the same way that Eastern European museums employ women of post-pensionable age to sit on a bench and stare blankly at a wall.

'First there are the beaches on the Summerstrand,' said the old lady in a very English accent, much better than mine.

I looked at the hideous greyness of the sky outside.

'The season hasn't started yet, and the weather isn't up to it,' she conceded, 'but we offer some of the best beaches in South Africa. Here's a brochure. Then there is Addo Elephant Park with the last remnants of herds of African elephant. Here's a brochure. If you want to go further afield, I suggest the Mountain Zebra National Park to see the unique Burchell's zebra that lives only in this part of the world. Here's a brochure. The city itself has some excellent colonial architecture around the Market Square down the hill on your left. We recommend a walking tour which you'll find very satisfying; the Dunkin' Heritage Trail.'

'Oh,' I knowingly grinned back. 'A doughnut on every corner! How thoughtful.'

The lady opposite didn't register.

'Your Dunkin' trail. It's sponsored by Dunkin' Donuts, no?'

The lady opposite blushed indignantly.

'The *Donkin* Heritage Trail,' she cleared her throat, 'is named in honour of Sir Rufane Donkin, governor of the Cape province, who, on 6 June 1820, named the settlement of Algoa Bay, Port Elizabeth after his wife Elizabeth, who died in India.' She took a deep breath and composed herself. 'Here's a brochure.'

I'd booked at the Edward Hotel after reading about its affordable colonial ambience. It overlooks the Donkin Reserve, a small, open space opposite the tourist office. Originally the King Edward Hotel – the 'King' bit was pettily removed in 1961 expressing the anti-British sentiment of the ruling National Party – this is an exceptional *art nouveau* building. It opened in 1904 when sixty gentlemen sat down for the inaugural dinner at the restaurant where I never had any meals, because a German holiday group occupied every conceivable nook and corner during lunch and dinner. It's amazing how easily a party of Germans takes over a place, even if there are no towels to put on deckchairs – hell, not even deckchairs to put those non-existent towels on.

The original King Edward Hotel offered 120 bedrooms and twelve suites specially adapted for doctor and dentist practices (don't ask why; I have also wondered about this). Each room had a gas lamp and an unusual innovation for its time: an electric bell. The hotel still has a lift which claims to be the oldest working in South Africa; I took a good look at it and used the stairs. There were two wings, each one with a large glass-roofed atrium spanning all floors, where tropical flowers and trees planted then blossom to this day. From my window I could see across the Donkin Reserve to the decaying Grand Hotel, an even older edifice, dating from 1885. That's where

Cecil Rhodes and Mark Twain lodged when they visited the city. It's now advertising cut-price rooms for backpackers.

The wind appeared to have subsided. People were folding their umbrellas. Maybe it was time for that heritage trail.

After the Union Buildings in Pretoria, Port Elizabeth's Market Square is the most architecturally cohesive ensemble I saw in South Africa. As I was facing the City Hall (gutted by fire in 1977) the mock-Gothic public library stood on my right with its terracotta façade sent from England to be reassembled here. This was where ships moored in the nineteenth century and goods were exchanged and sold, before reclaimed land pushed back the marine frontier. This was also where the 1820 English settlers – all 4,000 of them – first set foot on African land in the greatest colonisation project of its time.

The place felt strangely familiar and yet exotic: soothing, chummy Home Counties surroundings populated by black faces and foreign accents. I walked across to Prester John's statue. This is a strange choice for a monument, for Prester John was a mythical figure whose lore drove the Portuguese to explore Mozambique: his is the tale of a Christian priest who had ascended the throne of an African tribe, allegedly lording it in the jungle like Marlon Brando as General Kurtz in a kind of *Apocalypse Then.*

I walked up the steep slope of Castle Hill past the Opera House – this is a cultured city – to the Donkin Reserve and the pyramid next to the town lighthouse. I stood back and looked at this pre-Victorian folly. A dedication is inscribed to *'one of the most perfect human beings who has given her name to the town below'* by *'the husband whose heart is still wrung by undiminished grief'*. Taj Mahal it ain't, but any monument to love, however naff, is moving. We know little about Elizabeth Donkin – her best portrait was destroyed in that City Hall fire of 1977 – but we do know that her husband loved her so much that he ensured her name lives on in the town she never set foot in. Although the combined conurbation of Port Elizabeth, Uitenhage and Dispatch is now called Nelson Mandela Bay, renaming Port Elizabeth itself is thankfully out of the question. Love is still politically correct.

Way back from the ocean, deep into the more sheltered avenues of the modern town where Parliament Street meets Cape Road, I came across a quintessential English oddity. Forget the inspirational singularity of the statue of Prester John or the emotional anguish of the Donkin pyramid: I stood there looking at a monument to a horse. And not just any horse, but to the Unknown Horse that helped the Imperial cavalry during the Boer War. It was unveiled at a grand ceremony in 1905 and bears an incongruous inscription, given the history of this country: *'The greatness of a nation consists not so much in the number of its people or the extent of its territory as in the extent and justice of its compassion.'*

I hope we can all agree on *that*.

26. The secret tree bird

In desperate need of a break from the drizzle that engulfed Port Elizabeth, I took a trip to Addo Elephant Park with Callum and Caz, whom I met in the Edward Hotel bar under its prominent sign, *'Tipping is not a town in China'*. They were a perfectly matched couple at the start of their round-the-world trip. They were English through and through, with the minor mutation that they could tan: their faces looked carved out of a close-grained smooth brown wood – a week's diving course at Kosi Bay had seen to that.

Callum had been working for a well-known management consultancy. When he turned thirty, he realised that he wanted to see the world.

'So he resigned,' said Caz.

Very impressive.

'And you know what happened?' she continued. 'You won't believe it.'

Go on.

'They gave me a year off, unpaid leave,' said Callum, 'with a promise that I could go back to my old job when I returned. I said make it fourteen months and you have a deal.'

Caz continued to tell me their life story as we drove on the N2 through a landscape teeming with orange groves. This is one of the most pleasant highways you are likely to drive through: the section from Port Elizabeth to Cape Town has earned the nickname 'Garden Route'. At springtime it was fragrant, the blossom of citrus trees scenting the air. The Eastern Cape is where those oranges we used to boycott in the 1980s came from.

Only once did a haphazard huddle of huts interrupt the spectacle. We stretched our necks.

'Over there is Motherwell, a *bleck* township,' Gert, our guide, informed us with annoyance in his voice, 'and that's the spillover of the squatter camps. They should do something about it. People who travel to Addo get the wrong impression.'

Caz and I looked at each other. *What was the right impression?* We let it pass.

'What are those tall masts with the things like lampshades on top?' I asked instead.

'Street lights,' piped up Gert. 'You know, for the night.'

'They can't be,' Caz countered. 'They must be more than a hundred feet tall.'

'It's to illuminate a wider area. You build fewer of them this way.'

I tried to imagine the muted glow that must prevail in a township at night: it couldn't be more than having the TV on with lights off. Was it dark enough to sleep? Was it bright enough to read?

'Just enough to see where you're going,' said Gert, as if guessing my thoughts.

I exchanged glances with Caz again. Did the residents of Motherwell deserve no better?

Not long afterwards, we reached the park entrance. Addo is situated in the Sundays River Valley at the foothills of the

Zuurberg mountains. Although it was established back in 1931 as a small reserve of 2,000-odd acres to protect a herd of just eleven elephants, these 'charismatic megaherbivores' – as the park authorities like to describe them – have since multiplied to 350. As a consequence, the park has had to be extended in order to accommodate their voracious appetite which threatens the survival of other species.

The park is set to expand further and become a tourist magnet for the Eastern Cape in an area stretching from the barren desolation of the Karoo to the coast of Algoa Bay. Lions were recently introduced, so, like the Kruger, it can boast the 'Big Five' but, unlike the Kruger, it doesn't suffer from malaria. Plans are afoot to do even better: when it encompasses the marine reserve that includes the small offshore islands of Birds and St Croix, tourists will be able to experience the 'Big Seven'. This is a newly-invented term: the 'Big Five' plus sharks and whales. I can't imagine the great white hunters arming themselves with harpoons like Captain Ahab to add a stuffed whale's head to their trophy room, but historical details and a grasp on reality are too much of an encumbrance to the magnificence of marketing concepts.

Gert had an impenetrable accent – compounded with a lisp – which led to many an enigmatic utterance.

'Over there, you can see the secret tree bird,' he told us soon after we entered the park premises.

We turned.

'Which is the secret tree, then?' I asked, puzzled.

Callum and Caz looked embarrassed.

'No,' said Gert, 'The secret-tree-bird. No tree.'

I was lost. Gert turned red.

'Secret-tree-bird. S-E-C-R-E-T-A-R-Y!'

Oops. There goes another Dunkin Donuts moment. I pretended nothing had happened as I contemplated the oddity that is the secretary bird – only the hamerkop can match it in weirdness. It looks like a four-foot scraggy chicken on stilts with a distinctive crest of sparse, sharp black feathers like quill pens stuck at the back of clerks' wigs. It fascinated nineteenth-century biologists so much that it's depicted in the coat-of-arms of Cape Town's South African Museum along with Pliny's proverb: *semper aliquid novi Africa affert* (Africa always brings forth something new).

Some useless facts about secretary birds:
1. *They have nothing to do with personal assistants – or quill pens. Their name comes from the Arabic saqr-et-tair which means 'hunting bird'.*
2. *They eat reptiles and poisonous snakes and for this reason they were a protected species early on. By the 1830s the fine for killing one was 500 rixdollars.*
3. *Like ostriches, they have a strong kick and stamp their prey to death.*

Gert turned around. 'There are two species which have right of way in the Addo,' he said with a barrister's aplomb.

We could guess the first.

'One is, of course, the olifant,' Gert continued with a giggle. 'You don't want to crash on one of them. Can you guess which is the other one?'

'The secretary bird?' I ventured.

'No, it can happily run away,' said Gert.

'The rhino?' I continued.

Gert was jubilant. 'NO! It's the flightless dung beetle! It's an endangered species and the Addo is the only place in the Cape with a substantial population. It can't fly away, because it's *flightless*, as I said, so cars are supposed to give way to this tiny insect.'

And with that he screeched the car to an emergency stop. 'There's one,' he shouted triumphantly, as we checked ourselves for whiplash.

Some useless facts about flightless dung beetles:
1. *The dung ball is pushed by the females at about 25–30 feet per hour. Males follow close behind to protect them.*

2. *When the dung ball is buried, mating takes place underground and a single egg is laid by the female. The larva hatches in a few days and feeds on the ball.*

3. *As elephants like to walk unhindered on man-made roads rather than the bush, they deposit their dung there. It attracts the beetles, which get run over by tourist cars.*

4. *Dung beetles actually prefer buffalo dung. But, I suppose, you eat what you can find.*

We first encountered the elephants by the Rooidam waterhole. The Kruger has elephants – but they are solitary. In the Addo the animals are living, feeding, drinking and playing in *herds*.

Caz commented that some of them were tuskless.

'It's the nineteenth century hunters,' explained Gert. 'They shot and killed the olifants for their tusks and speeded up a Darwinian selection process. You were more likely to survive if you had small tusks, or preferably no tusks at all.'

And if you think that's an exaggeration –

'You've been to the Kruger, you said?' Gert turned to me.

'Yes, I have.'

'You saw buffaloes grazing during the day?'

'Yes, I did.'

'You won't see any here. As a result of the hunting, buffaloes have become nocturnal in the Cape. They come out to graze at night, like hippos.'

About time for...

Some useless elefacts:

1. *Elephants are so plentiful in South Africa that in the Kruger Park they are being culled (up to 300–500 per year).*

2. *There is evidence of right- and left-handedness of tusks. Most elephants use their right tusk for digging and stripping bark off trees.*

3. *A female's breasts are positioned between her front legs – unlike in other mammals where teats are situated on a line between the front and the hind legs. In this respect elephants resemble humans and apes.*

4. *Elephants dig up termite hills and eat the soil. The latest conjecture is that it's because they have a high sodium content.*

I had been dismissive of Addo when we started ('a single-animal park'), cocky 'cos I'd been to the Kruger and no one else had, but by the end I'd been won over, if only by the superb birdlife. A colourful bee-eater sang its *tee-dadadada* song in front of us as we started marching on the Spekboom Trail and, as if summoned telepathically, a fat red bishop, a weaver-like bird stunningly scarlet on its back and totally black in its face, perched itself next to us and watched us with curiosity.

We became just a tad nervous by a waterhole when we saw a large elephant herd of about a dozen charging down the hill towards the water – and ourselves. Thankfully, they stopped in time. They drank and hosed themselves; the little ones played tag; the *Ndlovukazi* used her trunk to scratch herself under the arm. It sounds so banal on paper, but nothing can be as exhilarating as observing animal behaviour in the wild. As a special bonus, a family of meerkats sporting large, moist eyes, elegant, black-tipped noses and slender bodies stood on their toes observing the surroundings from a rock. On the charmometer scale these ferret-like creatures come second only to rock dassies (of whom a lot more later). I have been an avid watcher of meerkat documentaries for years and sure enough, the ones in our Addo group didn't disappoint, stretching themselves up cutely on two feet to stake out in vain for predators that have been hunted to extinction in the Cape.

Maybe someone should tell the meerkats.

27. *The sixth kingdom*

It was the third consecutive day of the drizzle, the mist and the low cloud; it reminded me of English winter. (No, it was warm; make that English *summer*.) Back on the Baz Bus at the crack of dawn, I was reunited with Robert and Wendy, the Australian couple who had travelled with me to Swaziland.

After the initial buzz of excitement, I sank into my seat sleepily. The rest of the passengers were red-eyed and uncommunicative, but at least we were leaving Port Elizabeth for the Garden Route. The bus was full; like the Spanish Armada, ours was a backpacker horde routed by the weather.

Our first stop was the surfer's paradise of Jeffreys Bay. I'm sure it is delightful in season; but while I was there, the deserted, wet beach, the incessant drizzle and the hotel sprawl reminded me of Bournemouth. The difference is that J-Bay has supposedly the perfectly-angled coastline to catch the wind and create the best right-hand point break in the whole world. Typically, the main backpacker hostel was called 'Supertubes', after the long, hollow wave you see in the *Hawaii Five-0* opening sequence, a staple feature of the surf in J-Bay. The structure looked leaky and exposed to the elements, but then surfers love it wet: *real* surfers come here during the winter when the wind is strongest – just the thought made me put on a windcheater.

We rode back on an exposed section of the N2 to face more wind, Patagonian wind, wind that caused trees to grow at an angle: we were surrounded by woods permanently bent. The gales upon us were the notorious southeasterlies, hitting us sideways with gusts of untempered force. I anxiously checked the bus for ballast. Everyone was thin; they'd been in Africa for a few weeks, all right. The bus was so precariously balanced, if I but farted, I'd create a deadly torque.

Then, as we had all resigned ourselves to the grim conditions, a small miracle occurred.

Slowly and imperceptibly the N2 narrowed to a point where the bus was travelling under the shadow of large Outeniqua hardwoods and, in time, the Baz Bus became silent. The rain magically subsided while the wind was reduced to a remote hiss. Only Robbie Williams was left bellowing over the speakers about angels, as we were drawn into the sixth floral kingdom.

I have the unenviable task of trying to describe the indescribable, because to most people who have not seen what I saw, I might as well be describing the landscape on Mars: blue clouds made of ice, pink skies – because of the dust that floats – mauve sunsets, because the sun is further away, and dusk that lasts for two hours even on the equator. I am at an equal loss to convey to you what, for a human, must surely be one of the most extraordinary sights still left on our planet: the encounter of new life forms one never knew existed. Suppose you had not seen birds before; you weren't even aware of their existence. Now suppose that all the different species were concentrated in, say, Portugal. Imagine sitting on a train cruising through the plains of the Iberian peninsula, when suddenly you first catch sight of these feathered creatures – thousands and thousands of species of life you have never heard of.

That's what Tsitsikamma turned out like.

Guidebooks tell you that the Cape floral kingdom is the sixth floral kingdom in the world, but none mention the other five. Well, I will. There is the Boreal kingdom, the largest, comprising the vegetation in Europe, the Mediterranean, North and Central Asia and North America; the Paleotropical (sub-Saharan Africa, South and South-east Asia); and the Neotropical (Mexico, Central and South America). As usual, Australia merits a kingdom by itself. Then we have the Antarctic kingdom, which includes the Patagonian cone and, remarkably, New Zealand. Finally, comprising an area only as large as Portugal, is the sixth: the Cape floral kingdom. The British Isles are home to about 1,500 plants. There are 1,700 on Table Mountain alone. There are four families of heather in Scotland, 26 in the rest of the world, and an astounding 600-plus in the Cape, called ericas. It's this incredible concentration of new species one is confronted with in Tsitsikamma that grips and silences even the most casual onlooker. The major components of the flora are the *fynbos*, which means 'fine bush' in Afrikaans. These are: the proteas, which are shrubs with large waxy leaves; the aforementioned heather-like ericas; and the reeds or *restios* that are used for making thatch or teas, like *rooibos* tea, the best-known *fynbos* export.

But it is the proteas that define this land – pincushions, conebrushes, bottlebrushes and the giant red protea, itself the symbol of South Africa – and it is the proteas that face extinction from imported, killer flora. In times past, most of the Cape was covered in aromatic sugarbushes, proteas whose sweet nectar could easily be obtained just before dawn by squeezing the dew off the flower into a jar, as much as a teaspoonful per head. A hiker might also come across the ethereal, snow-white petals of another protea, the 'blushing bride'. This is a flower steeped in folklore: it used to be worn on the lapel of a male suitor, as he paid a visit to his future in-laws to ask for the hand of his beloved who blushed, since their affair was now in the open. It is a plant that was thought extinct throughout the nineteenth century, until it was spotted by chance in a Franschhoek flower show in the early 1900s. Its seeds, cultivated under guard in Cape Town's Kirstenbosch Gardens, have now spread around the world so much so that extinction is happily out of the question.

No such luck for the mace pagoda first described in 1922 by the absent-minded Mr. Thomas Stokoe who inconveniently forgot where he found it. Three years later he recognised it again in a Cape Town market; the flower-seller took him to a spot where a colony of mace pagodas were thriving. The exact location was kept secret, but in vain: by the 1960s only a single specimen remained and a tripod was erected to protect it. It was not a good idea, because the formidable Cape winds crashed the tripod on the plant and killed it.

Our indomitable Thomas Stokoe also made headlines in the 1940s when he came across a population of the rare diminutive powerpuff in the Palmiet River Valley. This was a plant that had not been seen since 1800 when its seeds were brought to England and grown in someone's back garden in Clapham.

Unfortunately the diminutive powerpuff is extinct today, because in 1985 Stokoe's grove was uprooted to make space for – wait for it – an apple orchard. I don't know whether I should laugh or cry. Nowadays there are rewards for a confirmed sighting of such extinct proteas – and, frankly, you could do no worse than have a stroll down Clapham Common. If it's at night and a policeman approaches and asks you whether you are loitering with intent, tell him that you are looking for the elusive diminutive powerpuff and see how he reacts.

The apple orchard incident aside, people didn't consciously intend to wipe out proteas in South Africa; it's just that the conservation authorities were simply at a loss as to what to do – these plants defied all established knowledge.

The turning point involved the cultivation of the blushing bride. After it was rediscovered, the romantic connotations of the name ensured that everything possible was done to preserve the species. Yet within a decade the irrigated and carefully weeded plants were dying, scraggy and weak, and to top it all, an accidental fire killed them all off. To the surprise of the horticulturists, seeds long thought to be infertile started germinating and within three years sixty new plants were flourishing. A massive project was started to protect the remaining blushing brides from other competing plants and predators. Once more, the plan failed and the population declined, until another adventitious fire whisked the area clean. It was then that the penny dropped: when strong, sprouting blushing brides started growing in large numbers once again.

You see, the most interesting aspect of *fynbos* is how they have adapted over millions of years, not to a varying climate from winter to summer like other plants, but to occasional destruction and devastation. Lightning is very common in South Africa and the dry, Mediterranean Cape climate connives with the storms to produce many a *veld* fire. So the *fynbos* have evolved *depending* on the occasional conflagration for their survival. Many species sprout from seeds that have fallen, or been cached underground; others only germinate after a fire.

It would be like humans adapting to volcanic explosions, and even depending on frequent eruptions for their survival.

The Baz Bus stopped.

Imagine the waves of the Indian Ocean crashing on the sharp rocks of a concealed cove, with the Outeniqua yellowwoods, as tall as any California redwood, covering the surrounding slopes. Imagine those new floral species of *fynbos* you've just encountered sheltering on the cliff sides all the way down a steep drop from the Tsitsikamma forest. Imagine waterfalls, rest camps with log cabins and scenic trails.

You may be imagining, but I'm not; I'm describing the most magical spot in my South African diary: Storm's River Mouth. I'm told that, in season, one can go snorkelling, scuba diving and swimming with dolphins. But I'm glad I saw it wild and imposing in colours dark and doom-laden, as Caledonian in character as the opening scene of *Macbeth* – only the three witches and their hurly-burly were missing. I saw it as it should be seen: surf-pounded in stormy weather.

The Baz Bus dropped off a couple in their fifties who had obviously done their homework. Many more stayed on impulse. A guy from Holland passed around a spliff. The rest of us dispersed to the chagrin of our driver ('We have a long way to go') who, in the end, decided to chill out and join our silent staring at the sky, at the sea, and at the dense forest around us. That wind all the way from the Antarctic whistled in my ears a song I could not decipher, but I smiled contentedly for I felt that serene, seeping, privileged satisfaction of being alive.

Splendour turns me soppy.

28. Cartoon Paradise

The Garden Route is rainy. Hey, if you want dry weather, go to the Med.

Knysna is a town dressed in British chintz and steeped in New Age consciousness: flaky like a chocolate twirl and nutty like rapeseed oil. For the English accents, focaccia breads, and smoked *bok* delicatessens – plus the downpour – you might have thought you were in Islington and the Blairs were your next-door neighbours. I found shelter in Macintosh's deli, where I bought four cans of paté: kudu, impala, ostrich and crocodile. Oh goodie, were those pink peppercorns? I had to have them. I could also not resist the Persian pickled garlic. I bought a jar despite my fears of leakage in transit and I still have only used four cloves in four different stews. I can only unscrew the jar with an open window and even then the big dog in the ground flat starts barking. The label says that, traditionally, Persian pickled garlic is kept for fifty years and served to honoured guests. The delicacy is obviously a ploy by the clergy in their campaign to abolish the sex drive. Never underestimate those mullahs.

I was staying at an idyllically situated B&B, the Yellowwood Lodge, that was operated by an expat couple from Yorkshire. This was an old manor house with wooden floors and high ceilings, furnished in landed gentry chic. The *Complete Fly Fisherman* was one of the periodicals on offer, the soap was lavender and a mighty English breakfast was included in the price. There were doilies everywhere: a doily on my teacup, a doily on the biscuit tin, a doily on the spare roll of toilet paper on top of the doilied toilet cistern. I only had a slight problem with the vicious guard dogs roaming the garden. Whatever the weather, I always came back after midnight and had to throw stones at them to prevent them chomping off my bollocks.

Idyllic or not, it was wet. This was not a downpour like Swaziland or the Kruger, but a good old-fashioned English shower.

'They don't call it the Garden Route for nothing,' said my landlady, happy to talk about the weather like back home. 'It rains a lot. Knysna can have four seasons in a day. Would you like your breakfast in the veranda?'

'In this weather?'

She shrugged her shoulders.

'I thought you might like to join the Scots,' she replied. 'They like to breakfast in the rain.'

I looked at an elderly couple eating under the balcony who waved back, smiling.

I ate a lot in Knysna, and I blame the weather. My favourite eatery was a small restaurant on Thesen's Island, in the Knysna lagoon which comes complete with its own shipwreck spread all over the sea floor. (Nowadays, the island is connected by a short, shallow levee with the mainland.) The restaurant was owned and occupied by the Knysna Oyster Company that farmed and served oysters larger than a size A1 French *ouitre*, and mussels whose fleshy heart was larger than the shell of a single Belgian *moule*.

I ate and also laughed a lot. The sky might have been drab and it might have turned people grumpy, but I had giggling fits. I stayed in and read two *Madam and Eve* volumes that I bought in a browser-friendly bookshop. This comic deserves an introduction, as it is hardly known outside the country except by cartoon cognoscenti.

Bushman cave paintings and a few Nobel literature prize winners notwithstanding, *Madam and Eve* ranks among the best art to have originated from South Africa, and I use the word art with the full connotations it carries. Truly great art encapsulates the Zeitgeist and renders it immortal. The format depends on the artist, and a cartoon strip is no less valid as a medium of expression than an aquarelle sketch. If anyone wants to learn about life in the South Africa of today and its interactions with the world at large, one need go no further than read the daily publication of this cartoon strip. It is the brainchild of an American writer, Stephen Francis; a South African copy editor, Harry Dugmore; and a Vienna-born illustrator, Rico Schecherl. I find it hilarious.

The inspiration for the cartoon came from Stephen Francis' mother-in-law, in Alberton, Gauteng, and her maid Grace. Their wacky relationship, burdened with history and preconceptions, fascinated Francis. He had arrived from the States in 1988 for a short sojourn that became a lifetime after he bumped into Dugmore and Rico who were already collaborating on a pioneering satirical magazine called *Laughing Stock*. The threesome offered their combined strip to the *Weekly Mail* – now the *Mail & Guardian* – and the comic was born in June 1992. From then on, it was plain sailing. The strip is syndicated around the world, with the French – those connoisseurs of comics – its greatest admirers. President Mbeki is also supposed to be a devotee, although he has been the object of much of the strip's lampooning.

Just a quick word about the title: a 'madam' in South Africa is not a brothel keeper; this is the sarcastic sobriquet of a housewife who doesn't do any housework but employs domestic staff instead. There are three main characters: Gwen Anderson, the white 'madam', her black maid Eve, and Gwen's mother, cynical gin-swilling Grandma Edith Anderson, one of the best cartoon personalities of all time alongside Dennis the Menace, Garfield or Dilbert. The comic satirises modern South African situations leaving nothing intact in its wake. Whereas in the US and in the UK cartoonists may have to bow to the specific offensivities and political correctness of our times, Francis, Dugmore and Rico poke fun at everyone indiscriminately. In a country with such a strict, censorious past, there are no sacred cows; writers are aware that any self-censorship is tantamount to weakness, and that a society in which *Madam and Eve* can be published is a healthy society, because the ultimate freedom is to be able to laugh at oneself.

The happening place in Knysna was a first floor saloon called 'Tin Roof Blues' with a large, wrought iron balcony. Robert, Wendy and I found it on my last night. Someone called simply

'Matt' was playing the blues. Now, I didn't come from London to Knysna to hear the blues – I have seen Eric Clapton, I have, albeit in one of his less divine incarnations. Hell, I don't even *like* the blues, what with people singing how they got up this morning and went back to sleep again, but – *but* – it was the only entertainment on offer. Excepting, of course, our stories.

'When did you two meet?' I asked them.

Blank stares.

'It was '91,' said Robert.

'No, '92,' said Wendy.

Blank stares.

'Ahem,' I said, 'I know couples who don't remember anniversaries, but they *do* remember the year they met.'

'We met at a festival,' said Robert helpfully.

'We're not arguing about *that*,' said Wendy.

'In '91 or '92,' Robert added.

Moving in to pacify the couple, I recounted the horrors of the hostel in Mbabane, the delights of St Lucia and my clubbing experiences in Durban.

Wendy shook her head.

'I can believe anything about Durban. In the hostel we stayed at there, people were having sex in the dorm. In fact, they were having sex in the bunk below ours.'

'Tsk, tsk,' I said, appalled. 'Bonking in the bunk! Bring back single-sex dorms!'

More beer.

'Are you staying tomorrow?' Wendy asked. 'We're going to see the elephants around Knysna. They're so tame you can touch them. I'd love to stroke an elephant.'

'The skin will feel wet,' I said. 'It will rain tomorrow.'

'It *has* to be dry, mate. It's been pissing for five days,' said Robert.

'I checked the weather forecast in the *Cape Argus*. It will be raining everywhere except the Karoo, which is where I'm heading to,' I retorted and went to buy my round.

When I returned, Robert had followed two leather-clad, biker-looking guys into the balcony outside. They had been standing next to us and – now that I thought about it – had been trying to attract our attention.

I looked at Wendy questioningly.

'I don't know,' she said. 'I hope it's all right.'

We tried to make out what was happening.

'I think they're trying to sell something. I don't like it,' Wendy said and walked over. I could hear, faintly, some verbal altercations between my two Australian friends. When Wendy dragged Robert back, he looked sheepish.

'Do you know what they tried to sell him?'

What?

'*Dope*,' said Wendy. 'They were trying to sell him *drugs*!'

I was delighted. 'How wonderful! Let's roll one right now. Any skins?'

'She didn't let me have any, mate,' said Robert.

'You don't know who they are. This is a foreign country. We shouldn't dabble in drugs with people we don't know,' said Wendy sensibly.

Erm, yes, of course. I sobered up and looked at the balcony. Empty.

'Excuse me for a sec,' I said, as I ran down the staircase, already out of breath.

The two bikers had disappeared. The main street of Knysna was deserted. The rain had ceased, and the cool, clean air made the blues guitarist sound crisper. I checked a few blocks further. Nothing. Funny, it was the first time I'd walked the streets of a South African town at night and felt safe. It's in places like Knysna where you're reminded that the cauldron of South Africa boils mainly in the big cities.

Someone made a noise next to me. I checked my right. A black guy was tapping his foot listening to the 12-bar melodies emanating from Matt's guitar. We exchanged glances. He chanced a wistful smile and shivered. He must have been standing there for quite some time.

He couldn't get in? Is that it? Or he *wouldn't* get in?

I rewound and played back my memories. There were no black faces in the 'Tin Roof Blues'. There were no black shoppers in the New Age food shops. There were no black guests in the Yellowwood Lodge, no black hikers in Tsitsikamma, no black surfers in J-Bay. In the anglicised Cape province where everyone knows their place, they kept out of sight. Or rather as petrol station attendants, housemaids, drivers, or street drunks they blended with a background I had got so used to, I barely noticed. Now that I thought about it, there was a black man in the blues joint: the empty glass collector.

So John, I asked myself, what about you? You've been in South Africa for so long and what do you know about how the majority lives? You didn't go to Soweto, you didn't go to KwaMashu, you were scared of Kahle. Granted, you may have met up with Swazis and Zulus – so what? You're living *separately*. That's what they want you to do, for that's what they designed: to keep the black faces out of sight. If the locals could, they'd put a doily on them, too, in this New Age cartoon paradise of Knysna – all feng-shui furniture covered in Laura Ashley fabrics. The Garden Route is the tourist route; visitors can spend their time driving through the N2 without seeing the shacks, without having to feel guilty, only occasionally *getting the wrong impression* – by accident. Now at last I know: the reason F. W. de Klerk surrendered his powers is because things were already so far apart that it would be impossible to bolt them together. Was this new South Africa a sham?

I didn't have much time to find out.

Chapter Nine

Ostrich Operetta: Oudtshoorn, Klein Karoo

Overture (flashback to Pretoria's Club DNA)
ME [dancing and addressing a stranger]: *These disco biscuits are fan-tastic!*
FUZZY FACE: *They are produced by the South African police, man. Guaranteed quality!*
ME [shaking from laughter]: *Yeah, and I'm a banjo!*

plonk!

29. Act One

Setting: 8, 9 and 10 June 1998, the Truth and Reconciliation Commission of South Africa, Chemical and Biological Warfare (CBW) hearings under the chairmanship of Archbishop Tutu. For the state: Mr Hanif Vally, Mr Jerome Chaskalson and Dr Fazil Randera. Testifying are scientists on biological weapon research: Dr Johan Koekemoer, Dr Mike Odendaal, Dr Schalk van Rensburg and Dr Jan Lourens.

MR VALLY: Doctor Koekemoer, what was your occupation prior to joining Delta G?

DR KOEKEMOER: Prior to joining Delta G, I was Professor of Organic Chemistry at the Rand Afrikaans University. I have a BSc in Chemistry, MSc in Organic Chemistry and also a DSc in Organic Chemistry.

MR VALLY: How did you come to join Delta G?

DR KOEKEMOER: I was recruited by Doctor G L Lourens who was, early in 1986, head of the Research Unit at Delta G Scientific. I had worked with him previously at a private company and I also knew him as a student.

MR VALLY: Did you know what Delta G was?

DR KOEKEMOER: I was informed that, when I joined Delta G in April 1986, that we would be developing an analytical capability, defensive analytical capability, towards Chemical Warfare Agents and that we would be doing some work on potential... [indistinct]

MR VALLY: Were you aware that it was a military front company?

DR KOEKEMOER: Yes, I was aware. I only actually became aware at a later stage when I was asked to sign a document relating to the Official Secrets Act.

MR VALLY: What was your function at Delta G?

DR KOEKEMOER: I started in April 1986 as a Chief Researcher and at that stage I reported to Doctor Lourens who was the head of my department. [...]

MR VALLY: What was the nature of your daily interaction with Doctor Philip Mijburgh when he was the Managing Director?

DR KOEKEMOER: Well, Doctor Mijburgh was Managing Director of Delta G Scientific initially and then when Medchem Consolidated Investments – I don't know the history of Medchem, but when Medchem Consolidated Investments was established in 1990, he became Chairman of this group but he still retained what he called being Chief Executive Officer of Delta G Scientific. And we, I, did my research work and we reported this to Doctor Basson [Author's note: this is Dr Wouter Basson, the manager of the South African chemical and biological warfare projects, nicknamed 'Dr. Death'.] *in his presence normally and at a certain stage, I believe it was in 1990 about May, I was asked to develop a pyrethroid synergist*

and this was apparently a prelude to making MDMA Hydrochloride, developing a process for making MDMA Hydrochloride for them.
MR VALLY: Who was this who requested it?
DR KOEKEMOER: This was Doctor Mijburgh that requested this.
MR VALLY: Now let's just understand what the MDMA analogue is.
DR KOEKEMOER: Well, MDMA Hydrochloride is commonly known as Ecstasy. I was relatively reluctant to develop Ecstasy for him for the simple reason that it's a Schedule One drug in the United States and a drug of abuse, but he insisted upon this. [...]I then went back and eventually developed quite a novel process for making MDMA Hydrochloride. This was implemented on a plant scale, and it was very high purity, it was 99.5 per cent-plus pure material and it was delivered by myself over a period from 4 February 1992 to about 5 January 1993 to Doctor Mijburgh's offices at Henopsmeer – that is Medchem Consolidated Investments. [...]
MR VALLY: Do you know what happened to this? First of all, what quantity of Ecstasy was delivered by you in this period between 4 February 1992 and 5 February 1993?
DR KOEKEMOER: 5 January 1993.
MR VALLY: 5 January, I beg your pardon.
DR KOEKEMOER: I believe it was about 912 kilograms.
MR VALLY: Do you know what happened to the – sorry, in what form did you deliver this?
DR KOEKEMOER: This was delivered in pure crystalline form, white crystalline form. It was not in encapsulated form at all. It was pure white crystalline material packed in white drums that could contain about 12 kilos at a time.
MR VALLY: And how did you deliver this?
DR KOEKEMOER: I delivered it by car, because they insisted that we keep a high confidentiality about this project, so they didn't want other people involved. Except in one case, where we had quite a lot – I think it was about 200 kilograms – where I used transport: a bakkie from Delta G; and at that stage I think that Mr Philip

Mouton helped me to transport the material there and pack it into a sub-basement store.

The Outeniqua Choo-Tjoe is a steam-hauled train that operates between Knysna and George twice a week. For the trainspotters among you, I left at 9.45 a.m. with number 33706, which was sporting a class 24 locomotive from the 1940s. Like the United States, the railroad turned South Africa into a cohesive country from the centre to the coast. Sea transport had been cheap, leisurely and practical; but the 'iron horses' straddled the interior and connected Cape Town with the diamonds of Kimberley and the gold fields of the Transvaal.

The Choo-Tjoe, like the Garden Route itself, had many German passengers in it, including Ute and Herman whom I had first met on the Baz Bus to Mbabane. Ute was a short, wide-eyed, blonde in Bermudas and sandals brandishing her travel guide like a Bible. Ever-smiling Herman was a tall, amiable, gentle giant; the only information I got out of him was that he was a high-precision machinist in Cologne. 'This is the end of two whole months in southern Africa,' they said with aplomb. 'The only thing we're missing is the Kalahari!'

Where were they heading next?

'We're going to Oudtshoorn to ride the ostriches. My travel guide says we must,' Ute said. 'And you?'

'Me, too. Have you called for a lift from the backpackers' hostel?'

Ute and Herman shook their heads. It's not often that I feel more organised than German tourists, so, with a whiff of self-satisfaction, I savoured the explanation: neither the Baz Bus nor our train went to Oudtshoorn which was forty-five minutes' drive north; you had to call one of the hostels there and arrange a pick-up. Oasis Backpackers would be collecting me from the station at George, a town originally – and less confusingly – named Georgetown after King George III.

'That's great,' said Ute. 'We'll come with you. We were going to the same hostel. My travel guide says that they organise mountain biking trips.'

'They do?' I asked, with a pang in my heart.

'Are you coming mountain biking?'

I should explain.

I own a Marin Palisades mountain bike and used to cycle to work come rain or snow, until that unfortunate morning when a car hit me in Clerkenwell and knocked me out for twenty minutes. Truth is, I would *love* to do some mountain biking in the Karoo. I was, however, afraid: afraid of cars and that I was too old and unfit for all that nonsense of adventure holidaying.

I gazed moodily out of the window.

The two-and-a-half-hour train journey passes through some of the best Cape landscapes – among flowering *fynbos*, under tall Outeniqua trees, and over picture-postcard river crossings. A photo of the steam train on the bridge over the river Coukhama, with its model railway appeal, is used in all the tourist brochures. For a change, the weather colluded to make it look as striking as possible: beyond the beach at Wilderness – another beauty spot – the rain slowed to a drizzle and the clouds began to part. By George (I can't resist the pun), the sun was out. As the first rays of sunshine hit my wet clothes, I led a collective sigh. I had not seen the sun since Durban.

We arrived at George around half past twelve and ensconced ourselves in the Signalman's Arms conveniently placed across the arrivals hall. Herman and Ute wanted a stroll, but I don't leave a bar that easily, especially with Castle beer on tap. By 3 p.m. when George (I am not making this up) from the Oasis arrived with a mini bus, I was quite tipsy. George (the driver) picked us up and took us to the main backpacker hostel in central George (the town, this getting ridiculous) to await the Baz Bus from Port Elizabeth as he had to ferry more backpackers to the hostel. When it arrived, we saw two of Ute's roadmates get off, Dirk and Daniel.

Dirk, a civil engineer from Karlsruhe, was tall, dark and athletically built – the type who wins Olympic competitions for Germany and has three Weetabix for breakfast. Daniel was blond with a leonine countenance and sported a chiselled goatee; in another era, he would have been called a ladies' man. He charmed the tits off every girl he met, especially the freshly-formed tits of a young Dutch girl called Emma. She was only eighteen, exuded Baby Spice innocence and had left the Baz Bus on impulse because of Daniel.

MR VALLY: Do you have any knowledge whatsoever as to what happened with the 912 kilograms of Ecstasy?
DR KOEKEMOER: No, sir, I don't.
MR VALLY: Have you ever enquired about it?
DR KOEKEMOER: Well, I just heard that it probably would be eventually destroyed in the presence of police but whether this was ever executed or not, I don't know. And I've also then read some aspects, some recommendations from these TRC documents, and I don't know whether you want me to comment upon them.
MR VALLY: No, but have you ever even talked informally among your colleagues, asked: 'Whatever happened to all that Ecstasy I produced?'
DR KOEKEMOER: Yes, I have asked things like this, but I never got any answers.

The Oasis Backpackers was a very efficiently run hostel. George had been managing it for six years like clockwork and was in the process of checking us in.

'How long are you staying?' asked George.

'One night,' I said.

Daniel turned towards me. 'Aren't you coming to the Swartberg Pass tomorrow?'

'No, I just want to visit an ostrich farm and leave,' I said.

Dirk looked reproachfully at me. 'We're all going to the Swartberg Pass for mountain biking. It's only 1,600 metres up.'

'Do what you want,' I said, inebriated far too early as I was after that encounter with Castle on tap. 'I am *not* climbing up 1,600 bloody metres. That's – that's about 5,000 feet! It only sounds less in metric!'

George corrected me: 'You won't have to climb.'

'No?'

'No. We take you up there in a car, give you the bikes and the helmets and let you cycle down. It's mostly downhill.'

I was still undecided until, over a few more cool beers, I met Nicole, Marion and Tanya. They were three young, pretty German nurses who lived and worked in Cape Town. Marion was the alpha-female of the group: sensible, assertive, practical, with a commanding presence. Tanya was the youngest of the three: quiet, smiley with an expression of perpetual wonderment, as if she was permanently praising the Lord for blessing her with a trip to Oudtshoorn – needless to say she fell for the charms of Daniel big time. Finally, there was Nicole. She was tall with long, zibeline, black hair, smooth, tanned skin and a toothpaste-commercial smile. I detected a glint in her gaze, similar to the spark in Tanya's eyes when stealing glances at Daniel.

Except that Nicole was looking at me.

'We're all going mountain biking,' she said, stabbing me playfully in the ribs. 'You *must* come tomorrow.' Germans use 'must' more often than considered polite, but I didn't tell her that, because I realised she was flirting with me. I flirted back: I offered her a beer which passes as foreplay in backpackerland.

Everyone was going mountain biking. In my fuzzy state it started sounding fun, and I'm not one to break a good party, so I caved in and informed George. After I signed a declaration that if I crash and die Oasis Backpackers would be totally blameless, I discovered what was in store.

'We take you to the top of the Swartberg Pass and you cycle down,' said George. 'The first ten kilometres are dirt road, very steep and stony, and the cliff face is right next to you, so be careful.'

I sobered up immediately.

'Then after another ten kilometres you reach the Cango Caves – entrance one kilometre uphill – where we recommend you take the Adventure Tour. It takes you potholing deep down into the caves.'

Gulp.

'A scenic alternative for the fit: seven kilometres afterwards you can go twelve kilometres uphill to the Rus and Vrede waterfall.'

Pass.

'Then it's eight kilometres of easy cycling to the Cango Ostrich farm. After that it's another fifteen kilometres on flat road back to Oudtshoorn.'

'How many kilometres altogether?'

'Fifty to sixty, depending on detours.'

That's London to Reading.

MR VALLY: Have you seen any studies or any projections by anyone involved regarding the possible usage of Mandrax as an indirect control mechanism by introducing it into certain areas which were possibly prone to political uprisings so as to create addiction to it?

DR KOEKEMOER: No, I was never given that impression and I doubt whether one can get addicted to Ecstasy, not as far as I know.

MR VALLY: I'm talking about Mandrax.

DR KOEKEMOER: About Mandrax, no.

MR VALLY: You haven't seen any studies or documentation in that regard?

DR KOEKEMOER: No, sir, no I haven't.

MR VALLY: Have you ever studied the literature on the issue?

DR KOEKEMOER: No, I have studied things like Mandrax and the analysis of that because that was part and parcel of our Incos

Data System, and we had permits to keep small quantities of *Mandrax for analytical purposes and for this purpose we, I, obtained quite a number of publications by the relevant authorities that analysed these sorts of drugs of abuse. I've got these papers in my possession, but I haven't seen any studies that relate to the other things you referred to now.*

MR VALLY: *Is there an issue of concern to you, as a chemist? The possibility that such an addictive drug, which has allegedly been responsible for fuelling a lot of the crime in this country, which has enslaved so many of our youth, was possibly produced in laboratories where you were head of research?*

DR KOEKEMOER: *It does concern me, although, as I said, I didn't know about large-scale production of Mandrax. It did concern me that we produced such a large quantity of Ecstasy and following the newspaper reports and so on afterwards, in hindsight, I could say it concerns me more now.*

MR VALLY: *The thinking prevalent in terms of being involved in a secret project in chemical and biological warfare programmes etc., within the parameters of that kind of total onslaught mentality – and I'm basing it on your experiences within Delta G and discussion there – is it possible that people who were in senior positions would consider using Mandrax on a large scale so as to neutralise the potential for rebellion amongst youth?*

DR KOEKEMOER: *No discussion has ever arisen in my presence which led to the premise that Mandrax for example would be used to calm crowds or anything like that, no.*

MR VALLY: *Well, I'm not talking so much about calming crowds as much as introducing it as a potentially recreational drug and thereby creating addiction?*

DR KOEKEMOER: *It would have gone against my grain. I don't like drug abuse, and I would not have approved of it in the first place. And secondly, it was never discussed in those terms in my presence, no.*

MR VALLY: *And when you raised your concerns with higher-ups, when you were asked to manufacture Ecstasy – I think you mentioned*

General Neethling. He, in fact, tried to get you to improve your production facilities, processes...
DR KOEKEMOER: *Well, he discussed the chemistry with me, and we differed violently where the chemical approach was concerned.*
MR VALLY: *The point I am making is that the issues which pricked your conscience – and you were thereafter overridden by more senior authority – would be issues which pricked the conscience of your seniors, that's the impression we have?*
DR KOEKEMOER: *I suppose it should have, but on the other hand if it was earmarked for the pure purposes of conventional incapacitation and chemical warfare context, I don't think it would have pricked anybody's conscience.*

Several Germans, a Dutch girl and I were walking around Oudtshoorn for the necessary supplies of alcohol with both Tanya and Emma vying for the attentions of Daniel. Someone remarked how different the black inhabitants were from KwaZulu/Natal: the males were skinny without that overdefined Zulu musculature, and the women were more slender yet still blessed with prodigious posteriors. I thought I'd seen enough of impossible behinds in Durban – how wrong can one be?

'Are these the Xhosa?' asked Ute.

We had a vote and decided they were. Always in a minority, I voted that they were Khoi-San or a mixture of Khoi-San and Xhosa. As I found out later, I was right. This was an area with a high degree of gene admixture between the Dutch, their Malay slaves and the original Khoi-San inhabitants; in times past, much further up by the Orange River, they proudly called themselves Bastards.

Emma was disappointed she saw no ostriches.

'In the streets?' I asked in disbelief.

'You ride them like horses,' Emma said, eyes wide open. 'I've read about it.'

'Yes, but in the streets? They do that on farms.'

'They *race* with ostriches. I've read it,' she insisted, stamped her foot and left.

The boys looked at me reproachfully.

'I don't think she likes you,' said Daniel.

I caught Nicole's eye, which definitely signalled 'but I do'. She offered me her arm; Nicole was becoming very touchy-feely.

Later at the hostel *braai*, she became even more tactile after a few glasses of wine.

'It's red,' I said.

'What's red?' she asked.

'The meat. Ostrich is a bird, but its meat is red, like beef.'

'Too dry for me,' she answered. 'I have to drink a lot of wine to compensate.'

That was an excellent excuse.

What about the Cango Caves? I asked around. What was this Adventure Tour?

'It's more like potholing,' said a backpacker.

'You need to crawl through slits,' said another. 'And kneel through corridors on your hands and knees.'

I looked up at the sky which was more star-spangled than all the world's US Embassies' stock of Stars 'n' Stripes. In other circumstances I might be moved to quote a poem. But not now.

What exactly had I let myself in for?

30. Act Two

The testimony of Dr Lourens.

MR VALLY: This research into fertility and virility, can you tell us more about this?

DR LOURENS: I can't tell you a great deal. What I can tell you is that the work that was done… was done by a scientist by the name of Dr Riana Borman, and she was working on primates – baboons, I don't know if the work ever moved onto the chimpanzee level – into ways in which she could influence the virility and fertility of the animal. Speculation has it that a part of this work was directed at an ethnic issue in terms of to be able to possibly manipulate ethnic virility or fertility rather, but I know no more than that, as far as that specific project is concerned.

MR VALLY: Referring to the speculation you're referring to – and to be more direct – was the speculation that this work was aimed at reducing the birth-rate amongst black people?

DR LOURENS: Well, Mr Vally, I assume so and again it's one of those situations that we never ever discussed a project in detail. You know, I would, for example, in this particular case I was responsible for the manufacture of a stimulator that is used to stimulate and draw sperm from the male animal and in this discussion with some of the junior scientists, you know, you discuss it vaguely, but I was never briefed formally and said this is the project, this is the extent, this is the scope, this is the objectives, etc, so please accept it as speculation.

I woke up wimpily hoping for rain. I had slept badly, dreaming of humiliation by the Germans in the athleticism stakes. Maybe, exhausted, I'd have to call George to pick me up; trying to inspire us he had said that he'd charge taxi fares if we wussed out. When I looked through the window grilles, I bit myself. The day was my brightest and sunniest since St Lucia.

No getting out of it.

Two minibuses drove us up to the saddle of the Swartberg Pass, imaginatively called Die Top, where we could survey, I supposed, Die Bottom: on one side lay the Little Karoo with Oudtshoorn in the distance and on the other, the vast, apricot-coloured expanse of the Great Karoo. It was only fifteen kilometres to Prince Albert, the town that was named after a penile piercing. I remembered Jane's comments on the flight from London: *'I love the Karoo. It's so quiet, so empty, so clear. Try to get there.'* How long ago was that?

Jane had been dead on. It was quiet, it was empty and it was clear. It reminded me of the wide spaces in Victoria and New

South Wales in Australia where you drive and drive for hours without seeing a single living thing (except trees and they don't count). Yesterday's showery weather had completely cleansed the atmosphere of any dust and the view from Die Top was as near perfect as can be: you could even see the curvature of the Earth if you squinted.

'Remember: do *not* keep your brakes on all the time,' said George. 'I know that when you go down this steep slope the temptation is there, but you will only wear down your disc pads.'

I chose an 18-speed Shimano Rough Rider while George psyched us up: 'Gain some speed and slow down; I repeat: gain some speed and slow down. Do *not* press the brake all the time.'

No chance of that, mate! I rode down terrified, my arms permanently braking, while my balls were painfully pummelled by the uneven rough terrain. The nurses sped by like a breeze – unruffled, unperturbed and elegant. And me?

Whoops! Is this a whoosh of adrenaline down my spine? It's as good as any drug I've had. There's a nasty-looking stone! Will I be able to avoid it? Will I? OUCH! Hey, this is great fun! Let's dodge that car. I said *dodge* it, dammit! Now *you* are tag! Look, a ravine! Brake now! Oh, I *am* braking. Phew, that was close.

The worst was over in about twenty minutes. Once on the paved road, the ride turned smoother and less scary; I even started enjoying the view. At a vista point, we stopped to take some pictures together for posterity. It was the clicks of those cameras that started a chain of events which would completely change my travel plans: a few more miles downhill, Daniel went pale.

'I think I left my camera up there,' he said.

Oh, no, I felt *so* responsible! Daniel had left his Canon compact on the ground to take our picture with mine and forgot to pick it up, because I had insisted that he take several shots. It's not my fault I look terrible in photos – I lack those sharp, photogenic zygomatic bones.

We looked up towards Die Top.

'You won't be able to climb up there,' Dirk said, practical as ever. 'Forget it.'

Daniel acquiesced, visibly upset, but perked up immediately when a car turned the corner in front of us. I was relieved – Daniel had his lift. He asked us to proceed slowly; he'd catch up with us soon.

We continued at a leisurely pace and soon reached the bottom of the Swartberg, immersing ourselves into the Karoo, the South African equivalent of the Central Asian steppes. Its Khoi-San name means 'land of great thirst' – and this is exactly what it was: a sweeping, dry plateau with only the occasional tree or homestead interrupting the uniformity of its terrain. Intermittently, the glossy, black plumage of a group of ostriches peppered the landscape, but such scenes were uncommon. We mostly rode on an empty, narrow road, sometimes in line, sometimes next to each other, crowding instinctively together as a reaction to the overwhelming sense of isolation. It was a relief when Daniel joined us again shortly before the turn-off to the Cango Caves.

'Any luck?' asked Dirk.

Daniel showed us a piece of paper. It was a message with a telephone number: 'I have your camera. Call this number to get it back.'

'That was smart,' I said. 'Why didn't he leave it there?'

Daniel waved his arms dismissively. 'At least I'll get it back. I have his number.'

Dirk, ever the engineer, was not so sure. 'We didn't see any cars going our way. That means your camera was picked up by someone going up. They're on the other side, maybe kilometres away.'

'The nurses have a car,' said Ute.

Daniel's face lit up. 'No problem then,' he said and rode off smirking waggishly.

'I didn't know the nurses had a car,' I said.

'Yeah, a family Toyota. How do you think they came from Cape Town?' asked Ute mounting her bike. 'They're returning tomorrow.'

I climbed back on the saddle thinking, *a trip of five hours instead of two days.*

I was in competition with our own Mr Charming.

MR VALLY: Sorry, maybe it would be opportune to show you some of these instruments. These were obtained by the office of the Attorney General, with your assistance.

DR LOURENS: Yes.

MR VALLY: And we'll come just now as to where they were buried. If I could take one of these instruments, and you took us through it – here we have what looks like a screwdriver.

DR LOURENS: Yes.

MR VALLY: Can you tell us about it?

DR LOURENS: Well, the principle in all cases had been exactly the same. You have in the front end the needle-like section and at the very tip of it there would be a hole. In the handle there would be a cylinder that would be spring-loaded. The principle always was the following: you would suck the substance into the cylinder via the front end and then you would lock it into position; now it would be spring-loaded.

The operator that uses the piece of equipment would stab the person being attacked, and in the stabbing process, the piston would be released and the chemical substance would be injected into the individual, and those would all to a lesser or greater extent work in the same manner. In terms of those particular units that you have in front of you, there were two varieties. The one variety was a basic screwdriver, the other variety was a needled unit; so what it would have at the front was, rather than a screwdriver, a single probe. It would have a number of needles, but the principle would be exactly the same.

Assembled for the Adventure Tour at Cango Caves, we were a party of about twenty-five from all corners of the world in all shapes and sizes. Our guide checked us to weed out the fat, downright unfit and demonstrably gravid.

'There was this eight-month pregnant woman once,' he confided in me. 'I wouldn't accept her despite her protestations. "Darling," I said to her, "it will be more convenient for all of us if you have the baby now."'

I was surprised he left me in. 'You'll fit in fine,' he replied casually, when questioned. I touched my love handles; I wasn't as confident.

The Cango Caves are one of South Africa's natural wonders. As the tourist brochure says, they started forming millions of years ago, when the limestone beds were displaced laterally. Rainwater and carbon dioxide percolated through the fractures to the limestone and the solution crystallised into an underground, multicoloured display of stalactites and stalagmites.

... but you and I know all that. The bitter-sweet news is that the psychedelic pigmentation inside the caves is due to recent light pollution. Light-sensitive algae form on the walls, discolouring them in the process, which is why the large compartments are kept in darkness and are lit only for a few minutes per hour for the tours. One can't help but whistle in awe over the fact that their discovery and subsequent exploration on 11 July 1780 by Jacobus Van Zyl (and a discovery it was, since the locals were too frightened to enter) was made with the light of a candle. Apart from the original Cango I, there are Cangos II to V, discovered in the 1970s and kept in relatively pristine condition: no tourists and no lights.

Cango I starts with three enormous phreatic chambers: first is Van Zyl's Hall, a whopping 350-by-115-foot arena, with a roof 55 feet high. Van Zyl's Hall is the location of a 150,000-year-old, 33-foot-tall stalagmite called Cleopatra's Needle, and a horizontal pipe formation, like a gigantic church organ. This is where concerts for a capacity of 1,000 used to be held and led to the aforementioned light pollution, now all too evident. Next comes Botha's Hall with an example of a heligmite – a stalagmite growing into a stalactite joined up from the floor to the ceiling 42 feet above.

The fun really starts in the third, smaller hall, called Lotz's Room. Six hundred steps lead up to the Love Chamber where your body must contort to Kama Sutra specifications in order to get through to the Lumbago Walk: a 30-inch-high, 100-foot-long tunnel which has you growling and swearing on all fours. Then, after the Crystal Palace, past King Solomon's Mine and the Devil's Workshop – who names these places? – you arrive at the seemingly impossible climb of the Devil's Chimney. This is a 10-foot upright cleft, 18 inches at its narrowest, which stands at an angle of 80 degrees to the horizontal. Oh, and it's slippery, too. The trick is to use bits of your body – like your bum and your ribs – to push the rest of yourself upwards.

It all culminates in the Letterbox where you slide through a horizontal 14-inch slit and slip through to the other side like a parcel. Daniel was the one who pushed me through and delivered me ignominiously, head first, to the merriment of the crowd.

'I told you you'd make it,' said the guide.

I giggled with relief.

'Has anyone ever been stuck in?' I asked.

'A few,' he admitted. 'But no one longer than two, three days.'

Oh, they wait until you're thinner. Cool.

MR VALLY: What did you understand that these screwdriver applicators were being used for?

DR LOURENS: Mr Vally, I was never told what it was used for, but it was quite obvious in terms of, you know, the sort of thing that was devised, I mean it was never told – I was never again briefed and said, you know, give me a screwdriver that can inject a poison into whoever, so that was never discussed with me, but from the job that, I mean, from the weapon that you have there, it's quite obvious what it was used for.

CHAIRPERSON: Excuse me, you said there were two varieties, ordinary screwdrivers, and then the other variety?

DR LOURENS: The other was exactly the same type of unit, but instead of it having the screwdriver end, it would have a number of needles, syringe needles, at the front end of the, let's call it the piston end. Now, what I need to say is, well, that these units were packed in different formats. In other words, for example, there was an example of a needled unit packed into what looked like a bicycle pump.

So, in essence what you would have in your hand would be a bicycle pump. You'd have the ability to slide it back and then you would expose the needles. It was packed into a walking stick, into an umbrella, so there was a number of different ways in which it was packaged.

CHAIRPERSON: Rather like a James Bond movie, wasn't it?

DR LOURENS: Unfortunately.

By early afternoon we were out of the Cango Caves, sweaty, dirty and very, very excited. It's not very often hindsight catches up with you in the present and you realise you are having the time of your life and what comes next will surely add to your delight; we still had to reach Cango Ostrich Farm.

Ostriches are what Oudtshoorn was and has always been famous for. Now, I have been to boomtowns before: Manaus in the Amazon, where the rubber trade created an opera house in the middle of the jungle; eerie, abandoned, nitrate ghost towns in Chile; gold-mining towns in California and Australia which, like South Africa's own Pilgrim's Rest, had to reinvent themselves in tourism to survive. But this one was different.

Oudtshoorn had no natural resources – it was fashion that boomed it and put it on the map; the demand for ostrich feathers for the ladies of the Western *beau monde* who were experiencing the thrill of the froufrou and did not feel complete unless adorned in plumes, jewellery and dead furry animals. As Rob Nixon writes in his *Dreambirds,* between 1870 and the First World War, tons and tons of feathers were exported to find themselves on top of ladies' hats from Italian opera audiences to the crowds of the Kentucky Derby. A pound of plumes fetched £500, which was forty times the price of the sea voyage from London to Cape Town. A million ostriches dotted the Karoo, bred mostly by Lithuanian Jewish settlers, who built their 'ostrich palaces' with the proceeds. You can visit those baroque follies around Oudtshoorn and marvel at the ostentatious exhibition of wealth expressed through the profligate waste of water through fountains and irrigated gardens. In this arid area, the ostrich barons behaved like modern oil sheikhs.

Like all booms it bust.

For a start, there was the motor car: no more open horse-drawn carriages high off the ground. Your headgear would be squashed in a Model T Ford and your feather boa or long scarf could dangle into the wheels and choke you, as happened tragically and most famously in the case of dancer Isadora Duncan in 1927: ironically, the year the last Model T rolled out of production.

Then there was the Great War that did away with the upper classes, dissolved empires and destroyed towns, Oudtshoorn amongst them. Communications were hit (if not London, then Vienna or St Petersburg) and exports plummeted. Great sacrifices by the young men who gave their lives in Flanders and elsewhere demanded stiff upper lips, not foppishness; mourning not flamboyance. The royal families of Europe started dressing down and led by example; the last good ostrich feather year was 1913.

The post-World-War-One heroes were exemplified in Charlie Chaplin's movies: they were the common man and recently enfranchised woman, dancing the Charleston. Taking her cue, Coco Chanel redefined fashion as inverted snobbery. 'How,' she asked, referring to the old millinery creations, 'could a brain function normally under all that?' Movie directors agreed with her: how could you fit these extravagant mad hatter's contraptions in a single camera frame without positioning the camera far away from the actress? Where Coco Chanel's liberating jerseys were photogenic, the old petticoats, outrageous hats and curvaceous dresses looked simply awful. Thin was the word – and still is, as many a budding actress can testify. By the 1930s, the only use for ostrich feathers was for dusters.

Today, there are about 100,000 ostriches in the Karoo and there is a renewed interest in their farming. You can buy online all-ostrich products like massage oil (originally mentioned by Pliny), skin toners and moisturisers, lip salves, shampoos, conditioners – and you thought it was all eggs and feathers?

MR VALLY: All right, let's just go into the screwdriver that you were asked to take with the two ampoules to Britain, what happened there?

DR LOURENS: What happened is, I met the man, by the name of Trevor. I was just introduced – I was told that his name is Trevor, and I met him as Trevor. [Author's note: 'Trevor' was a South African operative in Europe – now an estate agent.] *We went to a cottage that belonged or that was rented by Doctor Basson, just outside Ascot, that little place called Warfield. I drove him there, and at the cottage I demonstrated to him how the mechanism worked. I opened the vial, one of the vials, sucked the substance into the unit, and locked it into its safety lock mechanism.*

I somehow spilled some of the substance on my hand and I don't know how it happened, but I wiped my mouth and I lost consciousness very quickly. There was a bathroom, I recall going into the bathroom, and I recall there being a bottle of Dettol, which I drank. Again, in hindsight, I have absolutely no idea why I drank the Dettol. At that stage, I, to a large extent, lost sight, and of course the Dettol induced a lot of vomiting etc, etc, and I woke up a period later. [...]

MR VALLY: All right, after your delivery of the screwdriver, did you have any other mission in Britain, or did you return to South Africa?

DR LOURENS: I returned, yes.

CHAIRPERSON: And did you report this?

DR LOURENS: I reported it to both Doctor Basson and Doctor Mijburgh, and the reaction was one of great skepticism about my story and their response to it was that it was highly unlikely that even if I had only a drop in my mouth that I would have lived, and we never discussed it again. Not that particular incidence, the poisoning of myself, no.

Back at the Cango Ostrich Farm, I sat down on a spectator bench above a large round pen. A couple of male ostriches entered the enclosure uneasily. Two teenage Coloured farm workers placed hoods over the birds' heads and they calmed down at once: out of sight, out of mind works for them, too.

'Anyone want a ride?' asked one of the farmhands. Of course, this was a must-do in Ute's guide.

The birds twitched as Ute and Daniel were helped to climb on their backs.

'Hold on to the feathers and don't try to sit up,' advised the farm workers. 'Just lean back. Ready?'

Ready.

The farmhands removed both hoods at once, and the birds darted forward. Ute and Daniel were holding on for dear life, dangling from the soft, white tuft of the tails. The teenagers kept the birds on the track for a few rounds before they directed them to the finish. If the poor birds were not traumatised by the riders, they must have been shocked by the high decibel laughter of the spectators. When it was all over, both birds urinated from fear. Take it from me, the ostrich pisses like a horse.

I was next chosen to demonstrate how hardy their eggshells are by standing on top of a nest. Blimey, how do the chicks get out of these eggs? (Answer: with a heel kick which is one of the strongest found in Nature.) Our minds still hyper-impressed, we entered the shop where the struthious paraphernalia you can buy are legion, though two stand out: the feather boas (every single male tried them on, believe you me) and the painted eggs, which are as unique a souvenir as you are likely to bring from Oudtshoorn. Don't worry about transporting them; one thing they're not is fragile.

Beyond the farm, there was a final stretch of ten kilometres to negotiate. My German companions went via the scenic route – read 'unpaved' – but I continued on the main road to the hostel, stopping occasionally to delight in the majestic stillness that enveloped me. African wilderness had honed my senses to perfection and yet no flap of wings, no trot of feet and certainly no rattle of a motor engine disturbed the absolute silence that reigned around me. But for my own breathing, I could have been deaf or dead or maybe Adam himself, dulled in his desolate existence, longing for Eve.

31. Act Three

I presume that the only reason Jesus used loaves and fishes to feed the 5,000 and not, as he could have done, a single ostrich egg, is that he was thinking about the cholesterol. We don't want converts with clogged arteries, do we?

That evening in the hostel kitchen, I was trying to bond with Emma, the Dutch girl, by helping her prepare an omelette. She had bought a fresh ostrich egg for food. You can hardly serve ostrich eggs fried, because you can't crack them. (I wondered what kind of sperm penetrates and fertilises such an egg; if you see two ostriches mating, take cover.) After a lot of effort, we drilled a hole with a sharp screwdriver and started filling a frying pan with the yolk, for yolk is all an ostrich egg has. I have no idea where the white has gone; maybe to reinforce that concrete which masquerades as a shell. This would be one hell of an omelette – when the first pan was full, I filled another one, which I had difficulty hanging on to because a French party arrived and hijacked the kitchen. Four of them – almost militarily drilled – started chopping fresh vegetables, boiling noodles, cutting thin chicken strips and cooking what smelled like chop suey. But their eyes, like everyone's, were on Emma's egg, which they dismissed as the culinary equivalent of a soundbite: all show, no substance, gets all the attention.

'I'm going to Beaufort West tomorrow with Pascal,' Emma told me and smiled amorously at the master chef. Daniel must have been concentrating too much on Tanya.

'You *are*? How will you get back on the Baz Bus route?' I asked. 'Beaufort West is way up north.'

She looked at me for one whole minute; I had interfered with her daydream. 'I hate you,' she finally mumbled, stamped her foot and left me draining her egg.

Daniel walked in shaking his head.

'I spoke to the guy who has my camera.'

'Good. And?'

'He lives far from here,' he added, dejected.

'George?'

'No, Prince Albert.'

Those names.

'I meant our driver. Won't he give you a lift?'

'Oh, right. Erm, he said no. It's three hours away.'

I felt sorry for Daniel. The trip of a lifetime with no camera and all because of me. The nurses were his only hope. I gave up on Emma's *oeuf surprise* and followed him to the common area. Daniel ensconced himself close to Tanya with an expression that could wheedle a tortoise out of its shell.

I sat next to Nicole who described to me how the three of them were volunteering in South Africa through a German aid agency, being paid only expenses, lodgings and food.

'Our first posting was Kosi Bay. All of us were living in a room three metres by three. For one month. We ended up having *such* arguments.'

'You must have dived a lot,' I retorted. 'Kosi Bay is supposed to be a snorkelling paradise.'

'We had no time at all. Busy, busy, busy. This was Zululand! Doctors and nurses were few, and we were working hard. But it was enjoyable.'

'You felt you could make a difference.'

'Exactly. If we weren't there, there would be *nobody*.'

'And Cape Town?'

'Fantastic place. We're returning tomorrow.'

The conversation was heading the way I wanted it.

'You too?' I feigned surprise. 'We should meet there. Perhaps, before you leave –'

'I'll give you our phone number,' she said.

Strike while the iron's hot.

'Or, as it's three of you,' I ventured. 'I could come with you. If you have any space, that is.'

Nicole didn't answer immediately and looked at Marion, who kept her silence. Tanya turned around, whispered something in Nicole's ear and led her away. Daniel smiled in the corner. I bit my lip. That was a no.

Emma's pretty head slid out of the kitchen. 'Anyone want some omelette?' she asked. 'Everyone here is full.'

I tasted the omelette out of curiosity. It was no different to any other. Perhaps a bit too eggy.

Ute rushed in. 'George is driving us to a waterfall tomorrow. Only ten rand each.'

'I'm in,' said Dirk.

'Me, too,' said Daniel.

'I thought you were trying to hitch a ride to retrieve the camera,' I said.

'The nurses are not leaving until later in the afternoon,' he replied.

I admitted defeat.

Dr van Rensburg gives evidence.

MR CHASKALSON: Can I refer you to another document which is TRC 52. And I was wondering if you might consider some of the substances listed on this document to be of a covert nature?
DR VAN RENSBURG: Is that the list of products?
MR CHASKALSON: That's correct, it's a document with a list of dates down the left-hand side, substances and then there's a gram measure and a price on the far column.
DR VAN RENSBURG: I've analysed these lists. […] The favourite was cyanide. It was issued five times, followed by thallium and botulinum toxin at three times each. A further thirty-six per cent of the so-called sales also involved the administration means of these agents.
For toxins, chocolate was the favourite, they issued thirteen doses on four occasions followed by laced beer tins or bottles. That was seven doses and whisky five doses. Also issued were orange juice, hypodermic needles, propane, which I think is a propellant probably for an aerosol, methanol and two snakes.

Next morning I woke up aching in places that I don't normally know exist when healthy, but sure give me hell when I'm stiff. My grip was weak since my thenar muscles at the base of my thumb had been in constant strain, I was sunburnt, and my bottom had an imprint of the saddle. I gulped some coffee at the breakfast table, where a deep-yellow lump of ostrich omelette was still refusing to be consumed, and boarded George's minibus.

En route to the waterfall, an Israeli who had been helping with odd jobs in the hostel gave Dirk an earful, while the rest of us listened, rather embarrassed.

'Do you know what' – and he mentioned a prominent Israeli personality – 'said about the Holocaust? That however many years pass and however many generations pass we shall never forgive it.'

Dirk kept nodding while focusing at infinity. He was on auto-pilot, fending off his country's guilty past to which he was tied by association. I wondered if the next generation of South Africans will adopt the same defence mechanism about apartheid. How long will the sins of the fathers haunt the sons? Clearly, the vast majority who voted National Party could not possibly believe that their laboratories would be manufacturing Ecstasy and putting it in capsules, nor that Mandrax and cholera were produced on an industrial scale. The covert operations veered from cheap James Bond: a scientist flying to England with a poisoned screwdriver to hand over to a mysterious stranger; to the grotesque: laboratory workers masturbating baboons in order to conduct research on reducing the fertility of the black South Africans. The operations were so covert, F. W. de Klerk found out about them from the British and Americans and closed them down promptly afterwards.

Soon the past faded away, and we were able to enjoy the ride to Meiringspoort, the other pass north through the Swartberg mountains that wends its way through a narrow, leafy valley. When we arrived, the sun was blazing hot, and the lagoon under the waterfall appeared far too tempting to ignore – but ignore it we did, for the water was freezing. Despite this, Daniel and Dirk dived from a large boulder into the ice-cold pool, while the rest of us sat admiring their chutzpah.

So, where were we all heading to? Ute and Herman were off to Hermanus to see the whales. Daniel and Dirk were stopping at Mossel Bay.

Daniel?

'I thought you were going with the nurses,' I asked him.

He shook his head. 'If it was up to Tanya... but 150 kilometres is a tall order.' And after a short pause: 'I thought they were going back with *you*.'

'Me? No, they never asked me. I made arrangements with a hostel in Swellendam.'

'In that case, let's all meet in Cape Town next Wednesday,' said Ute. 'Nine o'clock, at the Hard Rock Café. My guidebook says there's one on the Waterfront.'

I benignly agreed. These things never work, but who cares? The day we had spent together yesterday was carved in our memory and it guaranteed that we'd remember each other at our best and most jovial, when all else would wither away in time. Was that not enough for a bunch of strangers?

MR CHASKALSON: Thank you, Doctor. Are you aware that two of the substances we discussed, Brodifacum and Menensim, cause acute heart failure in the human and also have the dubious merit of not being traceable?

DR VAN RENSBURG: That was a very highly sought after merit, Mr. Chaskalson.

MR CHASKALSON: Can you elaborate as to why you say that?

DR VAN RENSBURG: The most frequent instruction we obtained from Doctor Basson and Doctor Swanepoel was to develop something with which you could kill an individual which would make his death resemble a natural death and that something was to be not detectable in a normal forensic laboratory. That was the chief aim of Roodeplaat Research Laboratories covert side.

MR CHASKALSON: That's quite a startling admission or statement.

DR VAN RENSBURG: That's the most frequent repeated need that I heard or instruction given.

'We're late,' said George, as he parked outside the hostel. 'In fifteen minutes we must be off to meet the Baz Bus.'

I bid my goodbyes to the nurses, who were sunning themselves around the pool.

'I thought you wanted to come with us,' said Nicole, with mock juvenile disappointment.

I stood there speechless.

'Really?' I said.

They all nodded, each one more prettily than the other.

'Oh, thank you!' I jumped. 'Thanks very much!'

The goodbye arrangements were reversed. I ran to Ute, Herman, Dirk and Daniel, who were already on the Baz Bus.

'That's it,' I said. 'I'm going with the nurses.'

'Where are you staying in Cape Town?' asked Dirk.

Details, details…

'I've no idea,' I said. 'See you all Wednesday at nine p.m. in the Hard Rock Café.'

I ran back and opened my bag. I took out my gay accommodation guide and started phoning the numbers. I tried the Kinnert and Oliver Guest House ('full'), the Lady Victoria (engaged), the Little Lemon ('full'), the Quarters ('We're booked for three weeks solid'); how about this last B&B in the Gardens?

'Yes, we have a single room,' said a female with a musical contralto voice. 'How long for?'

'Nine days.'

Silence. Oh, *please*.

'It's fine,' the voice replied after a few minutes.

Yes-s!

'Under what name?'

I spelled my surname carefully. 'And yours?'

'My name is Vanessa,' said the voice. 'May I ask how you found our number?'

'Through the Spartacus guide,' I replied.

'Oh, that's fine, then,' I heard her say with a tinge of relief.

Dr Odendaal's cross-examination.

MR VALLY: Are you aware of these cigarettes prepared with anthrax?
DR ODENDAAL: Yes, I was asked to do that.

MR VALLY: So you personally put drops of anthrax onto these cigarettes?

DR ODENDAAL: Yes, I was given a packet of Camel cigarettes, and I was requested to drop some of the drops onto the filter of the cigarettes.

MR VALLY: And what would it have – what would have happened to the person who smoked these cigarettes?

DR ODENDAAL: Well, it's difficult to speculate, but I can imagine that it might have fatal results.

MR VALLY: Were you aware of that at the time you did it?

DR ODENDAAL: Yes.

MR VALLY: Were you aware of who it was intended for?

DR ODENDAAL: Well, once again, it was put to me that it was going to be used to test some of the filters that Dr Lourens was developing at Protechnic.

MR VALLY: Surely you didn't believe that! I mean you don't test the filter by putting anthrax on the cigarette.

DR ODENDAAL: Perhaps I did not believe it, but I had my own thoughts about the situation.

The drive from Oudtshoorn to Cape Town lasted five solid hours. It was an uncomfortably hot day – what can it be like when summer hits the Karoo for good? Despite my protests, the nurses had insisted I sat at the front, while Nicole and Tanya curled up at the back among all the luggage, mostly mine. They didn't even let me contribute to the petrol; I tried frantically to make it up by buying drinks and food from the various filling stations. Marion drove most of the way, as we kept each other amused with anecdotes about our experiences in South Africa.

We opted for the scenic route on the R328 via the Robinson Pass where the descent through the bare Outeniqua mountains provides a striking, gaping view of the ocean. The road has many steep and dangerous hairpins; a bus full of Dutch tourists would fall off these same corners a week after we drove down.

The soundtrack for the final drive was provided by Depeche Mode's *Greatest Hits*. Eighties electropop reverberated through the speakers as we swept past Albertina (yawn) and Riversdale, much more picturesquely situated at the bottom of the Langeberg mountains. At Swellendam, Marion swapped driving with Nicole, occasioning the scariest moment of my trip, and it had nothing to do with any muggings or, indeed, Depeche Mode.

We were heading westwards; the sun was setting and was hitting us horizontally in the eyes, blinding us despite our sunglasses. Nicole was cruising in the middle lane of the N2 up the Houhoek Pass, when, unavoidably, she had to drive into the amorphous, black void of the contrasting mountain shadow. Only once we were inside did we notice that we were heading for the back of a slow-moving juggernaut at 80mph. Tanya shrieked. Marion shouted 'BRAKE!' Nicole instinctively obeyed and nearly stalled the car. Our approach to within a few yards of the lorry's rear bumper seemed in painfully slow motion.

'That was close,' whispered a shaken Nicole. 'Did *you* see the lorry?'

I hadn't either.

'Is everyone all right?' asked Marion.

We were fine.

'I'll drive to Sir Lowry's Pass, and we'll swap back,' said Nicole, still rattled.

Twenty-two hushed miles later, with only Dave Gahan belting on unfazed, there was a panorama point where Nicole parked the car for Marion to take over. We stretched our legs and shook off the memory of the incident by walking towards the crowd that was congregated on the edge, gazing across the hazy sunset. Below us I had my first glimpse of Cape Town and absorbed the magnificence of its setting. The landmarks I had heard of were there: Robben Island, Lion's Head and that implausible flat-top of Table Mountain. Great view. No, I lie: *bloody* great view.

So there I was at last, in Cape Town, the Mother City – and a mother of a city it was, too.

CHAIRPERSON: Now talking about cholera, how would it have been administered, these cholera cultures?

DR ODENDAAL: There's basically only one way I would think, and that would be to contaminate drinking water.

CHAIRPERSON: Contaminate drinking water! For instance, in peace time, at election time in Namibia, these doses could have been administered in drinking water in Namibia. What effect would it have had on the election process?

DR ODENDAAL: Well, I think to start off with, I think the Department of Health would basically agree with me that if you have this organism in your environment, it can have a devastating effect on the health services. It can lead to disruption, because you need urgent medical attention to the people that are affected. You can disrupt a whole area. It can cause widespread disruption.

CHAIRPERSON: You are talking about the disruption of an election process, possibly even leading to some deaths.

DR ODENDAAL: Certainly.

CHAIRPERSON: And you agree that the quantities of this cholera culture that you produced were sufficient to have been able to produce an epidemic. Certainly that would have affected a population of one million plus in Namibia at this time; had there been a plan to do so?

DR ODENDAAL: That's possible, yes.

CHAIRPERSON: Did it not worry you that in peace time you were being asked to produce toxins of those proportions?

DR ODENDAAL: You see, at this stage, and as I mentioned it to you, there was a stage that we produced these organisms and that could have been in 1988 even.

CHAIRPERSON: Yes, but I'm talking what you are agreeing on. Here in 1989, which is peace time, you now know that certain of these toxins were being collected, certainly were being delivered to agents as you called them, did that not worry you. Or let me not talk about that time: now, with the benefit of hindsight, doesn't it raise a number of questions in your head that these things were being delivered through Doctor Immelman to whoever, CCB maybe, Armed – Special Forces. You were aware that these projects were associated with the South African Defence Force and linked in some ways to Special Forces, were you not?

DR ODENDAAL: It is disturbing, yes, but at that time it wasn't. You know, we had a lot of projects going, and when you get an order or a directive to produce something, you had to produce it.

I know you've been waiting for this.

Some useless facts about ostriches:
1. *The ostrich is monogamous. Over its reproductive period, which lasts up to 30–40 years, it only has the one mate.*
2. *The incubation temperature determines the sex. It's impossible to determine the sex of a bird before it is one year old. Until then, only via DNA testing may one ascertain who is Rachel and who is Richard.*
3. *It has a rather silly reputation. No, it doesn't bury its head in the sand, but it does lie face down and protrude its feathery bum upwards pretending to be a bush, which is even more daft.*

Still, as a paradigm of hypocrisy and reality denial, the ostrich is unique. It doesn't matter that it doesn't bury its head in the sand. For there are people who do, like the congeries of scientists testifying their blinding innocence during the Truth and Reconciliation Commission hearings in front of a world that had to pinch itself to accept the outrageousness of it all. Like those scientists who disregarded their country's laws, their own principles and ultimately their own humanity, in a hear-no-evil, speak-no-evil, see-no-evil comic ensemble performance befitting an operetta.

An ostrich operetta...

Chapter Ten

African Drama: Cape Town, Robben Island, Cape Flats

Deep down in every human heart, there is mercy and generosity. No one is born hating another person because of the colour of his skin, or his background, or his religion. People must learn to hate, and if they can learn to hate, they can be taught to love, for love comes more naturally to the human heart than its opposite.
Nelson Mandela

They should shoot all the kaffirs dead and then they'll all come back to work tomorrow!
Woman in Vanderbijl Park speaking after the Sharpeville massacre, where 69 black protesters were killed and 178 wounded.

32. The Gardens

The nurses left me outside my B&B, tired and exhausted from the sun and the heat and Depeche Mode's *Greatest Hits*, hugging me more than might seem morally proper in the petit-bourgeois Gardens district of Cape Town. When a slightly camp, affable elder guy with a blond, receding hairline opened the door, they were still blowing me kisses as they drove off. He had a good look at me and introduced himself as Piet.

'Were they your friends?' he fished elegantly leading me up the staircase to my palatial room, complete with balcony, floor-to-ceiling drapes and sturdy colonial furniture: shades of the Blue Angel in Pretoria.

'Yes, they're friends,' I said. 'Friends who gave me a lift. That's all.'

My host seemed relieved. 'I would be delighted if you could join me for a glass of wine outside.'

After I had freshened up and changed into something much less comfortable – I was going out after all – I walked down to meet Piet and his friend Teddy. They complemented each other so well, I guessed they were a couple. Piet was strikingly pale and thin, except for a twee beerbelly; Teddy was big and tanned with thick black hair, sporting a handlebar moustache that made him look like a nineteenth century explorer. Piet was quiet and sat there absorbing the conversation; Teddy was a master of small talk. They were sitting on a small patio – walled, like everything else in urban South Africa – drinking wine, a pastime which they pursued every night. We broke the ice talking about the ghastly weather on the Garden Route, but before long hunger overwhelmed me; I had hardly eaten anything all day.

'There's a new gay restaurant, Priscilla's, off Long Street, near our end. I recommend it,' said Teddy with the assured tone of a bon viveur. It was the first time the word 'gay' had been mentioned. Oh, the coded way things work.

'I'll pop in there then, I'm famished,' I said to put them out of their guessing misery.

'I'll call you a taxi,' said Piet.

'Can't I walk there?' I said.

'*Walk?*' They looked, astonished, at each other. 'I suppose you could.'

Map in my right back pocket, butterfly excitement in my solar plexus, I waltzed down the traffic-choked curve of Orange

Street with a feeling of fulfilment: I had reached Cape Town – and all in one piece! Still, the sun must have struck me hard in the car, or the elation must have been far too blinding, because I forewent my own advice: I was walking the streets of a big, bad South African city at night; only once in Durban had I dared walk unaccompanied and it was the short distance from the Galleon to the Tropicana.

At the top of Long Street there was a 7-Eleven with a large number of unruly guys outside. By now my responses had been conditioned sufficiently to make me change road sides and avoid the mêlée, but it is hard to look inconspicuous when you are the only pedestrian and the only white one to boot. I attracted the attentions of two well-built youths. I tried to lose them by going up Buitensingle Street, but they followed me. The neighbourhood was residential, deserted and unlit, so I made a turn at the next street going down. I checked. They were walking faster. I turned left nervously and – what's that? A restaurant! It was – was it? Yes, it was Priscilla's. I must remember to donate my cadaver to radar research.

I ordered a *bobotie* – the famed Cape spiced meatloaf – and was served the chicken pie instead. It was 10 p.m., I was relieved to be inside and I was the last client, so I did not make any fuss. I did note, though: Cape Town is a surprisingly early town for dinner.

For the short distance back, I took a taxi. The driver heard my story and didn't blame me for being tense. 'They should cut off the muggers' arms and bring back the death penalty,' he said.

'Well, they didn't *do* anything to me,' I protested feebly.

'Blacks. They're all criminals.'

The driver who said that wasn't white. Like most taxi drivers in Cape Town, he was Coloured. In the Cape there are whites, there are blacks and there are Coloureds. They are as indigenous as the Voortrekkers and with a settlement as long and chequered. They are descended from Malays brought to the Cape by the Dutch in the seventeenth century to work for the settlers – they are their masters' mixed progeny. Until their rights were eroded away by the post-1948 National Party apartheid government, they had the vote along with the whites, when suffrage was still subject to property ownership. The Coloureds aspire to be white and define themselves by negation: *we are not black.* In one of those turns of a history as puzzling as that of South Africa's, the Coloured vote made the old apartheid National Party the ruling regional party in the Western Cape after the country's first free elections.

'They're all criminals,' repeated the driver. 'Even Mandela.'

'*What?*'

'He was in jail, didn't you know?'

'He was a political prisoner!'

'He was a criminal. A terrorist. Like the lot of them.'

I was woken up in the middle of the night by a strange noise. I could hear someone moving furniture about. Where was I? Oh, Cape Town. What was this music? Opera? Yes, opera. Are Piet and Teddy listening to opera at, what's-the-time, three in the morning? This sounded like a modern, incoherent aria in monotone. Did Piet like Glen Branca? I put in my earplugs and went back to sleep.

As in Pretoria's Blue Angel, there was none of this breakfast-is-served-before-ten officious nonsense; breakfast was served whenever you woke up, which is how it should be.

A slim black maid came out of the kitchen and hovered around the breakfast buffet. She couldn't be more than thirteen or fourteen. Shit, I thought, aghast, child exploitation. I must have a word with Piet about this.

'Hello,' I said to her. 'I'll just have coffee, thank you.'

A woman came out of the kitchen. 'Are you John?' she asked in a recognisable, husky voice. 'Hi. I'm Vanessa. We spoke on the phone.'

Vanessa was a curvaceous young blonde with a fetching smile and a friendly, warm personality. In this country of beautiful busty females, she was a prime specimen of Afrikaner womanhood. We clicked straight away.

'Meet Jasmine,' Vanessa said and put a carton of milk on the table. 'She's next door to you.'

I looked at the black girl in astonishment. *Integration!* This is the new South Africa with a black middle class that can afford holidays.

Jasmine said hello to me. Or rather she hummed it.

'Jasmine, did you pour out all the other milk?' asked Vanessa.

'Falalalalala,' sang Jasmine.

Vanessa turned to me. 'Cooked breakfast?'

'Erm, no thanks. Just coffee will do.'

Jasmine took every single chocolate muffin on the breakfast table, put a finger through it and replaced it carefully on a platter. She poured a whole carton of milk in the big, serve-yourself muesli bowl and left it there. She started shrieking like a demented soprano. It sounded like an incoherent aria – so *that's* who it was.

'She's taking her time, is she not?' Jasmine asked me. 'Falalalalala – lala-lala.'

'Who's taking her time?' I asked, perplexed, in return.

'Her Majesty,' Jasmine said.

Vanessa came back.

'Jasmine, did you leave the fridge door open?' she asked.

'*No!*' cried Jasmine. 'Falalalalala!'

Vanessa brought me the coffee as a stunning, slender black woman made a grand entrance to the breakfast room like Sonia Braga in the *Kiss of the Spider Woman*. She was wearing a tight red dress that looked as if it had been sewn by Michelle Pfeiffer in her Catwoman incarnation.

'Her Majesty,' announced Jasmine. 'Falalalalala.'

'Well, *hello*,' the woman purred in my direction in a long-vowelled American accent. 'And how are *you* today?'

So they were not South African. 'Tired,' I replied, but she had already turned towards Jasmine.

'And how are *you* today, Jasmine?' she asked.

'You know how I am,' Jasmine snapped. 'I sleep in the bed right next to you.'

'What will you have for breakfast, Loretta?' asked Vanessa.

'A glass of mineral water,' the woman replied.

'Falalalalala,' sang Jasmine and set upon destroying the bananas.

I drank my coffee and split. Muggers or not, somehow it all seemed safer outside.

33. Prisoner 466/64

Robben Island is flat – its highest hill stands at only 80 feet above sea level – and windy (those dastardly southeasterlies) *ergo* inhospitable: a 1992 survey found 22 shipwrecks around its paltry coastline. Formed by the summit of a submerged mountain, it lies seven nautical miles – less than half an hour's sailing distance – from Cape Town. It commands a strategic location, and its first inhabitants were Dutch soldiers. When the British arrived – who ruled the waves and were not afraid of invasion – it became a place of exile, prison and later a leper colony. During the Second World War, when said waves became crammed with German U-boats, the soldiers moved in again. It was only in 1962 that the Department of Prisons of the Republic of South Africa took over, and that's how we know Robben Island today: as a prison, the place where the world's most famous political detainee served 18 years of a 27-year incarceration. He was prisoner 466/64 and his name was Nelson Mandela.

The lure of the name is such that the prison is now a museum and the erstwhile prisoners are guides. Every day there are several sailings, whereby visitors from all over the world call on the island to catch a whiff of the presence of the 466th prisoner admitted in 1964 who would become an international symbol of fortitude and forgiveness. The reason I went to Robben Island along with the hordes – and I am not embarrassed to admit this – was to walk the ground Nelson Mandela stepped on: a kind of mute pilgrimage. After the vicissitudes of its colonial fate, Robben Island has finally become a place of hope in the ultimate nature of Man.

I sailed there sitting on the stern ramp of the catamaran, watching the Waterfront disappear behind me. Ah, yes, the Cape Town Waterfront: a glorified shopping-mall-on-the-docks, a newly-built all-mod-cons cocoon with five-star hotels, pubs, shops, restaurants, post offices and banks amongst the quays. You have the Hard Rock and Planet Hollywood, the Sports Café and an English pub: all the trappings of Western culture in a safe, pretty, artificial environment. Yet, however false and feigned, one can't dismiss its appeal. Everyone gravitates there and, just like in Piccadilly Circus, if you sit on a Waterfront bench long enough, you'll eventually meet that long-lost friend. It truly is a delight at night with people strolling by in the balmy weather. A delight, that is, for the ones allowed in, since it is heavily policed to keep out the undesirable squatters sleeping under the nearby motorway bridge. As often happens in South Africa, the safest place stands jaw to jaw with the most dangerous.

We entered the prison camp through the main gate, walking under its original, grand bilingual sign: *Ons dien met trots* – we serve with pride.

Our guide was the one-time ANC political prisoner Theophilus Mzukwa, nicknamed Muthe. He was admitted in 1986 on a 25-year sentence, but he served only four; he was released in 1990 by F. W. de Klerk. He was small, scraggy and long-limbed with a permanently pained expression on his face; I don't know whether it was due to the baking sun, the memories of imprisonment or the unsightly spectacle of tourists invading his place of anguish. He spoke in measured, heavy tones. When you asked him a question, he turned, faced you and looked you straight in the eye when answering. I thought it was a result of his incarceration, but now I know it is the Xhosa way.

After some basic, dry island history, Muthe's account became more dramatic as he focused on the prison. 'The first period from 1963 to around 1969 was the worst. The conditions were bad and there were beatings and physical torture. In the seventies they improved but after the Soweto riots in 1976 they worsened again. In the eighties conditions were much better. One prisoner was even allowed a pet rabbit and another old inmate kept chickens.'

I should add here that Robben Island in no way compares to the much more brutal regimes of the Soviet gulags, Nazi concentration camps or even some American high-security prisons. It is doubtful whether Nelson Mandela would have outlived any of the above. Yes, it was harsh, petty and unjust – every political prisoner is held unjustly – but Dachau, Auschwitz or even Devil's Island it was not.

'Robben Island was a criminal jail and the authorities' – Muthe always said 'authorities' to refer to the apartheid government – 'put the political prisoners in here thinking that they were punishing them. But the criminals ended up politicised. And the guards – there were also Coloured guards initially – started sympathising with the prisoners. For this, they were replaced. Soon, there were only white guards and black prisoners.'

'Were there any white political prisoners?' asked someone.

'Not here. The white political prisoners were detained in Pretoria,' answered Muthe. 'When Nelson Mandela was arrested with his white comrades, the van carrying the suspects was segregated by a steel divider. Whites on one side of the police van and the rest on the other.'

Muthe took a long breath.

'There was racial division within the prison, too. Coloured prisoners received long trousers – black prisoners received short trousers; to remind us that we, even the old men, were "boys". For centuries they called "Hey, boy" and we answered "*Ja, baas*".'

He took a long breath.

'Food was also racially divided. We normally received porridge and coffee. Blacks received one sugar, the Indians and Coloureds two sugars. Blacks received four ounces of bread per day, but the Indians and Coloureds seven ounces. Only in the seventies was there some equalisation.'

Later as Harding and I were roasting some of the birds spitted on a ramrod, I informed him of my intention of sending to the bay for more substantial supplies, as much for ourselves as for our young Cafres who were squatting round the fire, staring into the flames. The little wretches were sniffing the smell of the fat as it dripped into the embers. I considered this means of sustenance poetical enough, but not very sustaining.

'Good Heavens,' said my companion, 'you are too kind to concern yourself in this way. Truly you are not made for travelling; you are too solicitous. Thank God we lack nothing and neither do our Cafres.'

'But our Cafres have absolutely nothing. They have been with us nearly two days and, just think, they have had not a bite to eat.'

'That is true; but they have an immense advantage over us: they can spend three whole days in this way without complaining. Look, their stomachs are only flat; when they are hollow, the time will have come.'

I considered these remarks to be just and true, and at the same time very droll on the part of a European. But Mr Harding, who had been longer in Natal than I, had had the opportunity of observing their customs closely...

Our Adulphe Delegorgue, reminiscing in the early 1840s. *Plus ça change*, as he might have pronounced.

What was a typical day in the life of the prison?

'We woke up at seven a.m. and went to our cells at four p.m. At eight a.m. we went to the lime quarries where we worked for six, seven hours. Food was millie rice or porridge. Vegetables were cabbage and carrots only. Don't ask me why. Just cabbage and carrots. We also got powdered egg and some fish. But the authorities were playing games. In the summer we had hot soup and in the winter cold drinks. The water we drank was not purified. It was not clear. It was brackish. Showers were cold until the seventies. Every day we received eight squares of toilet paper. You had to make do with eight.'

He pointed at the library.

'After work we could go to the library. Studying was a privilege, not a right, and could be withdrawn any time. But most of us studied. People came in without education and left with a university degree. So the prisoners won even before they were freed.'

We entered what seemed like a tennis court surrounded by long walls on one side and a series of cells on the other.

'This is where the Category B prisoners, the political prisoners, lived,' Muthe pointed out. 'And this is where they broke large stones to make gravel every day. Except once: when the International Red Cross arrived in the sixties, they were given clothes to mend. The observers found them sat around sewing. Later they were moved to work in the quarries. You will see the lime quarry afterwards.'

He stopped. In speech it is the pauses that are precious.

'The fourth window from the left was Nelson Mandela's. He lived in that cell all his time in this prison. Only once was he moved to cell number seventeen. It was when the white MP Mrs Helen Suzman arrived to check on the welfare of prisoners. The authorities put Nelson Mandela in there so that he would not have time to talk to her after she met the first sixteen. But everybody she met first said with one voice that the prisoner in cell seventeen is the one who should speak for them all. So she quickly moved on to meet him. It was

Mrs Suzman personally who was responsible for the first real change for the better in the prison. Other elements were international pressure and hunger strikes. The first hunger strike was the most successful because the guards imitated the prisoners. They went on hunger strike themselves for more pay. It was too much for the governor, and he gave in.'

Someone's mobile rang. The culprit – skin as thick as rhino hide – answered it and went to a corner of the yard, his loud yapping occasionally drowning Muthe's unhurried narration.

'The correspondence was all checked. There were no newspapers. Our letters were read by the authorities. They did not know African languages and they cut every bit they did not understand. What you got back was strips of letter that were unreadable. When we received a newspaper, it was so cut by censorship that only the classified section remained. And the sports pages.'

We entered the Category B wing and flocked in front of Mandela's cell, Number Four, which was the only one with bookshelves. Was he more privileged?

'No,' said Muthe. 'Just that Nelson Mandela's cell is as it was when he left it. The others have been emptied.'

I entered the cell where the light used to be on relentlessly, day and night.

'Do not look at this bedding. When he entered the jail in 1964, he only had a straw mat on the floor. Later felt mats were brought in.'

What about visits?

'One every six months lasting for half an hour. It had to be booked six months in advance. A guard was standing by at all times. You were not allowed to touch.'

I thought of Winnie.

Although Winnie Mandela is now demonised because of her excesses during the later years of apartheid and her association with the thuggery and intimidation of the Mandela Football Club, one should remember the pettiness and persecution she faced for decades. It was *she* who kept the Nelson Mandela legend alive. It was *her* life which was made impossible. It was *she* who had to work, bring up the children and fight for the release of her husband.

Let me quote just one example: Winnie visited Nelson in 1964, but did not return again until 1966, because she steadfastly refused to carry a pass. After two long years she relented for Nelson's sake. For that visit she was given permission to visit Cape Town but not the places in between. As a result, she could not go by car or train; she had to pay for an air ticket at her own expense – and there were no budget airlines in the sixties. She was obliged to use the shortest route between the airport and the Caledon police station where she had to report. There she had to fill in a form with her name and address. She had to fill in a form on the Robben Island ferry where she had to travel in the hold. After she met Nelson for half an hour, she had to fill in a form on the ferry on her way back. Then back to Caledon Road police station to fill in the same form again. She snapped and refused. We can all imagine her screaming that she had already completed three forms and that they knew very well her name and address. For that small gesture of defiance, she was arrested, she lost her job, and she received a one-year suspended jail sentence.

It is not difficult to see how a lone woman – however pugnacious – who dared stand up to a regime as draconian as that of apartheid, ultimately buckled. I suspect that, towards the end, she never expected that her husband would survive his long incarceration and that the spotlight would settle permanently on her, as she was being transformed into a saintly Mother of the Nation. When CNN and the BBC start treating you with deference, hang on your every word and record your slightest move, it is easy to exaggerate your importance and become imperial. We would all love her to have held up like her future ex, to have resisted the temptation of aggrandisement, to have emerged from all the turbulence with superhuman dignity and courage. She failed and ended up being convicted of fraud by the courts, a demagogue who sells soil from her Soweto garden to tourists – but let the one who would have shown more moral strength cast the first stone.

There is only one person who could do that, and he did. He divorced her.

There have been innumerable column inches written about Nelson Mandela by people much worthier than myself, but no South African travelogue could fail to comment on possibly the most popular politician on the planet. To celebrities from the Spice Girls to Bono of U2, a photo opportunity with Nelson Mandela is a confirmation of their status, and to politicians from Fidel Castro to Bill Clinton it is a guaranteed popularity boost. His greatness is the sum of his individual experiences and his personal philosophy. It is one thing to have Voltaire prepared to expire on paper in order to defend someone's right to disagree with him, but quite another to have a defendant in a trial facing a possible death sentence uttering: *'I have fought against white domination and I have fought against black domination. I have cherished the ideal of a democratic and free society in which all persons live together in harmony and with equal opportunity. It is an ideal which I hope to live for and to achieve. But if need be, it is an ideal for which I am prepared to die.'*

Mandela upheld the sanctions against South Africa, and supported the campaigns of defiance and the ANC's armed struggle as a defensive action against the violence of apartheid. For this he was portrayed as a militant hothead: a cross between Joseph Stalin and Che Guevara. To the white South Africans' great relief, astonishment and shock the man who emerged from Victor Verster prison in February 1990 to the glitz of the media was the exact opposite of his caricatures: a man who was erudite, insightful and kind-hearted.

If there are any who doubt Nelson Mandela's greatness, they live in his own country. For those who remain unconvinced – and there are a few – I will point out a specifically South African achievement. A few weeks before the 1994 elections, the brinkmanship between Chief Buthelezi and the ANC negotiating team had reached a flash point. KwaZulu/Natal might consider secession. Violence between Inkatha and ANC supporters was at its height. In a continent torn by tribal conflicts, other leaders – and as we have seen from the former Yugoslavia, not only African ones – might have bitten the bullet and gone for war to subjugate an independently-minded province. Mandela, however, despite the bedrock of his authority, despite having the world on his side, was prepared to compromise and accommodated Zulu pride with an explicit place in the constitution for the Zulu king. Many South African citizens may love their country, but that is not enough; in a country blinded by communal strife, Nelson Mandela loved its people, *all* of its people. Not only did he keep his multiracial and multicultural country together, not only did he provide the young of all races with a shining example, but he was also the first true South African *patriot*. For this attribute alone he deserves a seat in the pantheon of greatness.

Muthe accompanied us through the prisoner association rooms to the exit. The question was burning my tongue, so I asked him,

'How do you feel guiding tourists around here, Muthe?'

He paused, turned around and faced me. 'I feel good,' he said. 'This is history that you cannot sweep under the carpet. History that must be told and I tell it. It is good to be able to tell my experiences. You meet people with different backgrounds. And it is interesting. I like it.'

A blond, Scandinavian-sounding backpacker made him turn to his other side. 'Was it just ANC prisoners here or Inkatha, too?'

I don't know whether the backpacker was naïve or mischievous, nor did I see Muthe's face, but I heard him spit out: 'None. No Inkatha prisoners'.

'Why?' The backpacker was way too blond.

'Cos Inkatha were government in just another colour,' said Muthe and went silent, as did the whole group, who felt his discomfort.

This was our cue to leave.

We drove around the island: to the old guard quarters, to the hospital (where there were fifty-odd births although male and female prisoners were kept apart), to the cemetery of the old leper colony, to the island school with seven pupils but no teachers. And then to the bungalow of Robert Sobukwe.

Sobukwe was a Mandela without the media attention and his fate was far, far worse. He was President of the Communist Pan African Congress and the only political prisoner the apartheid government recognised as such. After the Sharpeville massacre, he was one of a wave of activists to be sent to prison. When his sentence was over, Prime Minister Vorster pushed through the South African Parliament – with only Helen Suzman voting against it – what became known as the 'Sobukwe Clause': the Ninety-Day Detention Law. Those arrested could be held without trial, charge or access to a lawyer for ninety days. Robert Sobukwe would be arrested and re-arrested back-to-back and held under this law, as Vorster boasted 'to this side of eternity'.

In solitary confinement.

When Mandela and the others marched on to the quarry, they silently saluted him; occasionally he greeted them back holding a piece of soil which he let run through his fingers. For six years he led a lonely, rueful existence tending his garden. In 1969, even the apartheid regime recoiled at the psychological damage it was inflicting upon the prisoner and put him under house arrest – in Kimberley, a place alien to him. He lived there with his family and was allowed out for twelve hours a day. He completed a law degree and started a small practice – but the damage had been done. Sobukwe's mental and general health kept deteriorating. He died of cancer in 1978, his dream of a free South Africa unfulfilled in his lifetime.

We reached the lime quarry. Only after two years of working in the blinding sun and the glare of the white lime were the prisoners allowed sunglasses – too late for Nelson Mandela who partially lost his sight. Yet for us tourists, the quarry ghosts of the past lost to the background of the present, where a perfect day exposed Cape Town and Table Mountain in all their grandeur. We marched to the lighthouse where we could marvel at the view. A bontebok stared at us lazily. A crown cormorant dived into the sea and a black oyster-catcher with its striking red beak hopped on the rocks; white egrets straddled the shallows and colourful teals swam further away. How cruel it must have been for those toiling in the quarry to see the birds soar above.

Back home Piet was frantic.

'Loretta and Jasmine were supposed to check out this morning. Where *are* they? I had to turn away customers.'

'Are they leaving?' I asked.

'Leaving? They'd better be leaving,' Piet said.

I sat with him in the patio. Table Mountain looked incredibly enticing. There was no 'tablecloth' today, the regular cloud and mist that covers its flat top. When exactly was the last cable car up? I looked at my watch. Could I still make it?

Loretta and Jasmine made up my mind for me, as they walked in carrying sackfuls of shopping.

'Well, *hello*,' said Loretta in a Marilyn Monroe feline purr.

'Falalalalala,' sang Jasmine.

This was definitely the day to visit Table Mountain.

Table Mountain is more than a natural landmark. It's not somewhere you climb up, take a photo and come down again. There are miles and miles of trails in its hinterland extending to the mountain range of the Twelve Apostles. One can spend a whole holiday hiking among the silver trees, the ericas, the red disas and the cutest creatures on the planet: the dassies. These are small furry mammals that look like fat, tailless squirrels. Not only have they been designed straight out of the Creator's stuffed toy department, not only do they make Furbies look as submissive as hungry ferrets, but they also advance towards you, look you straight in the eye, grunt plaintively and bat their eyelids like Chip and Dale with a winsome expression that says; 'Feed me *now*, you fucker, or I'll look even cuter!' Old ladies were reduced to tears having to part from them on the way down, and it is a very tight tourist indeed who heeds the *'Do Not Feed'* signs and does not rush to the retail store in order to buy peanuts, bread or chocolate to offer them. It's almost beyond belief to think that they were once killed to make tobacco pouches for the Xhosa – pass the hankie immediately.

Some useless facts about dassies:
1. *Their crystallised urine is said to have medicinal value. Honest.*
2. *They have a bad temperature-regulating mechanism which is why they snuggle amongst themselves when it's cold and sun themselves when it's hot. See what I mean about cuteness?*
3. *Although there are similarities in their teeth and their toenails, they bear no genetic resemblance to elephants, in spite of popular rumour.*

I hiked for a few hours in the back paths, watching orange-breasted sunbirds flap playfully until the wind picked up. I stayed as long as I could endure the alpine blow of the backdraft; at 3,100 feet Table Mountain has different weather than Cape Town, and I was still dressed for the salty fieriness of Robben Island. I stood on the edge until the Cape Town lights came on for I couldn't bear to take my leave from the view of Lion's Head and Table Bay. I looked directly down. There were surprisingly no houses in a location with what must be a priceless view. Maybe the area below Table Mountain was a nature reserve stretching all the way to the Technicon University I could see in the distance. But no, there was a mosque.

Funny, a mosque without any other sign of habitation.

I froze. I checked the map. Zonnebloem. I looked down again. This must be, this must be...

Yes, this was it.

This was District Six.

34. District Six

Mohammed from Legend Tours might just be the most extraordinary person I met in South Africa. He picked me up in his minivan from my B&B and within five minutes he knew who I was, where I came from, where I stood in the South African divide, my hobbies and disports, whether or not I was a vegetarian, even my mother's maiden name. (I told you he was exceptional.) Mohammed was cut from the same cloth as a Sufi *qawwali* singer; young, bright-eyed, intense, with a fuzzy black beard that appeared awkwardly stuck on his chin. He looked as if he'd just come off-stage performing in the retinue of the late, great Nusrat Fateh Ali Khan. He wore one of those Mandela colourful shirts, and, like the great man, he was a live wire.

We first picked up a Dutch guy from a hostel on Long Street – Marc, a policeman from Arnhem. Our small party was complete with a sagacious Colombian anthropology professor who was accompanied by a young, Turkish female researcher. Asia, Europe, Africa, America: we were all there.

'My friends,' said Mohammed, 'you want to see how the majority of the inhabitants of South Africa live, don't you? You've heard about apartheid, eh? Of course, you have! During apartheid, the law determined where you lived, what kind of job you could get, how much you could earn, even who you could have sex with. Everything depended on one single factor:

the colour of your skin. Did any of you come to South Africa during apartheid?'

No one had.

'Thank you for boycotting our country! It was international pressure that made the government yield and reverse the race laws. It's a simple story, the history of South Africa. The Dutch came to settle on the southern tip of Africa to grow fresh fruit and vegetables and open the first 7-Eleven in history because the sailors on long sea voyages were suffering from scurvy. But the nearest natives – the Bushmen or Khoi-San – were nomads. Imagine the horror of the Dutch when they realised that the Khoi-San did not know how to farm! So they imported Malays from their colonies in South-east Asia and brought them here. And what did they speak to them? Simplified Dutch – *kitchen Dutch* – mixed with Malay words to be understood. What do we call it today? Afrikaans. In South Africa it's not just the whites who speak Afrikaans. It's *my* native language. It's the language of the Coloured population. It was Malay Muslim scholars who wrote the first texts in Afrikaans.'

We stopped to walk the narrow lanes of the Malay quarter, the *Bo-Kaap*, marvelling at its Edwardian architecture mixed with the odd Dutch gable here and there. Brightly painted houses adorned the cobbled streets, as if van Gogh had been the shade consultant to the decorators. This was South African historical urban architecture at last; a visitors' must-see if only because this is the only neighbourhood with a non-European population in the centre of a South African town. It is such an old settlement, even the Group Areas Act respected its character and designated it a Cape Malay district.

'During the Napoleonic Wars the British came with their liberal values and started antagonising the conservative Dutch farmers, the Boers, who by then had been cut off from civilisation and modern thought and only studied the Bible for inspiration. They were living in a hostile land and in order to survive they had to kill or enslave the natives. So they developed this theory to psyche them up, that they were their God's chosen race and that they were superior. They fled the rule of the British and trekked to the interior where they beat the Zulu in the Battle of Blood River; the Zulu, whose leader Shaka had turned into the most feared of warriors. They beat them – and from then on they were sure they were superior and that their God was with them. Then they found diamonds and gold in their land. A lot of diamonds and gold. The British wanted the diamonds and the gold so they fought the Afrikaners. The British won the war but they lost the peace. Within ten years of the end of the war, the Union of South Africa was formed. It had a pro-British government and fought on the side of the Empire in the two world wars. But this involvement angered the Afrikaners and led to the victory of the National Party in 1948. The National Party was a party that hated the British, promoted its own people in industry and in government and formed an ideology of segregation of races, called apartheid.'

Thus spake Mohammed.

There are two sections of thought in South Africa in regard to the policy affecting the non-European community. On the one hand there is the policy of equality, which advocates equal rights within the same political structure for all civilized and educated persons, irrespective of race or colour, and the gradual granting of the franchise to non-Europeans as they become qualified to make use of democratic rights.

On the other hand there is the policy of separation (apartheid) which has grown from the experience of established European population of the country, and which is based on the Christian principles of Justice and Reasonableness.

Its aim is the maintenance and protection of the European population of the country as a pure White race, the maintenance and protection of the indigenous racial groups as separate communities, with prospects of developing into self-supporting communities within their own areas, and the stimulation of national pride, self-respect, and mutual respect among the various races of the country.

We can act in only one of two directions. Either we must follow the course of equality, which must eventually mean national suicide for the White race, or we must take the course of separation (apartheid) through which the character and the future of every race will be protected and safeguarded with full opportunities for development and self-maintenance in their own ideas, without the interests of one clashing with the interests of the other, and without one regarding the development of the other as undermining or a threat to himself. The party therefore undertakes to protect the White race properly and effectively against any policy, doctrine or attack which might undermine or threaten its continued existence. At the same time the party rejects any policy of oppression and exploitation of the non-Europeans by the Europeans as being in conflict with the Christian basis of our national life and irreconcilable with our policy.

The party believes that a definite policy of separation (apartheid) between the White races and the non-white racial groups, and the application of the policy of separation also in the case of the non-white racial groups, is the only basis on which the character and future of each race can be protected and safeguarded and on which each race can be guided so as to develop his own national character, aptitude and calling.

Statement by the National Party of South Africa, 29 March, 1948.

Mohammed stopped the car.

'During apartheid we all had to register into nine ethnic groups. Even the number of our *dompass* ended on a digit that signified our colour. If your number ended in zero, you were white. Now, let's try to classify people in this street shall we?' he said, school-masterish.

'No,' I said. 'Let's not.'

Mohammed ignored me.

'You, Mr Policeman,' he asked Marc. 'Perhaps you want to classify people according to their colour.'

'No,' said Marc. 'I don't.'

'Tell me, Mr Policeman, what colour is the woman carrying the groceries?'

Marc relented. 'White.'

'And the lady crossing the street?'

'Black.'

'And the old man with the hat?'

'Black.'

'WRONG!' shouted Mohammed triumphantly. 'He's Coloured!'

We winced.

'Exactly! The authorities' (that word again) 'also didn't know. Sometimes the classification was arbitrary. Do you know about the pencil test?'

The pencil test?

'Yes, my friend. If you weren't white, they put a pencil on your head and if your hair was curly enough to keep it there, you were black. If it was smooth and it fell down, you were Coloured. And this pencil determined the rest of your life.'

The Turkish woman was the first one to lose it. 'Is this how they classified you?' she asked, horrified. 'With a *pencil*?'

'No,' said Mohammed seriously. 'Sometimes they used a comb.'

We didn't know whether he was joking; we guessed not.

'Have you been to Table Mountain?' asked Mohammed.

Everyone nodded.

'Did you not wonder why such prime estate below de Waal Drive with a view of Table Bay is empty?'

Here it comes.

The Turkish woman spoke. 'Yes, we did. We thought it had something to do with the ground. Subsidence. Or falling rocks.'

'There is something wrong with the ground, all right,' said Mohammed. 'No one wants to live there. It's haunted. It used to be District Six.'

He parked on Buitekant Street and entered what appeared to be an Anglican church. It's now a museum, a living testimony to the fabric of a society that was wrenched forever.

It is a gruelling task even to recall that day in Cape Town which started in the District Six Museum. Although I was aware of the Group Areas Act – that cornerstone of apartheid legislation – I was ignorant of its human impact. District Six – originally called Kanaladoorp and renamed when the municipalities of Cape Town were officially established in 1867 – was a multi-cultural working-class community, differing little from a modern-day Arab *souk*: artisans, labourers and immigrants working off the sea, the port or the shops and factories of Cape Town proper. In 1966, under the Group Areas Act, it was declared a white area: this was prime land on the slopes of Table Mountain, situated between the expanding town and the airport. Between 1966 and 1982, sixty thousand people were forcibly removed from their homes, which were razed to the ground after a long and bitter struggle.

Outside the museum stood a plaque: *All who pass remember the thousands of people who lived for generations in District Six and were forced by law to leave their homes because of the colour of their skins.* The plaque was put up in 1971. It has been pulled off once and defaced twice.

Inside we met a group of astonished elderly American tourists who plainly didn't know what to make of a tragedy ('Hey Thelma, what happened to entertaining holidays?'). What was this map on the floor? Names of ghost streets like Hanover Street, Vernon Terrace, Harrington Street, Constitution Street, the beautifully named Vogelgezang Street, Rutger Street, De Villiers Street – English names, Afrikaans names, French Huguenot names. In a parallel universe, had it existed, this would be the place where backpackers would flock to, like the Medina in Fez or the old bazaar in Istanbul. What they get instead is the sanitised world of the Waterfront.

Street signs hung from the ceiling, donated by a worker whose brief was to dump them at sea but who didn't. Photographs from people's albums were exhibited on the walls. Personal things surrounded us: a carpenter's tools from a shop on Horstley Street; kitchen equipment from a restaurant; an archaic shop till that really ought to be in the Smithsonian. People still remember their days in District Six with nostalgia: one Coloured resident, Patric de Goede, carried a bottle of District Six sand with him for fourteen years until he donated it to the museum. There is a small bookshop inside with a photographic record of the old town, as well as a novel, describing life in District Six before and during the forced displacement: the semi-autobiographical *Buckingham Palace, District Six* by the late, murdered, Richard Rive. It is now a school text in the new South Africa.

The American tourists left pale.

We drove around the old District Six; empty blocks everywhere. The bitterest pill is that after the high-profile struggle no one dared build houses there and no one dared move in – all the pain for nothing. The 'authorities' built a university, the Technicon, hoping this would be non-controversial, but made sure that even the street grid had changed. Hanover Street with its New Year's Eve carnival has been completely obliterated; it used to run inside the Technicon compound parallel to the modern Kaizergracht Street. The main uni buildings were built on top of the Public Wash House, where collars were starched and ironed. The Fish Market, Maxim's Sweets, the People's Dairy, Dout's Café, Waynik's School Uniforms, Polliack's Original Music Store (est. 1896): all gone. The shoreline just below Sir Lowry Road where the old morning market stood (now the Good Hope Centre) has moved due to land reclamation. Every memory of an erstwhile community has been painstakingly eradicated. Only the churches and the mosques were not torn down: the Aspeling and Muir Street mosque and the diminutive St Mark's church, stubbornly inside the university perimeter, still draw their communities from miles away. In Searle Street around the Holy Cross church there are a few houses that were not demolished after a fierce battle with conservationists. They show how District Six used to look: two-storey Victorian buildings, with chimney tops and flat fronts. Yes, in the end – with the neglect shown by the absentee landlords and the hostility of the regime – yes, the area might have become a slum. But the New York municipality never bulldozed parts of Harlem or the Bronx – because it relies on the votes of their residents.

As the small photocopied museum guide said, this is truly the way Holocausts are made. Indeed, they don't occur out of the blue like cases of spontaneous combustion; they burn slowly in people's hearts like a cigarette behind an old, flame-retardant sofa: by the time you notice the damage, the fire is out of control, your house is burning down and your only thought is to save yourself. Which is what must have happened to the conscience of the white South Africans.

'Where did the people from District Six move to?' asked Marc.

'To formal townships like Bonteheuwel or Heideveld or a barren, sandy area: the Cape Flats,' said Mohammed. 'That's where we're heading, my friend.'

35. Ashes to ashes

So this was Langa, a township of anything between 30,000 and 80,000 people – no one knows exactly how many. Tens of thousands could disappear and no one would notice, for here even in death people are unequal. Langa has a hospital – I saw it – the size of a Surrey village clinic. Imagine a Langa grandfather having a heart attack in the middle of the night;

what are his chances compared to the wealthy pensioner of Belville, a few miles north?

'Langa means "sun" in Xhosa,' said Mohammed as he drove past. 'This is the original Sun City! Welcome to a township, my friends. How do I know it's a township? There, see? One way in, one way out and the rest carefully enclosed between railway lines and large motorways so that every movement can be easily controlled.'

Like Canary Wharf, I thought. It's funny that urban planners use the same design to keep people out as to keep people in.

'Look around you. This is how the majority of the people live. This is a legal settlement; wait until we go to the illegal ones,' said Mohammed and pointed at miles upon miles of disorienting shacks; puddles of brown water; corrugated iron and plasterboard dwellings with roofs out of every imaginable substance; grim, jail-like four-storey blocks of flats with grubby skylight windows criss-crossed by electricity wires hanging as low as wash lines; rows of terraced bungalows with makeshift rickety fences in peeling reds, blues and yellows; huts made out of planks unsure of the horizontal and the vertical and plastic lilos instead of doors. Housewives were bent over buckets struggling to clean dirty clothes with dirty water, for hundreds of thousands live without sanitation, water, power – you name it, they haven't got it.

I had seen my share of shanty towns, but three had stuck in my mind because of the proximity of the poverty to immense wealth: in Bombay, the centre of the Bollywood industry and provider of thirty per cent of India's tax income, where a line of wretches with palms open line up along the waterfront to a saint's mausoleum and where entrepreneurs give you change for one rupee so that you can give one worthless cent each to a hundred people to minimise your discomfort; São Paulo, the economic powerhouse of the world's fastest growing economy with *favelas* lining the motorway from the airport to the town – they seem temporary until you see the 'For Sale' signs and realise that that structure, which most of us wouldn't use to defecate in, is precious property to others; and the Cape Flats, because the combined forces of capitalism, colonialism and apartheid condemned people to a continuous struggle without hope. Take away the prospect of advancement or betterment in this life and what have you got? If not hell, then the desperation of purgatory.

'Are we in any danger?' asked the Turkish woman.

'Do you feel any danger, my friends?' Mohammed asked back. 'People here know Legend Tours and they know that we contribute part of your tickets towards community projects.'

No, we didn't feel any danger. But there were certainly strange looks from Xhosa teenagers along the route. I crossed eyes with a barefoot guy in his twenties. *That stare.* Was it hostility or shame?

The air stank. We closed the windows.

'One of the places we support,' continued Mohammed, 'is the Chris Hani school we will visit. It's run by a woman, Mrs Maureen Jacobs, whom I truly believe to be a saint. She has single-handedly created this school. The school choir will sing for us at eleven o'clock.'

Marc winced. I felt embarrassed. What is this, the Kruger Park? Why am I taking pictures of the squalour? Why am I here – on a *tour*?

'I don't like this "sing for us at eleven",' I said to Mohammed, searching for the right word. 'They don't have to... *perform.*'

'My friend, in order not to hurt the sensitivities of the schoolchildren the tours arrive at eleven during choir practice. The children are proud that you are here. They have been told that their choir is world famous and that people all over the world visit them to hear them sing. And, of course, we think of your sensitivities as well.'

Our sensitivities?

'Well, yes. We don't want to make you feel like a voyeur.'

I had never expected the citizens of Langa to care about *my* feelings.

Mohammed gave me one of his piercing looks.

'Don't feel bad. You have come and seen it, and in this you have done more than most residents of Cape Town,' he said, as he stopped in front of a long, L-shaped bungalow.

'It's a big school,' commented the Turkish woman.

Mohammed laughed.

'Your conditioning,' he laughed. 'The school is not this building. The school is that *room*. The rest are living quarters of the residents.'

We got off the bus, as these very residents eyed us with curiosity. They knew and we knew where we all stood in the pyramid of life and that none of us could make an iota of difference in theirs.

We were received by Maureen Jacobs. For a saint she was very plain-looking: middle-aged and bulky with a brown-orange Xhosa complexion, she could have been one of those housewives struggling with the washing in the township alleys. But when she started describing her school's aims with an unpretentious air of noble dignity, she seemed to grow in authority and fill the room with her presence.

'This is a school for Xhosa children who are so poor they have not even been registered,' she said.

What did she mean, *registered*?

'At birth. It costs one hundred rand to register your child and many people in the rural areas cannot afford to. Without a birth certificate you cannot go to school. Those you see here are from the Transkei or the Ciskei and have such low language and maths skills that they cannot even be admitted to a school. We register them and give them enough schooling so that they can be admitted back into state education.'

Inside there was a blackboard with subtractions:

$$7 - 1 = 6$$
$$6 - 1 = 5$$
$$5 - 1 = 4$$
$$4 - 1 = 3$$
$$3 - 1 = 2$$
$$2 - 1 = 1$$

Next to it hung another board with joined-up writing in Xhosa and some in English:

> *I eat with my mouth.*
> *I see with my eyes.*
> *I hear with my ears.*

The children were looking at us questioningly. They were mostly girls dressed in pressed clean uniforms: white blouses and brown skirts. (Their parents must have found the money to register their brothers.) I smiled at a tiny girl and was rewarded with one of the pearly white smiles only African kids can muster. I heard the choir sing a beautiful song in that uniquely South African antiphonal accapella style. I didn't know the Xhosa words, but it didn't matter, because music can take you to any world you want to imagine – yet, whichever image came to mind, it was imbued with infinite sadness. As if to clear our heads, a more upbeat song followed with two boys performing a little merry dance, kneeling on the floor with one leg and alternating the position. Finally, we were treated to a hymn written in 1897 by a Xhosa choirmaster, Enoch Sontonga. The original version contained only one verse; the poet Samuel Mqhayi added seven more in 1927. It was banned from being sung, performed or played in public during the apartheid era. It is one of the few national anthems the whole world can hum, one of the most stirring choral pieces ever: '*Nkosi sikelel' iAfrica*' – God Bless Africa, indeed, for it needs some serious blessing.

I think Marc lost it then. He felt compelled to say something and, in a broken voice, he thanked the children for us – but he was babbling. I kept my eyes pinned on the floor. This was my fifteen minutes of contact with a destitute way of life I couldn't help feeling personally responsible for, because of the colour of *my* skin.

Maureen gave me a small, pitiful, photocopied brochure containing the school's founding principles. I couldn't read it; I was gritting my teeth trying not to shed a tear.

'We need more funds,' she was saying. 'There are four teachers. All volunteers. We do not draw any salary ourselves. All money goes into registering those children. Else they do not exist.' I realised she was talking to me alone in the yard and that I was nodding mutely because it was clear that the land imbued with infinite sadness was not miles away but here and now.

'We have met some very nice people from Europe,' she was saying now. 'Last year three girls from Denmark came with Liberty Tours. They were only eighteen, but after they visited our school, they stayed and taught English for six months. We did not pay them. We only cooked for them. We cried so much when they left.'

I wanted a picture of her. She obliged. She wrote her address on the back of my crumpled photocopied brochure. She was struggling; her writing was disjointed – I thought she was dyslexic. When I leaned closer I saw that it wasn't her, it was the pencil she was using, if that could be described as a pencil: it had been ground to a small blunt tip, impossible to grasp and control. 'No money for school equipment,' she explained with a resigned smile.

'Are things better now?' I dared ask.

She didn't answer the question directly.

'We have suffered a lot,' she said unhurriedly, 'but like our president, we forgive and forget.'

I swear to you, she did say that.

From that point on, the trip was a blur. I remember barefoot kids in corners chewing on the laces of their tracksuits; bent-over women beating the dirt off clothes in buckets; kids kicking cans out of rubbish bins; huts only distinguished as shops by their signs: Stuyvesant cigarettes, Chamberlain's syrup, Njoy Coca Cola. Amongst all this, the waste, the human waste of talent: look, there is Langa Athletic Club with no money and few facilities. A town this size had only two athletic fields and they were being shared between the cricket club, the rugby club, the hockey club – in fact, every Langa sports club.

There was also physical waste: rotting vegetables, discarded broken seats, cannibalised shells of cars, white plastic bags, hollowed-out radios and carcasses of TV sets. Garbage seemed to grow like weed out of the ground. This was Guguletu, a shanty town of – how many? – 200,000? 250,000? 300,000? No one knows. These people don't really exist. Guguletu means 'our pride'. Was this a joke?

'Street signs,' said Marc.

We looked up at the wondrous sight. There were two signs at an intersection: 'NY1' and 'NY2'.

Mohammed laughed. 'Yes, my friends,' he said. 'Street signs. Do you know what they mean? No, it's not New York One and New York Two. Guguletu was a place built by the apartheid government to house forcibly removed black people. The signs mean Native Yard One and Native Yard Two.'

I crossed eyes with the Colombian professor. He was shaking his head vigorously. I knew he'd lost it then. 'Native Yard One,' he whispered. 'Just like pigs…'

'This is the Cape Flats,' said Mohammed. 'A useless piece of sandy soil which was used as a rubbish dump and was put to better use by the apartheid government by dumping its own people. Tourists come here and they see the rubbish and say: "Aren't black people dirty and ignorant? Why don't they pick up their rubbish?" But this whole place used to be the Cape Town rubbish dump. Look at this field opposite. Can you see the bottles buried underneath? Can you see the thick layers of compressed waste exposed by the blowing wind?'

We could.

'Look closer,' Mohammed said to me. 'What do you see?'

'People,' I said. There were people walking amid the litter.

'And?'

'They're carrying flowers. They're crying.'

I swallowed audibly. We all did. Among the rubbish, there were tombstones. This was the township cemetery.

This is where I lost it.

I closed my eyes unable to reopen them dry. I saw my father in his coffin, the lid open for that last, harrowing glimpse. Whenever I visit him with fresh flowers, I feel compelled to take a bucket of water and wash the gravestone clean. Oh, to have to bury him in a rubbish dump!

No, India, Brazil, you are forgiven. This was no Bombay or São Paulo; this was a conscious, authoritarian decision by an ethnically exclusivist government brandishing a philosophy which became a self-fulfilling doctrine. From the cradle to the grave, black people were condemned to live with rubbish, be treated as rubbish and die in rubbish, regulated within the great creationist pyramid of apartheid with white man at its peak. If, as the Afrikaners fear, the white man disappears in Africa – well, he may have had his chance and blown it.

'I know what you're thinking,' Mohammed said. 'How could they? How can they? The answer is simple. They've all been brainwashed. Black and white.'

'And Coloured,' added Marc.

Mohammed chuckled.

'You're learning, my friend,' he said. 'Yes, and Coloured. Your church, the Dutch Reformed Church, preached to us that the white man is superior. Our families saw the white man's technology and told us that they were superior. Our schools, our history, everything told us that white man was superior. And we believed them – even the Zulu believed them. That was our problem; that's where we went wrong.'

He was angry now.

'I've been doing these township tours for some time now and do you know what I want most?'

This was supposed to be a rhetorical question, but I butted in.

'I think so,' I said.

He waited.

'You want to show the white South Africans around, not just tourists.'

He didn't answer.

'Isn't it so?'

He nodded.

'How could they? How can they?' I repeated his words now coming out of my mouth torrentially, like a Swazi downpour. 'Simple. They don't know, and they don't bother challenging so-called truths and half-baked lies. It takes a lot of effort to think independently, to detach yourself from your blinkers and look objectively at something from a different angle. Most people don't believe in themselves enough to make that leap. Who am I to question centuries' old wisdom? Prejudice is based on arrogance, ignorance and fear and, believe me, I know a bit about prejudice myself.'

This plunged the car in total silence. It didn't occur to me then, but reading my diary later, I saw that I was just describing the process for breaking self-denial which is exactly the process for coming out as a homosexual. In South Africa, a whole nation needs to come out and confront itself.

We next drove through an endless landscape of identical and equidistant matchstick boxes, made out of the same materials, every one in the same shape and structure, like replanted trees, the individuality of the residents only revealed by differently coloured window curtains.

'These,' Mohammed informed us, 'are the Mandela dwellings.'

Explain please.

'These are the houses Nelson Mandela and Thabo Mbeki promised to the township residents.'

These?

'Yes, these, my friend. Don't you like them?'

Erm… no.

'You make me laugh, my friend. Yes, they look bad, but there are differences. They have electricity and water, and they are not made out of wood. They are solid. The people in them have not been displaced. They moved here willingly. And the houses have room to expand.'

I wasn't convinced. Were these the houses the ANC promised their voters?

'The government are not providing them with houses. They can't. They provide them with a solid start and they invite them to expand. They give them one room and challenge them to build a second, through their own efforts. And a third.'

I pointed at a house with a second room shabbily made out of cardboard in that characteristic shanty town manner.

'Unfortunately for the expansion they use several materials,' Mohammed admitted.

'How many of them are there?' asked Marc.

'The government promised one million. They built 750,000.'

'All like this?'

'All like this.'

'Are you in the ANC, Mohammed?' I asked to squeeze out the propaganda.

He shook his head. 'I was. Not any more.'

'Why?'

'I've realised that governments don't run a country. Money runs a country.'

Mohammed stopped. We had reached Bonteheuwel, a Coloured township.

'The Coloured people call this a Cape Town suburb,' he said. 'Look at the houses. Any difference from Langa or Guguletu?'

The houses were better constructed. There were front gardens, a petrol station, a supermarket. This was more recognisably a town, as I would picture it: fences professionally erected, houses with bricks and fresh paint, tended gardens, asphalt in the streets.

'But don't be deceived,' continued Mohammed. 'One way in, one way out, surrounded by motorways and railway lines: a township. The Coloureds have been conned.'

'But you are Coloured,' I said.

'Yes.'

'So?'

Mohammed's features darkened and his eyes flashed.

'So I'm aware that the apartheid system used us as a wedge between the black community and themselves. The abused became abusers as some ineffectual privileges came their way. By making us hate each other the apartheid regime could perpetuate its rule. What the Coloured people hate the most is to be considered black. Coloured people don't have any guilt complex using black women as maids – only whites do. Do you know who ran the province of the Western Cape after the first elections? Not the ANC but the National Party. The Coloured people voted the old oppressors in.'

The prejudice and mutual hatred between the two communities is legendary. During the 1950s debates raged whether just the Africans or all racial groups, including the Cape Coloured, should participate against the overthrow of apartheid. At the time, a young Nelson Mandela spoke against an integrated fight. The ANC adopted the policy of cooperation with all racial groups in spite of his directives.

'Do you think the blacks like other blacks?' Mohammed continued. 'There are seven million black illegal immigrants. They are chased away from the townships. They are the ones who live under the motorway by the Waterfront. But *they* are the ones who will hawk you matches or try to sell you something. They won't beg! *Our* blacks have a victim mentality. "Give me money 'cos I'm poor. Give me money 'cos I've suffered. Give me money 'cos with Mandela it's my turn now. Give me money or I'll kill you."'

Stop it!

Mohammed drove on.

'Do you know something else, my friend? Unemployment in Bonteheuwel is forty to sixty per cent. How do they counteract it? The Coloureds deal in drugs, *dagga* and Mandrax. Crime here is more rife than in Langa. This is where people have time and money and indulge in drugs. Here you get the drug addicts and the burglaries and organised crime.'

'Like PAGAD?' I asked.

PAGAD – People Against Gangsterism And Drugs – is a militant Muslim association which had been originally responsible for the vigilante murder of several high profile gangsters. Yet, several bombings on the Waterfront and other tourist areas later, the original anti-crime movement turned into an Islamic terrorist group. Thankfully it has been quiet recently and some point the finger at the rehabilitation of Colonel Qaddafi who stopped sponsoring the organisation.

'We all supported PAGAD in the beginning,' said Mohammed. 'Everyone knows who the top guys are, including the police. Its headquarters are in a mosque in Charlesville. They say that the police helped them by providing PAGAD with information about the gangsters' movements. But after that they became a destabilising factor. No one supports them any more, but apartheid created a dangerous fundamentalism amongst the Muslim community. Every racial group retreated to its traditions and rejected Western values.'

Indeed. If European civilisation and the Age of Reason led to colonialism, racism and apartheid, why is Western culture superior to our ancestors', who lived in relative peace and freedom?

Answer that.

Mohammed left us by common consent at the Waterfront. I was heavy-hearted and heavy-footed and slid out of the van with all the grace of a sleepy walrus. Mohammed thanked us all individually for attempting to see the other South Africa.

'Goodbye, my friend,' Mohammed said and shook my hand. 'The day was nice with you.'

I thought of Maureen. I thought of the Danish girls. I couldn't leave like that.

'I have to do something about it,' I told Mohammed.

He smiled.

'Many people say that,' he said. 'What the people of Langa need is jobs and education. What can you do?'

What could I do?

'I don't know,' I said.

'Well,' said Mohammed, 'if you think of something, this is my cellphone number.'

36. The Gardens (Reprise)

Vanessa brought me breakfast. 'Jasmine and Loretta have finally gone,' she said with relief.

'I know.'

'No, I mean from my flat.'

'What were they doing in your flat?'

Vanessa explained. Her flatmate, Dominic, was in the advertising business and Loretta was a model. His agency had paid for Loretta to come all the way from LA for a photoshoot.

'She said she was eighteen,' said Vanessa.

'And Jasmine? Why does she carry her little sister with her all the time?'

'Because she's her *daughter*.'

Buzz, buzz, mental arithmetic.

'Dear me, at what age do they menstruate in California?' I wondered. 'It must be those hormones they feed the chickens.'

Vanessa looked at me: 'She's *twenty-eight*! She's older than me!'

'She's not that old.'

'She's very old for the fashion business,' said Vanessa. 'And she lied. Which is why Dominic stopped paying their rent and sent them back to America.'

She sat down, her face drained with dread.

'But not before they stayed at our place for one night. That kid is something else. She screamed constantly. She opened every cupboard in the house while we watched TV. It was bad enough when she hung around the kitchen and destroyed all the food. When she started searching through my bedroom drawers, I flipped.'

I changed the topic.

'Vanessa, have you ever been to Langa?'

'No. Why should I?' she said, unruffled. 'I have a pretty good idea what it's like. I used to live a bit further out. Every day I used to come into town on the train. I was the only white face in the train station. Then one day these guys came up to me as I was standing there and said: "People like you," – they meant whites – "we throw them into the tracks."' She smiled a bitter smile. 'We can't undo the past. We now have this new South Africa. But what I find amazing is that they don't look after their own people. Their government has done nothing to improve their lot.'

'Vanessa,' I said. 'It's not *their* government – it's *your* government.'

There was a pause.

'I know,' she said softly. 'One of our guests once – a German – you know what he said?'

'No. What?'

'He said, "You white South Africans, you live behind bars. You live in prison and you don't know it."'

I looked at the high wall around the patio.

'I've been thinking about it in more ways than one,' she continued. 'I certainly feel like that. In my job, too. Piet leaves and I stay here, look after the house, cook breakfast, clean. I hardly meet anyone.'

'So why are you working here then?'

She got up. 'I'll tell you another time. Have you finished?' As she collected the plates, she had the last word.

'It all started with the British, you know,' she said. 'Everything started with the British.'

She was right, of course. Throughout my historical interludes, there has been a giant, silent character sitting motionless in the corner of this South African drama. Like Cape Town, I leave the best till last.

Enter the British...

Chapter Eleven

A Shrimp Learns to Whistle: The Cape

If there be a God, and He cares anything about what I do, I think it is clear that He would like me to do what He is doing Himself. And as He is manifestly fashioning the English-speaking race as the chosen instrument by which He will bring in a state of society based upon Justice, Liberty and Peace, He must obviously wish me to do what I can to give as much scope and power to that race as possible. Hence, if there be a God, I think that what He would like me to do is to paint much of the map of Africa British red as possible, and to do what I can elsewhere to promote the unity and extend the influence of the English-speaking race.

Cecil Rhodes

37. Die Boers

I was reading the papers on the patio, sitting opposite Piet, who was leafing through a family album. I chuckled as I read aloud the headlines about former Zimbabwean President Canaan Banana, the man with the best name in the world after Cardinal Sin of the Philippines. He had been hounded by Mugabe and had just escaped from his captors.

'Listen to this,' I said to Piet. 'They're having a ball: "Banana Slips into South Africa". Yesterday it was "Fruitless Search for Banana" and before that "No Record of Banana Entry".' I still remember the headline I read when he was indicted on sodomy charges: "Banana Forced Officer to Have Sex" – sodomy being a crime in Zimbabwe, but a constitutional right in South Africa.

The Chardonnay compounded the giggles.

'So these are your sons?' I asked, leaning over his shoulder as I poured us a second glass of wine. 'They're enormous. The one who lives here is rather cute.'

'The first and the third are big, *ja*.'

'This one looks like a Nazi,' I yelped.

'*Ja*, hmm, the older one,' said Piet without even glancing at the photo.

'And you're also enormous in this one.'

'Married life, see?'

The subject had been broached. 'How long ago was this?'

'About ten years ago. This is when I came out properly.'

'You mean all that time…'

'I married her on her eighth month,' Piet said, 'and she was eight years older than me. Funny thing is, I had only slept with her twice.' He stopped to sip some wine as if to emphasise the subject with an, ahem, *pregnant* pause.

'You're implying she tricked you,' I said awkwardly.

Piet was quick in his rebuttal: 'My family blame her for my unfortunate life. I don't. I didn't tell her I was bisexual until fifteen years later. That was my fault alone.'

We were waiting for Teddy, and he was late. 'Where is he?' Piet fretted, wanting to dispel the memories. 'The wine is running low.'

One more sip of Chardonnay and those memories returned.

'It happened in England, you know,' Piet recalled, eyes fixed on the patio wall behind me. 'I came out to her in the Lake District. Near Lake Windermere. We had a shouting match. I opened the car door and screamed at her: *"Get out of my car and out of my life!"*

A bit harsh.

Piet sighed. 'She didn't leave the car, but our life together stopped there and then. My eldest son, the Nazi, wanted to kill me when he found out. But everyone else in Hermanus was fine about it. I never expected that. Strange isn't it? People in the Cape are tolerant. Gay priests have crept into the Anglican church here without fanfares.'

The bell rang. Teddy walked in with that air of embalmed adolescence that envelops ageing gay men. He was wearing a carefully pressed safari suit and shiny walking boots, as if we were about to go on a shooting expedition accompanied by liveried servants.

'Fab,' I said. '*Very* Hemingway.'

'You like it?' he asked with a twirl. 'I call it my Lion Queen safari suit. It makes me feel like Katherine Hepburn.'

'You should go to Safari Camp,' I said and showed him a flyer for the Cape Town annual gay and lesbian celebration. 'It's a safari costume theme. Only eighty rand a ticket. Unfortunately, I'm flying out on the same day.'

Teddy turned to Piet. 'Well, girl, shall we go?' he asked.

Piet frowned. 'I don't know. I'm too old for that.'

'Look at him. *Too old!* The opera queen! I'm trying to take him to parties, and he won't come out with me. He's always sitting there like a Dora.'

'What's a Dora?' I asked.

'A drunk queen,' he replied.

While we're at it, what's the slang term for...

'A *moffie*. That's what you are in South Africa, doll. Unless you're black, in which case you're a *Natalie*. As in: look at *her*, she's a right Natalie!'

The bell rang and interrupted our linguistic class. It was Dominic, Vanessa's flatmate, the one in advertising.

'What happened to Loretta?' I asked after the introductions. This was the wrong question, answered by muted grumbles.

'I still can't understand why you had to import a black model from the States when you have so much cheaper indigenous talent,' I continued, unabashed.

'The Zulu and the Xhosa want their women plump,' answered Dominic. 'The indigenous talent is fat. Fat is unphotogenic.'

'But to whom? Should black adverts not try to appeal to black men and women?'

Dominic looked at me as if I had come from another solar system. 'The adverts are not for *blacks*,' he explained. 'The adverts are not even for South Africa. The weather, the locations and the wages attract European and American agencies. It's the timing, too. Adverts that are shot here in your winter appear six months later for your summer.'

As an afterthought, he added: 'We *do* use local models. But they are so unreliable. A shoot may take several days and in the middle of the shoot they don't come and send their brother or sister to cover instead. Can you believe it? Start the shoot with one face and end it with another?'

We all laughed.

Dominic asked me if I'd been out clubbing.

'Not yet,' I said. 'I'm in need of some chemical refuelling.'

'On a scale from one to one hundred, I stand at one thousand against drugs,' said Teddy. 'Totally against.'

'Me, too,' said Piet. 'I'm afraid I might get addicted.'

Dominic and I looked at him.

'So sweet,' I said.

'*Ja*,' said Dominic. 'Sweet aren't they?'

Teddy and Piet blushed.

After several post-prandial bottles of Chardonnay, Teddy started reminiscing for our benefit. 'I had a boyfriend in Kuwait, Ali. Still do. I'm trying to get him over here.'

'Oh,' I said, looking at Piet, 'I thought you two were...'

They tittered like teenage Japanese girls.

'That's what all people think,' said Piet. 'We certainly enjoy each other's company, but –'

'He's too old for me,' piped Teddy, breaking into laughter.

Piet sulked queenly.

'But we'll grow old together,' added Teddy hastily.

This seemed to placate Piet. 'You know,' he said, 'I often dream of the two of us in an old people's home, senile, holding each other's hands. I get some comfort from that.'

'Aaaah,' I said. 'The ones we *really* love, we don't sleep with.'

They both shifted buttocks uneasily.

How come Teddy ended up in Kuwait?

'I left South Africa because of apartheid,' said Teddy. 'I first went to England, but couldn't stand the weather. Then I moved to Kuwait. I stayed away for twenty-four years. I only returned when the Iraqis invaded.'

Did he lose a lot in the war?

'I had a nice business doing interior design for hotels. I invested $800,000 and was making a lot of money. The Iraqis took it all: money, equipment, materials. I have a formal claim against them. So what? Some niece of mine will probably inherit a lot of money in forty years' time.' Teddy looked at me jovially, his rosy cheeks aglow, and pointed at his head. 'Now I'm back, representing beauty products, like Grecian 2000.'

I looked at his dark, black hair and laughed.

'So many people leave South Africa,' I said. 'Funny you should return.'

Teddy's jovial expression faded.

'I'm a South African! I'd never miss a chance to live in this country if democracy ever began in my lifetime,' he said with a quiet, determined intonation. 'But the unthinkable happened. Like the fall of communism. Do you know what Nikita Khrushchev once said? "Those who wait for the USSR to abandon communism must wait until a shrimp learns to whistle."'

Teddy took a deep breath.

'Well, it did learn how to whistle! And you know what? Not only did I return, but *as a South African*. I fought heavily to retain my nationality. They wanted to take it away from me, but I fought tooth and nail not to lose it. *And I won!*'

Teddy looked fiercely at me for a moment. Then his expression gradually mellowed as he lost his halo of newly-acquired sagacity. 'It was so easy,' he added nostalgically, 'Kuwait beach, Ali, my job... It's harder here.'

He sighed. 'But it's a lot more just,' he added.

Some useless facts about die Boers:

1. *President Kruger believed to the end of his days that the Earth was flat.*
2. *In the crucial election of 1948, the winning Nationalist/Afrikaner Party alliance under Dr Malan ('Die Doktor') took 443,719 votes. The future opposition took 624,500. The single member constituency electoral system ensured that the Nationalists won more seats, and they went on to build the apartheid structure based on a minority of votes.*

38. Die Blacks

It was the turn of Vanessa to sit opposite me at breakfast, have a sip of water and tell me her story. Simple one, really, as it revolved around a man.

'His name is Grant,' she said. 'I met him working in Piet's bar. You know Piet had a bar back in Hermanus, don't you?'

I did.

'Back when –'

He was married. Yes.

'Grant had a British passport. He went to London and I followed him. I worked in various bars for three years, but neither of us liked it there. Too expensive. Too grey. By then

Piet had started this hotel business in Cape Town, so I stopped with him here.'

And Grant?

'I first shared a flat with a Greek.' She avoided the question. 'Very unlike you. You're more British than Greek. Let's say, my Greek had very fixed ideas about women. Surprising we got on at all, even for a short period.'

And Grant? Why didn't she stay with Grant?

'Because during the time we were in London, he met someone else.'

And?

'And, well, he married her.'

I struggled to find the right thing to say. 'Vanessa,' I said eventually, lost in Clichéville, 'Grant doesn't know what he is missing. It's *his* loss, OK?'

'Oh, I'm over it now,' she said without conviction.

'How long has it been?'

'Six months.'

I shook my head. 'That's not long. It takes as long to get over a relationship as it lasted originally. Where does Grant live now?'

'Here, in Cape Town.'

'Vanessa…' I started reproachfully.

'I'm *over* him,' Vanessa repeated and stood up ending the conversation abruptly.

I felt uneasy and looked at the sky outside. It was a scorcher of a day. 'How much would a taxi to Sandy Bay cost?' I asked her – Sandy Bay being Cape Town's nudist beach.

'Eighty, ninety rand,' Vanessa answered distractedly.

That was less than the money I usually spend in London for a taxi home on a Saturday night. That was it, I was off.

My Coloured taxi driver was Isu. He had a large four-wheel drive and plans to become a guide.

'But you need qualifications for that,' he said. 'I must go back to school. I didn't know I need to study. So I'm still a taxi driver. Before, I was a minibus driver, but they force you to join an organisation, a so-called union. But no, what they want is *thugs*. Because when a bus slips in the wrong route they expect you to join in.'

'Join in what?'

'The shooting.'

Explain.

'The companies have a gentleman's agreement on routes. If one of their minibuses strays, or if a new one tries to squeeze in, you go out and shoot them.'

At least the etiquette is simple. And the police?

'The police are on the take, too.'

We had reached Camps Bay emerging from the M52 by the other side of Table Mountain. At the bottom of the Twelve Apostles lies Llandudno – yes, I also chuckled at the name – and from there, a tortuously narrow road took us down to a car park where a drinks vendor was lying oblivious in the sun.

'How are you coming back?' asked Isu.

Oh, so many hours ahead. Who cares?

'Shall I come back and pick you up here?' he insisted.

I had to concede that this was really out of the way. 'Three hours?' I proposed, hoping it wasn't too long; yet somehow I didn't think Isu would object.

I made my way on a narrow path, winding through dense bushland until I saw Sandy Bay. Just before the main beach, I perched myself on the highest spot. The surrounding area was full of naked bodies. I stopped staring like a British tourist and descended from my position to freshen up in the sea for the proverbial cold shower. I nearly fainted when I put my foot in. It was as if Death himself had gripped my ankle and cut it off with his bony fingers. I knew that the South Atlantic was cold, but I never expected Cape Town's beaches to feel like Ostend. On the other side of the Cape peninsula the water is warmer and people venture into the sea, but on this side, I could only shiver. I scooped water to cool my face, and it felt like rubbing icicles on my cheeks. Needless to say any naughty thoughts I might have entertained disappeared forthwith, so I worked on my tan which, by now, had reached Durban surfer standards.

Three hours later, Isu was still waiting for me.

'I wasn't here all the time,' he said. 'I decided to take it easy,' he said. 'I went to Hout Bay and had lunch.'

'You did nothing but wait?'

'*Ja.*'

'So, my trip to Sandy Bay and back was enough to pay for your day?'

'Two hundred rand? *Ja*, sometimes I don't get that much during a whole shift.'

'How long is your shift?'

'Twenty-four hours.'

'*Twenty-four hours?* You work twenty-four hours non-stop?'

'I share the cab with another driver. Twenty-four hours on, twenty-four hours off. If I don't work through the whole of my shift, I'll lose my share. There are many people who want to be taxi drivers.'

I shook my head.

'You think it's too long?' Isu asked.

I left the question pending. This was not the time or place to expound on ILO work directives.

'All you taxi drivers are Coloured,' I said. 'It's like a minicab Mafia.'

Isu grimaced dismissively. 'Blacks don't drive. They can't drive. And they don't want to work.'

'Not true,' I said, 'in KwaZulu/Natal I met Zulu bus drivers.'

'The Zulu are the Zulu,' said Isu. 'I have a lot of admiration for the Zulu. But here, all over the Cape, we have the Xhosa. They can't drive. And they don't want to work.'

People believe that globalisation is a twentieth century feature. False: the global village was well in place in the nineteenth, albeit rather spread out. The proverbial butterfly rubbing its wings in the Philippines really did cause a storm in Canada, as events unfolded with international consequences. In this way, the Xhosa nation was irreversibly affected by the Crimean War.

By the middle of the nineteenth century the Xhosa had fought no less than seven frontier wars against the encroaching, land-hungry Brits and Boers. The early ones were no more than cattle raids; the later ones were far more serious affairs. In 1850, a teenage weakling called Mlanjeni claimed that he could cure witchcraft by making the afflicted walk through two poles he had erected outside his tent. Remember, in the Nguni world all sickness and adversity has a cause and that cause is a human who has been unwittingly bewitched by an evil spirit; after a disaster, scores of witchdoctors would 'smell out' the witches and drive out the evil spirits by impaling the 'possessed'. Mlanjeni's cure was understandably popular, as it eschewed the previous forced anal penetration, and that popularity had a predictable side-effect: since evil was caused by witchcraft, and since Mlanjeni could cure it, he had power over good and evil. Maybe power to drive the whites out into the sea where they came from?

Mlanjeni accepted the responsibility placed upon him and demanded that the dun-coloured cattle (the colour of the white settlers) be sacrificed to the Xhosa ancestors who would help them in their struggle. There was an eruption of slaughtering and a bitter holy war – the Eighth Frontier War – which ended in 1853 with the complete subjugation of the Ciskei Xhosa. The Cape Governor at the time was Sir George Cathcart, who was promoted and dispatched to fight in the Crimea.

In September 1853, a Dutch ship bringing Friesland bulls to Mossel Bay introduced the dreaded bovine lung-sickness to South Africa. Cattle started spewing green vomit and could not eat. Bulls died on their feet – as they were in pain lying down – weak and starved; cows dried from the inside out. By March 1855, the disease had spread to King William's Town and was responsible for the deaths of 5,000 cattle a month: the Xhosa had lost their land, now they were losing their livelihood. Then came the astounding news: their ex-governor, Sir George Cathcart, had been killed in a faraway land by 'Russians'. (Incidentally, Sir George died because he charged the wrong way and was surrounded by the enemy; his last words were the epitome of English sangfroid: 'Gentlemen, I fear we're in a mess.') Who were these Russians who had defeated the British? The Xhosa dismissed the notion that they were a white tribe; no, they had to be the spirits of their ancestors who had been placated by the Mlanjeni offerings and punished their oppressors. If only the Xhosa had been more pious and had followed the instructions of Mlanjeni...

The stage was ineluctably set for the suicide of a nation.

It started simply enough. In April 1856 two strangers appeared to a young girl called Nongqawuse and told her that the Xhosa should get rid of all their herds that were now impure and would die of lung-sickness in any case. Their ancestors – who had killed Sir George in the Crimea – would rise from the sea, drive the whites out and bring along healthy cattle and golden crops. In other times, she would have been laughed off. In the desperate times of 1856, however, her apocalyptic vision – bearing the influence of confused, creeping Messianic Christianity – was embraced by many chieftains. They included King Sarhili, the king of all Xhosa; a king who was accessible, courteous, pleasant and much-loved. But he was an embittered king who had lost all his sons to disease and was now losing his cattle in the lung-sickness catastrophe. He was also a guilt-ridden king who had had his chief medicine man slowly roasted on an open fire to make him confess that he was the malevolent spirit causing the royal misfortunes. King Sarhili personally needed to clutch at the straws Nongqawuse was offering. After visiting her in July 1856 and allegedly glimpsing the fleeting image of his diseased elder son, he decreed with a royal *imiyoleto* that she should be obeyed. Many more visited her and saw their ancestors and the cattle waiting inside the ocean. If you consider such mass hysteria freakish, just ask yourselves how many Americans claim to have been abducted by aliens.

Thousands of cattle were sacrificed in the three months that followed. The big day was set for the next full moon, when two suns would rise in the sky and collide over the mountains, plunging the earth into darkness. A great storm would blow, and only the newly-built huts of the believers would withstand it. The dead would arise, new corn would grow and the English and their fellow travellers – translated in Xhosa as 'the ones who wear trousers' – would disappear back into the ocean.

The full moon was due on 18 August 1856. Need I say, nothing happened.

The reaction of the Xhosa justifies the theory that Man is an emotional rather than a logical animal, using reason to justify irrational opinions. The dead did not rise, the argument went, because the Xhosa did not sacrifice all their animals in atonement for their sins, *but some sold them to the whites instead.* Therefore, all the remainder must be slaughtered without exception: the new, clean cattle the ancestors will bring must not mix with the old, impure beasts.

The Xhosa were divided into the *amathomba* (the believers, or '*soft*') and the *amagotya* (the unbelievers or '*hard*'). The most fanatical believers were the ones who had lost most of their livestock already. The believers leaned heavily on the unbelievers telling them they were greedy, preventing the ancestors from providing heaven on Earth, not sound enough to follow their brethren to the glorious future. The ancestors would punish them! Look what happened to the main unbeliever, chief Bulungwa: his testicles developed a scrofulous swelling which turned into an abscess. Hell, even I would kill all my cows if there was a chance in a billion my balls might fall off!

The first death from starvation occurred in late September 1856. By the next putative date, the December full moon, people were very hungry indeed and, as nothing had been sown, the Xhosa were on a rollercoaster to catastrophe. By January's full moon – where *were* those ancestors? – the horrible possibility that nothing might happen started to dawn on the famished population. Sarhili visited Nongqawuse again. He remained convinced: *all cattle must be slaughtered*. The unbelievers must be smelled out by the witchdoctors. They, not the prophetess, were the cause of the ancestral procrastination. The king personally pledged that the ancestors would finally arrive by 16 February 1857, within eight days of his return back to his *kraal*.

Need I say, nothing happened.

About one quarter of the Xhosa died and two thirds were displaced in the famine of 1856–57; around half a million cattle were killed and left to rot while their owners perished from hunger. Like the Irish famine, this episode irreversibly changed a whole nation's consciousness. And like in Ireland, the British looked coolly on. Plans for a famine relief were laughed at: wasn't this what the Kaffirs deserved? The new Cape governor, Sir George Grey, suspected a conspiracy. He jailed the chiefs and aided the Xhosa the only way he knew: by appropriating land, spreading British government and educating the natives through hard work.

To this day, some Xhosa believe that the prophecies were the work of the colonial government. No such evidence exists, and even Sir George's extensive private correspondence has been scrutinised to death. It is the great misfortune of South Africa that the superstitious Xhosa were unable to accept that their twilight was their fault. Instead, they manipulated their remembered history to blame a 'scheming' colonial administration, incapable of learning from the lessons of their collective mistakes, which set them back a century in their fight against colonialism.

The long-term effect of the killing of the cattle was typically unpredictable. Unlike the highly territorial Zulu who remained in KwaZulu/Natal, the Xhosa – as Isu pointed out – were now spread by necessity all over the Cape Colony, well before the general migration to the diamond and gold mines. It was thus that the Xhosa became the first true black South Africans – and it was from their ranks that sprang the eventual democratic leaders of the country: Oliver Tambo, Govan and Thabo Mbeki, Nelson Mandela, Steve Biko.

Such are the vagaries of history.

Some useless facts about die Blacks:
1. *Pointing with the index finger among the Zulu is equivalent to clapping.*
2. *Poets used to sing the praises of the king (and nowadays of political parties or trade unions) in triumphal poems called imbongi. One such imbongi was composed for the Prince of Wales on the occasion of his 1925 visit to South Africa by Samuel Mqhayi, of 'Nkosi sikelel' iAfrica' fame. It starts like this:*
   Ah, Britain! Great Britain!
   Great Britain of the endless sunshine!
   You can tell he never made the voyage.
3. *In Xhosa foreign words are amalgamated by sticking the prefix i in front. It is thus that toothpaste is called* iColgate *and deodorant* iMomu *(from Mum). Cast your mind back to the 1980s for the etymology of the word for those small, fast minibuses used for commuting:* iZolaBudd.

39. De Beers

I don't care whether Cape Agulhas is the most southern point in Africa and whether, geographically, it is there that the Indian Ocean meets the Atlantic. What I know from experience is that on one side of the Cape peninsula it is cold and people don't swim in the sea (the South Atlantic) and on the other it is warm, and they do (the Indian Ocean). Geography be damned: it is the Cape of Good Hope that has captured the popular imagination. We don't even have to say 'Good Hope'

– saying 'the Cape' is enough; we all know which one we're referring to.

It is the Cape of Good Hope – *the* Cape – which fuels so many fantasies and provokes Wagnerian legends such as that of the Flying Dutchman. This was a ship that disappeared in 1680, whose captain, a historical figure called Hendrick van der Decken, tried in vain to circumnavigate the Cape during a storm and asked for the Devil's help when God seemed to have forsaken him. He was punished forever, roaming the seas; a mariner's version of the Wandering Jew, fated never to round the Cape.

In the immortal words of Cartman from *South Park,* this is a place that kicks ass.

I went there with a Dutch couple who had just arrived from Amsterdam for a computer conference and had a few days to spare. Our guide was the spitting image of Teddy: Kitchener moustache, safari suit, ruddy, world-weary complexion. He was called Kurt and for once someone's name matched his nature: Kurt was built like a Transvaal outhouse and was gruff to the point of abrasiveness. He was born in *Rhodesia*; we quickly learned not to dare him with Zimbabwe.

Kurt was now gazing down from Chapman's Point.

'Isn't Cape Town the most beautiful city in the world?' he said somewhat oddly, since we were not looking at it. We were admiring the splendid curve cut by Hout Bay against the backdrop of the towering peaks behind Table Mountain.

'Yes, Cape Town is probably the place I would choose to live in South Africa if, and that's a big if, I wanted to settle here,' I replied wistfully, 'but I fell seriously for KwaZulu/Natal.'

Kurt took this as a personal affront.

'Durban, pfff,' he said. 'The blacks have overrun the beaches. They kill white people and kick the bodies afterwards. All the Transvaalers who were holidaying there are starting to come to Cape Town. We have much more to offer than Durban *and* we're safer.'

Kurt stopped, collecting his breath, and changed the subject.

'You know, I'm full of admiration for those explorers like Bartolomeu Diaz and Vasco da Gama who sailed around the world with primitive technology and even less information. They were brave and self-reliant. Think of this: when Magellan circumnavigated the globe, many people thought it was flat!'

'Magellan didn't circumnavigate the globe,' I said. 'He died in the Philippines. The voyage was finished by his second-in-command, Elcano.'

Kurt opened his eyes wide.

'And since Elcano wasn't the first-in-command when the voyage started, the first commander to sail around the world and survive the ordeal was, of course, Sir Francis Drake.'

Kurt didn't like that.

'Hm, but can you tell me a country that's named after an individual?' he asked me as we got back in the car. 'And don't say America, it's a continent.'

'Colombia?' I asked.

Kurt didn't like that either.

'Another one.'

'Bolivia?'

Kurt gave up.

'No, a country in the *Commonwealth* that's named after an individual.'

'If you mean Rhodesia, it was never in the Commonwealth, strictly speaking,' I replied. 'It was a colony and then a federation with Zambia and Malawi until Ian Smith's declaration of independence in the sixties. It was admitted to the Commonwealth only after it became Zimbabwe.'

I knew that Kurt hated me there and then. 'My friends,' he shouted, turning to the Dutch and ignoring me, 'after Cape Point, we'll visit Muizenberg to see the house where Cecil Rhodes died. He had a whole country named after him, Rhodesia.'

I didn't tell Kurt that Cecilia had also been seriously considered. What a pity. Imagine all those rugged Rhodesians having to be called Cecilians: they'd never be taken seriously. I'm sure they'd change it to Zimbabwe before you could say Canaan Banana.

The drive from Cape Town to Cape Point is a winding oceanic ride high above sea-level with views far-reaching and spectacular. Every curve is a picture frame: there are soaring cliffs above sheltering the narrow highway and majestic, wave-swept rocks below to add to the splendour of the scene. Combine this with the unique flora of the *fynbos* and you have an unmatchable combination. There are a staggering 2,600 species just in the Cape peninsula, shorter and thicker than those in Tsitsikamma, including no less than 52 species of wild orchids. The sun, the ocean, the clarity of the air and the strange, distinctive vegetation made the trip down the M6 one of the most memorable moments of my days in South Africa and there's considerable competition of the stiffest kind.

We drove across the Cape peninsula from its Atlantic, western side, towards Simon's Town that stands in the middle of False Bay, and continued south to Cape Point down its eastern side. En route we stopped by a colony of noisy jackass penguins at Boulders Beach. They deserve their name: their cries sound totally unbirdlike; they bray like donkeys. Poor sweeties, they were moulting and waddling on the sand, ragged and hungry. Without their plumage that protects them from the cold water they could not dive and feed, so they looked as miserable as a posse of Sheraton waiters hanging outside for a fag who have suddenly been told they can't light up.

Some useless facts about jackass penguins:

1. *There were more than a million jackass penguins in southern Africa in 1930. There are only 120,000 left now. The reason the population has collapsed is the mining of the mounds of guano fertiliser where they built their nests. This forced them to nest in the sand, making their eggs and chicks easy prey.*

2. *They have more feathers than any other bird: about 70 per square inch. I told you those waters were cold.*

3. *They cool off like dogs, by opening their beaks.*

The Cape peninsula consists of a nature reserve of over seven thousand acres and thirty miles of coastline. Its (introduced) wildlife includes the bontebok and eland antelopes. The signs in the visitors' centre by the Cape Point Lighthouse warn you that baboons are a big menace. I was reminded of that when I posted a card gloriously stamped from the Cape Post Office into a litter bin. *A litter bin?* Yes, because the bins are sealed to avoid scavenging by the baboons, with only a horizontal slit for depositing the refuse, so that they look just like postboxes. Well, to me, anyway.

The view north from the lighthouse is as incomparable as you expect: on your left lies the Cape of Good Hope and the cold waters of the Atlantic; on your right, the warm waters of False Bay. It's here, when you face south to witness the endless watery expanse all the way to Antarctica, that you feel the visceral awe of Bartolomeu Diaz, of Vasco da Gama, of the Flying Dutchman and its crew: that of being at the edge of the world. Centuries and millennia may come and go, but the Cape has the ability to elicit the same raw and rough response from every visitor.

The Cape is schizophrenic and splits in two equally majestic rocky outcrops: Cape Point and the Cape of Good Hope; after we walked the short distance between them on the lookout for baboons, we drove through the Smitswinkel flats back to False Bay and Simon's Town. Because of the prevailing wind patterns, nineteenth century marine underwriters would not insure any ship unless it took shelter in Simon's Town for six months of the year and in Table Bay the other six during the obligatory anchorage on its way to India. As a result, settlements around False Bay are rich in Victorian architecture, culminating in the Historical Mile in Simon's Town. But we were running late and Kurt was keen for us to complete our catalogue of sights: he drove on and stopped in front of a small, insignificant-looking bungalow.

This was the house where Cecil Rhodes died.

It is hard to talk about South Africa without mentioning the colonial British rule and yet I pride myself in having written ten chapters with only the occasional hint. And it is hard to talk about the British in South Africa without mentioning Cecil Rhodes, the man who became simultaneously Bill Gates and Bill Clinton: the richest and most powerful man in a continent; the chairman of de Beers, Consolidated Gold Fields and the British South Africa Company; the Prime Minister of the Cape Colony; the man who extended British rule in Africa from Cape Point to Lake Tanganyika, an area the size of Western Europe; the man who planned and launched the Boer War; a man of charm, wit, intelligence, immense drive and a racial supremacist like they don't make them any more. Oh, and, and...

'It's commonly thought that Cecil Rhodes was homosexual,' said Kurt as we entered the empty bungalow and were greeted by a polite elderly guard. 'But I don't believe it. There's no evidence for that. I myself believe he was asexual.'

No evidence, indeed.

No evidence except that he was inseparable from Neville Pickering for four years, until Pickering – who must have been the love of his life – died falling off a horse, sending Rhodes to tearful paroxysms. Let's also discard his predilection to employ handsome men in their twenties as private secretaries, men who also shared his house and his cabin in the long sea voyages to London. (Philip Jordan? Frank Johnson? Gordon le Seur? Harry Curry? Johnny Grimmer? How many do you want?) Let's ignore the fact that his closest friends, Alfred Beit and Dr Leander Starr Jameson, were also confirmed bachelors who died childless without the whiff of a female presence in their lives. Forget that even Queen Victoria asked him directly: 'Is it true Mr Rhodes that you are a woman-hater?' (To which he replied obliquely: 'How could I possibly hate a sex to which Your Majesty belongs?')

I wonder what evidence some people require – an *in flagrante* photograph? I mean, when Rhodes put an advert for a private volunteer army to capture the land of the Matabele that would later bear his name, he sought 'good fighting men who would be able to form the nucleus of a civil population'. As one of his biographers, Antony Thomas, pointedly comments: *'The one oversight – the exclusion of women – does not seem to have occurred to Rhodes.'*

No, there is no concrete evidence since all of his letters and papers were burnt by Dr Jameson after his death, but, hell, if it walks like a duck and quacks like a duck, it ain't the arctic diving skua. The reason men want to call Shaka Zulu and Cecil Rhodes asexual is because they run against type. Rhodes' life was a macho adventure straight out of the pages of *Boy's Own*. Like King Shaka he's an example of how cruel men can become when love, or worse the hope of love, is denied them and like Shaka he requires us to redefine masculinity itself: it matters not what you do in bed or how you behave or look (for who looks more manly than a gay tattooed, muscle hillock with a number one crop?) and it certainly has nothing to do with virility or procreation. Masculinity is about inner strength and courage and respect; it is ultimately about how brave you feel inside, which is why some straight men are terrified of reassessment, for they may be found wanting.

'Here you can see the extent of the British Empire – mostly the work of Rhodes,' said Kurt, and he led us to a large, old map of the southern African cone hanging by a wall. The whole area was coloured pink transcending borders around lands with names lost to the shifting sands of history; names like Nyasaland, Griqualand or, indeed, Rhodesia and Transvaal.

Rhodes came to the Cape Colony from Bishops Storford at seventeen and started a cotton plantation in Natal before the lure of the newly-discovered diamonds brought him to Kimberley. Slowly but surely he bought out or incorporated everyone else and created a monopoly. He fuelled his expansionism with private capital (he used to boast that Rhodesia cost nothing to the Exchequer) to render that map area pink except for the Boer republics.

When gold was found in Johannesburg he wanted it – the Kruger government with its mercantile restrictions was anathema: in Rhodes' eyes this was a state that had a lot to learn from British law and efficient government. He clandestinely – and without the knowledge of the Colonial office – sent his friend Jameson to raid the Transvaal, having organised a fifth column of local militia which would come to the latter's aid. The fifth column was betrayed, its members arrested and Jameson's people defeated. The two Boer republics of the Transvaal and the Orange Free State realised that the best defence was attack and invaded the Cape Colony and Natal in 1899, thus sparking off the Boer War or, since hostilities embraced the four main constituent parts of South Africa, the South African War.

The conflict claimed seventy thousand lives. It gave the world the word *commando,* the concept of the guerrilla raid and, lest we forget, Baden-Powell and his Boy Scout movement which has delighted generations of sporty brats since. More sombrely, it gave the world the first concentration camps. The British army cut off the commandos from their supplies by incarcerating their women and children. It is hard to imagine how popular the Boers were in their resistance one hundred years ago: Sinn Fein and Rosa Luxemburg, Keir Hardie and Franklin Delano Roosevelt, even Pope Leo XIII supported the underdogs. An international brigade fought on their side, amongst them Prince Louis d'Orleans, Count Zeppelin (killed in action) and Vincent van Gogh's brother, who committed suicide after being captured.

Despite all this, the British won because they cold-bloodedly did the unthinkable – what the Americans didn't dare do in Vietnam, and the Serbs tried in vain to carry out in Kosovo: uproot the local population. But it was a pyrrhic victory that could not be sustained for long; within ten years the self-governing Union of South Africa had been born along with an Afrikaner sense of nationhood founded upon bitterness and revenge.

Rhodes had health problems throughout his life, which came to an early end here, in this unvisited villa, two months before the Boer War ended. In his time as member of the Cape Parliament and Prime Minister, he and his predecessors laid the foundations of what was to befall South Africa under the National Party of Malan, Strijdom, Verwoerd, Vorster and Botha.

Robben Island? Lord Somerset first incarcerated there the blind prophet Nxele in 1819. Nxele tried to swim to the mainland and got swept away by waves, thus ensuring him a place in the pantheon of the Xhosa memory; he was to have led the ancestor troops that killed Sir George Cathcart in the Crimea. Indeed, after the Cattle Killing, eight Xhosa chiefs were confined on the island and had most of their lands confiscated for the Crown.

District Six? In 1901, 500 males were sent to Uitvlugt (Ndabeni), the first group to be legally displaced from District Six. The number reached 5,000 in one month. No strangers were allowed longer than twenty-four hours, women couldn't stay overnight and alcohol was banned. The men stayed in corrugated iron dorms, *Gastarbeiters* in their own land. For this service they were charged rent by the British authorities.

Non-representation? Rhodes was the first to raise the property qualification in the Cape to exclude the Coloured population who owned small, though derelict, houses. The Voters' Registration Act 1887 further disqualified voters if any of their land was communally owned: the remaining Xhosa lands had finally been annexed and, since land in traditional villages was – surprise, surprise – communally owned, 2,500 Xhosa (out of a black population of half a million) could vote, and that would be the thin edge of the wedge.

Group Areas Act? The Glen Grey Act was passed quickly in an all-night sitting by Rhodes in 1894 to set out the first native reserve. Rhodes' plan was that the natives should be kept in these native reserves and not mixed with white men at all. In the Glen Grey area blacks would be allowed to farm an eight-acre allotment, pay a hut tax ('*A gentle stimulus to these people to make them go on working*' as Rhodes himself admitted) and could not subdivide it. In this way, all their children but the first-born would have to leave and seek work in the mines, thus converting the black masses into a submissive proletariat.

We came out of the bungalow in time to see a black traffic policeman write a sixty-rand ticket on our van. Kurt couldn't park in front of the house, so he'd parked impatiently on the other side against the traffic – illegally, and as we were at the bottom of a hill, dangerously, too.

'A ticket? We're leaving now. LEAVING!' exploded Kurt. 'Sixty rand? You know where you can stick your piece of paper! This is racial harassment! *Harassment!*' he shouted again as the policeman left on his motorbike, surprisingly unfettered by Kurt's temper. 'HA-RASS-MENT!'

Kurt's cantankerous mood turned the rest of our day ugly. It spoiled the drive through elegant Constantia, whose residents include Earl Spencer and, until recently, Mark Thatcher, and the visit to Kirstenbosch Gardens where we had a leisurely hour's stroll amongst orchids, proteas and paradise-bird flowers.

In the end the Dutch and I had the same idea. We gathered together behind Kurt, who was barking directions out of the *fynbos* alleys, and decided to give him a sixty-rand tip to offset the fine.

One has to do everything possible to improve race relations.

Some useless facts about de Beers:

1. *'A diamond is forever' was a 1950s advertisement for de Beers, an indication of how successful slogans can enter the vocabulary of daily clichés.*

2. *The original de Beers brothers were the owners of the Vooruitzigt farm, where diamonds were found in May 1871. They were simple folk and couldn't handle it, so they sold out for £6,000. They were never involved in any diamond mining.*

40. Die Backpackers

I can't believe this is my last excursion in South Africa – still, I'm glad it was with Caz and Callum, my mates from Addo whom I met again in Cape Town, and that it was the wine country. It is there that visitors are exposed to the country's full European heritage and there is plenty of it in Stellenbosch and Franschhoek. This is a mountainous domain where every small ridge and valley has its own microclimate resulting in many different grapes. It even has its own varieties: the Steen, responsible for many sweets or semi-sweets; a local Riesling; and the most famous (and unique), Pinotage, a cross between the Pinot Noir and Hermitage varieties that tastes like a bitter claret without the tannin. 'Stellenbosch' is an *appellation controlleé* of such international quality and renown that the Villiera estate in neighbouring Paarl asked for reclassification to the Stellenbosch region (and succeeded). This is the only area where reds, mostly Cabernet, Merlot and Pinotage, outnumber the whites and where estates such as Rust en Vrede, Saxenburg and, further out, Thelema and Tokara regularly produce award-winners.

But to South Africans, Stellenbosch is a university community in the manner of say, Cambridge, with a student population of 15,000 out of a total of 65,000. This makes for a lively and pretty town with oak trees shadowing the streets, earning it the nickname *Eikestad* – Oaktown – only this is Cape oak, a porous wood which, ironically, is not good for storing wine. The oak barrels have to be imported from France.

Stella, our guide, parked by die Braak, an open space surrounded by gabled manors in the old Cape Dutch style. 'In the early 1800s the inhabitants ran here during an earthquake and made a pact with God,' she told us. Every Boer town seems to have made a pact with God but this one was easy: Save Us from the Quake and We Won't Build on This Square. You call that a *pact*?

Stellenbosch is enchanting in an Old World, fey sort of way. There are cheese shops selling a range of Mrs Ball's chutneys made with a secret recipe. There are stalls advertising pick-your-own strawberry farms. There is the Oom Samie Sewinkel algemene Handelaars, an Olde Curiosity Shoppe, with gadgets and bric-a-brac galore: mid-twentieth century gramophones, weaved baskets, military paraphernalia, wine racks, parrot cages. I surprised myself in that I left the Shoppe with only a set of witchdoctor's bones and a pamphlet on the art of African fortune telling. Now I, too, could order someone impaled.

Throwing bones is easy: there are two large chicken bones (man and woman) and four small ones (the children). There are two red stones symbolising the negative forces (called 'crocodiles'), two brown shiny ones (the positive forces of the ancestors) and two brown rough ones (the eyes of wisdom and perception). Everything comes in twos, the larger item being the male and the smaller the female. You take the bones and stones into your palms, intone 'I breathe my soul and the soul of my guiding spirit upon you' and throw them like dice. The final positions of the bones and the angles between them are then interpreted; whether they land face up or face down is an indication of good or ill luck. Sometimes the fortune telling is easy: if you ask 'Will I have offspring?' and all four children fall between the man and the woman, well, I give you only one guess. In more complex questions, you count the bad versus the good forces between the man and the woman or draw imaginary lines between the good and the bad influences and see if they intersect with any of the human characters. As soon as I got back, I threw them on the floor and breathed my soul and the soul of my guiding spirit upon them to check out my sex life. One of the children bones stood upright which I took as a positive sign of a boner.

For our tastings we had to drive over the Drankenstein mountains to Franschhoek (literally: French corner) where the Huguenots settled in 1688. At the time there were only about 600 Dutch residents, so when the 250-odd French came, Governor Simon van der Stel – he of Simon's Town fame – allowed them to settle but forbade them to intermarry. This was a far-reaching decision because the French asylum seekers mixed with the Dutch settlers so as to become indistinguishable; Piet Retief himself was of French descent. Just like the Voortrekker monument in Pretoria, there is a Huguenot monument in Franschhoek – also inaugurated in 1948 – and a nearby museum which contains the names of the original immigrants: this is where surnames such as Laroux, du Plessis and de Villiers originate. The slender three-arched Huguenot monument with a sun and a cross is elegant and much more aesthetically pleasing than its Voortrekker equivalent, with which it is coeval, and with which it also shares the spiritual symbolism. In line with its policy of fostering white nationalism, a memorial was built around the same time to the Afrikaans language in Paarl: the National Party built monuments, celebrated anniversaries and created heroic myths like other governments cut red ribbons.

By then we were rather thirsty. Callum reminded Stella diplomatically that this was a wine tour, wasn't it, before I had the chance to tell her what I *really* thought of the National Party's erections. She complied with decorum and drove us to Boschendal, our first vineyard – and a stunner it was, too.

Dating back to the late eighteenth century, the Boschendal estate contains one of the most photographed buildings in South Africa: the Boschendal manor, a Cape Dutch architectural gem in an idyllic setting under the shadow of the Drankenstein Mountains. It feels like visiting a British stately home, with walnut cabinets, rococo-style rosewood tables and chairs, ornamental brass birdcages, wall paintings, gilded mirrors and family portraits of the Villiers family. But this is where similarities end. In 1897, Cecil Rhodes bought the estate

– he really *did* have his finger in every pie – and Boschendal Manor became part of Rhodes Fruit Farms. It's now a part of the faceless Anglo-American Corporation.

What about the wine, then?

Callum thought the Boschendal Chardonnay first-rate and Caz and I readily agreed. But, but...

'What's this?' asked Caz pointing at the wine list, which bypassed the expensive Chenins and Sauvignons. 'It's a *blend*.'

I read 'Blanc des Blancs'. 'You're right,' I said, my heart sinking.

'And this?' asked Callum, surprised, pointing at an entry.

This was Blanc des Noirs, and we were so intrigued by the name we ordered it. It was neither *blanc* nor *noir*, but a bland, blended *rosé*.

We didn't expect a rare vintage uncorked for our pleasure, but, as we had been eating and drinking in South Africa for so long, we knew there were better wines than the ones we were offered. At least the plonk was free, so we basked in the warmth of the afternoon in the Boschendal gardens half-merrily and half-grumpily. We were of one mind: scrimping on visitors' tastings is a short-sighted policy.

It was a policy not only in Boschendal, but also in the KWV complex in Paarl, a huge industrial site processing wines from thousands of producers, involving hundreds of thousands of employees. The tour of the cellars was conducted like an army drill, as several multilingual groups followed each other with Teutonic efficiency. Whether allowed to admire a prized barrel of sherry for the designated number of seconds – donated to the South African cricket team by the MCC – or allowed a photo each in front of Mrs Bill, the largest of the vats, we were all subjected to the same commentary: this was a cooperative founded by Afrikaner farmers in 1918 to pool resources and dominate the wine industry. In this they have succeeded because the power of KWV (producer, distributor and marketer in one) is formidable: fifty per cent of South Africa's brandy originates from this plant. This is also where much of the UK's supermarket wine and the cheaper, more common South African brands come from: Cape Blush, Cape Horizon, Doornberg, Mymering sherry and Cavendish Fine Old Ruby.

The wines I liked best were the ones I don't normally drink: the sweet and semi-sweet such as the KWV Muscadet. The famous Pinotage also leaves me cold; I like more body in my reds and have found most examples I've tasted rather thin. I suppose you want some tips: Chateau Libertas claret, Boschendal Chardonnay, Vergelegen Red, any Merlot or Cabernet from Stellenbosch, Pinot Noir from Walker Bay plus that cheap, tasteful Graça. And to anyone who knows of a good, affordable Pinotage: write it on the back of a postcard and keep it to yourself.

'Are you watching the rugby on Saturday?' asked Callum, interrupting my musings.

'What rugby?'

'In the Sports Café at the Waterfront. South Africa v Ireland and England v Australia.'

'Will you be there?'

'Yes. On Sunday we're off to South America. We need your advice about Brazil.'

'We'll buy you a few beers,' said Caz.

Deal.

At this stage we were driving through Paarl, past the tall Afrikaans Language monument and past Nelson Mandela's final place of detention. Is that Victor Vester prison? Hey, I hiccuped merrily, why all the rush?

We were late, Stella told us. We were heading to the airport so that a passenger could catch her evening flight back. *Hmm, other passengers.* I had forgotten about the rest of the coach. One of them made a joke regarding the punctuality of South African Airways that didn't go down well with Stella.

'Absenteeism in the SAA has been increasing lately,' she said. 'One executive started sending flowers to people who had called in sick, but not out of politeness. He wanted to check if they were in the house or not! It's this new positive discrimination. Everything else being equal, the company will choose a black employee. And you know what happens?'

I felt I wouldn't like what happens.

'There is a real story that goes like this,' Stella continued, looking ahead as she drove. 'A plane was about to start and the door was still open. The captain shouted to the crew to close the door. The black stewardess didn't know how! Apparently, she'd arrived to cover for her sister!'

Some passengers laughed, but I didn't. I remembered Dominic's exact same joke about black models. I caught Caz and Callum's poignant looks. They too had heard this before. They knew that this was no real-life anecdote, but blind regurgitation of a stereotype. And, though it may sound far-fetched, I think I heard Caz telepathically whisper to me: *Yes, they're racist; but they're missing the experiences of our society. Deep down they're good people and they will learn in time.*

That sounded patronising, Caz.

So was the joke.

We're missing *their* experiences, too.

They might have to learn the hard way.

It's so easy to be judgmental.

When you visit this country, it's difficult to hold back.

And with that, Caz looked away and broke the link.

Maybe now is the time for my final tale, darker than a moonless *veld* night. I started with a Hallowe'en party; I'll finish with the horror of the real thing.

Brace yourselves for the story of Marike de Klerk.

F. W. de Klerk's family were fundamentalist *Doppers*, belonging to the most intransigent of Afrikaner churches, where white supremacy was an essential condition for the survival of the *Volk*. De Klerk was well connected: his family had been politicians for four generations. He was the nephew of J. G. Strijdom himself, the 'Lion of the North', the hard-line

Transvaal politician who wrested the National Party from the control of the soft, Anglophile Cape administrators. Strijdom became Prime Minister in 1954 until his death four years later. During Strijdom's time, F. W. De Klerk, affectionately called 'Frikkie', studied law at the University of Potchefstroom where he met Marike Willemse, a deeply religious woman who once described the mixed-race Cape Coloureds as 'non-persons, the people that were left over after the nations were sorted out.'

Strijdom passed the *Hoofleier* torch to Dr Hendrik Verwoerd, the architect of *grand apartheid:* an insurmountable mountain of laws to control land, labour and internal migration for the benefit of the *Volk* and the *Volk* alone. It was during that first year of Verwoerd's premiership that Marike and Frikkie married.

F. W. de Klerk was practising law in Pretoria when a gunman shot Dr Verwoerd in the head, at close range. Amazingly, Dr Verwoerd survived. Everyone spoke of a miracle. When, after a few months in hospital, he gave a speech in Parliament in a clear, booming voice, like Moses returned from Mount Sinai to lead his flock, a friend of the Progressive Party MP Helen Suzmann asked her, astonished: 'Good God, didn't that bullet do anything to Verwoerd?' 'Sure,' she replied, 'it cleared his sinuses.' Divine intervention seems to have been tried sorely in Verwoerd's case for he did not survive a second assassination attempt, this time by a Greek immigrant, Dimitris Tsafendas. Maybe mindful of the effect the gunman had achieved, Tsafendas stabbed him in the heart four times instead.

The 1960s saw the de Klerks settled in Vereeniging with three children: boys Jan and Willem plus a daughter, Susan. Milking his father's last political influence, F. W. de Klerk entered Parliament in 1972 as the member for Vereeniging and became Minister of Posts and Telecommunications under John Vorster, who succeeded Verwoerd.

Under Vorster the state turned into a paranoid securocracy hungry for high-tech, giving Frikkie a high profile: he circumvented sanctions and supervised South Africa's advance into the digital age. But then came Muldergate – the scandal whereby millions were siphoned to secret accounts for the bribery of foreign opinion makers – and the return of the Cape 'moderates' into the fold in the shape of 'pragmatic' P. W. Botha: the choice between *verliegte* moderates and *verkrampte* conservatives being one between Tamerlane and Genghis Khan.

Strijdom, Verwoerd and Vorster were ethnopurist, interventionist Transvaalers who wanted to secure colonial-style privileges for the Afrikaners; P. W. Botha (*die Krokodil*) and the Cape industrialists wanted an end to sanctions and more labour competitiveness, which meant cheap African labour for positions reserved for Afrikaners. To the Cape functionaries, if that meant a relaxation of petty apartheid rules then so be it: the headline-grabbing Immorality Law was one of the first to go, though the Group Areas Act stayed so a mixed married couple could not live together – smart, huh? Those early Botha reforms split the National Party; in 1982 the Transvaal President, Dr Andries Treuernicht, formed the Conservative Party to join Eugene Terre Blanche's neo-Nazi AWG in forming an opposition coalition, which, cliché or not, could *truly* be described as being to the right of Genghis Khan.

With the defection of Treuernicht, the National Party Chairmanship was empty: F. W. de Klerk was voted in and Marike led the women's wing of the party. Around that time, the de Klerks were introduced to a Greek shipping tycoon, Tony Georgiades, and his wife, a radiant beauty called Elita. The couples became close friends – but at some future point Elita and Frikkie became lovers.

Here some paths start to intersect to make our story more complex, because that's how real lives are.

During Botha's rule, a boy called Luyanda Mboniswa was born in Motherwell, near the orange groves of Port Elizabeth – that township you can't miss on the way to Addo. He grew up with his mother Cynthia, who had raised him alone. The little child went to school during the escalating violence of the

1980s – war in Angola, intervention in Namibia and Mozambique, states of emergency – and every Sunday accompanied his mother to church. In 1989, they heard that P. W. Botha had died and someone called F. W. de Klerk had become President of South Africa.

Chic Marike became First Lady and accompanied her husband to Downing Street where she met her idol, Margaret Thatcher (who dismissed her, oh so cruelly, when the de Klerks arrived in Downing Street: 'You can go shopping now, Marike.') Yet, history was on its course and de Klerk freed Mandela to start negotiating the end of apartheid, which would eventually earn them both the Nobel Prize.

Meanwhile back in Motherwell, Luyanda Mboniswa tried to be accepted for a male nurse course; his application wasn't even acknowledged. He was the eldest son and had to earn money for his mother, his two teenage siblings and his 85-year-old grandfather: he moved to find work in the Western Cape.

Marike hated Mandela who, she was sure, was trying to humiliate the de Klerks by what she considered petty arrangements. Worse was to come: in 1998, when he didn't require any more political propping by familial stability, Frikkie divorced Marike after 39 years to marry Elita Georgiades. When Frikkie finally packed his things to go and live with the younger model, Marike's pleas to start again were typically biblical: she would forgive him 'seventy times seven'. His response was blunt: 'I'm certain about my decision. Stop hoping.'

Mandela also divorced Winnie and married Graça Machel with a *lobola* of sixty cows; he retired and Thabo Mbeki became President. Marike met a businessman on the rebound: Johann Koekemoor, 13 years her junior. They were engaged to be married until he was exposed by newspapers as a conman. Under the glare of the newspaper spotlight, and fraud allegations, the affair disintegrated, and it seems, Marike did as well.

Now well in her sixties, she lived alone in Flat D 102 of the gated, exclusive Dolphin Beach luxury apartments north of Cape Town where Koekemoor had helped her relocate. She had lost the buzz of high office, the contacts, the bodyguards, her family. She became heavily depressed; she cried and sobbed, frightened of loneliness. Friends who met Marike at the local supermarket were shocked at how unkempt she was. She had financial problems and was considering becoming an estate agent in a development at False Bay.

Luyanda, now 21, handsome and athletic with a shaven head, finally got his big break: a job. He could now afford to rent his own wooden shack in the township of Khayelitsa at 100 rand a month. It was only big enough for a bed and a table. The only decoration was a poster of a football player, but the bed was double, for he now also had a girlfriend, a local Khayelitsa girl. His job – his big break – was with Securicor Gray as a guard in the gated, exclusive luxury apartments of Dolphin Beach.

On Tuesday afternoon, 4 December 2001, Marike de Klerk was found dead by her hairdresser. At first everyone assumed she had taken her own life, but then word got out that she had been murdered. Reading the reports, you wish you could take that simple statement at face value. Marike had first been beaten savagely; then she had been sodomised and sexually assaulted with two vaginal injuries consistent with non-consensual sexual intercourse; finally she had been stabbed with a broken steak knife which was still stuck in her back when she was discovered. Even that was not the cause of her death: she had been strangled with such force that four neck vertebrae had snapped and one eye had split from the pressure. She had died on her knees.

There was no sign of forced entry; Marike had been murdered by someone she knew. From the records of two phone calls on her stolen mobile phone, the police homed in on Luyanda Mboniswa who confessed, trying to implicate her dance instructor and, bizarrely, her son Willem. Mboniswa later retracted his confession, but the evidence was overwhelming. Apart from the calls, a wristwatch and two torches found in Mboniswa's shack were identified as Marike's. Mboniswa's DNA was found on a pair of yellow rubber gloves stained with Marike's blood.

Marike's death united South Africa in a way her life had divided it. She was a political celebrity and if she could die so violently, what hope was there for anyone in this new South Africa? Thabo Mbeki described her as 'strong, charming and dignified'. Winnie, now Madikizela-Mandela, poignantly declared: 'As a woman I can identify with the exhaustion of her emotional resources in shaping her former husband's career.' She attended Marike's funeral, embraced a sobbing F. W. de Klerk and rallied out against crime, calling the murder a 'wake-up call for the country'.

In May 2003 Luyanda Mboniswa was convicted for Marike's murder and received two life sentences. He will first be eligible for parole in 2028. He didn't give evidence in his trial, and he never explained why he killed Marike de Klerk.

The Sports Café was packed; South Africa v Ireland would be on soon and the Springboks were on cue to beat all five Grand Slam nations. It was impossible to meet anyone in there, let alone Caz and Callum. My free drink was in danger.

I was wrong. I saw Vanessa. With a bloke!

'Vanessa – hi,' I said and sat on the stool next to her, as my eyes posed the obvious question.

She appeared embarrassed.

'John,' she said, 'this is Grant.'

She turned to the man next to her.

'This is John. John is a guest – a friend – at the hotel.'

We shook hands and Grant offered to buy me a drink.

'A Castle,' I said. Let's have some product placement for the lager that kept me afloat all this time.

When he left to get the drinks in, I turned to Vanessa.

'Vanessa,' I said, 'is this *the* Grant?'

She nodded yes – I mean *ja*.

'He's married now, Vanessa. Forget him.'

'We're just friends,' she murmured.

'No, you're not. *He* can be friends with *you*, but *you* can't be friends with *him*. You're still hoping, aren't you?'

She was silent.

'Vanessa,' I said. 'Nobody loves a doormat.'

She looked away.

'His wife?'

'She doesn't like rugby.'

'Does she know you're here?'

Vanessa shrugged her shoulders.

'So what *is* he doing meeting you behind her back?' I said, shaking my head disapprovingly, before I turned around politely to pick up my drink from Grant's extended arm.

We watched the first half of the rugby – throughout which Vanessa was cheerful but remote – and when my round came, I made my excuses to find my other friends: I wasn't buying Grant a drink. Caz and Callum were into their second wheelbarrow of Castle beer when I joined them on the balcony. South Africa won and England beat Australia in two long, uneventful hours, but not once did I move from my seat to check on Vanessa inside.

Some useless facts about die Backpackers:

1. *By popular acclaim, it seems that the best backpackers' hostel is the Cintsa Buccaneers, outside East London. It's in the middle of a coastal forest next to an unspoilt Indian Ocean beach, offering double rooms in single cottages with hand-painted curtains.*

2. *The most 'cool and happening' backpackers', again by popular acclaim, is the Oasis in Oudtshoorn. My own description of my time there should be convincing enough.*

41. Die End

Today I started to pack. Was this my T-shirt smelling horribly or was the pickled Knysna garlic jar leaking? Thank the Goddess it was just plain old sweat: memories returned from the time I brought back some French cheese on the Eurostar in a hot July (I know, whatever possessed me?) and had to wrap it up in bags upon bags while the other passengers stared at me, annoyed, thinking; 'Does he *never* wash his socks?'

I walked down to the breakfast room reading a magazine advertisement for Project P, that stood for 'Penile Development, the World's First Phallic Fitness Programme (Take Your Penis to the Gym)'. The programme involved an exercise to enlarge the scrotum, three exercises to enhance sperm production, an exercise to develop natural foreskin and eight exercises to strengthen the penis, as well as client endorsement letters, before and after photographs, and an introductory video. I read aloud to Vanessa: '"The penis is a very important, yet neglected organ."' *Neglected?* Speak for yourself, mate.

I looked up, expecting a giggle.

Vanessa wasn't laughing. 'I've resigned,' she said.

'What?'

'I've resigned. I'm fed up. I'm going back to Hermanus, to my family and friends. You were right. I should forget Grant and get on with my life.'

And Piet?

'I'm not packing up tomorrow and leaving him on his own. I'll stay until he finds someone else.'

I drank my coffee slowly. Vanessa sat in front of me and rested her head on her elbows.

'John,' she said, 'the reason I still go out with Grant is that I don't know any people in Cape Town. I lived with that Greek guy for some time, but we fell out. Dominic is nice – very nice – but he has his own circle. I stay here all day, alone, looking after the house. I want a job where I can meet people and make my own friends. So that if Grant calls and invites me out to a bar, I can tell him that I have something else to do.'

She got up and left the room.

I finished breakfast alone and went to settle my account. Piet was in his office. He refused to charge me for any of my drinks or for the *bobotie* he cooked for me last night.

'You'll be pleased to know that I will be going to Safari Camp after all,' he said. 'Teddy finally convinced me.'

Yes! I nearly punched the air, but then I thought of Piet alone, without any domestic help.

'What about Vanessa?'

Piet was philosophical about it. 'I've known Vanessa for a long time,' he whispered. 'I care for her.'

'And she cares for you,' I added clumsily. I'm not good at emoting in tandem.

'It's all going to work for the best,' he said, as his shoulders went heavy. 'I can see that a young girl like her wants to meet people and go out, but she knew all about this when she came to work here. Why such a sudden change of mood?'

'Do you know I saw her with Grant in the Sports Café?' I asked.

Piet's eyes widened as the penny dropped.

'Grant? Are you sure? She's *still* seeing him?'

The inevitable dawned on him. He paced up and down, an expression of determination on his face.

'*Ja*, this is – this is the end of the road,' he concluded.

No, this is *truly* the end of the road.

I tried to get into Club Zone, but that Saturday was its grand opening night of the summer season and the queue seemed endless – not to mention stationary – wrapping around the nearby City Lodge Hotel as it doubled up on itself. I went to Detour instead. The club was a heaving muscle mass: the topless male crowd were sweating it large. Just like Club DNA in Pretoria and Club 330 in Durban, this was techno-house of the hard diamond kind. I took off my T-shirt and joined in, waiting for my rush, my mind working overtime about the new South Africa.

The images of Langa still hovered in my mind.

Like everyone else I feel the need to blame someone. Before I came here, it was easy: it was the fault of those nasty Afrikaners. But the miracle in the new South Africa is that no blame need be apportioned any more, and the revelation is that the blame itself is shared. Yes, the racist structure of apartheid with its monstrous excesses is the top culprit, leaving all others distant seconds. But the colonialism of the Brits who came, scoffed, plundered and left, having laid the groundwork for an inhuman society for one hundred years to come, is equally responsible. And would all this have been possible without the wedging-in of the Coloureds who willingly accepted and aided this pyramidal social construct as long as they weren't at the bottom? The racism of the whites draws cries of shame, but is the racism of the Coloureds, outspokenly provocative at best, wildly offensive at worst, above criticism? And while we are politically incorrect, what about the black peoples themselves? In the Great Cattle Killing the Xhosa were the victims of their own superstition, which took years to shed – and did not the pride and superiority complex of the Zulu split the land, and render the opposition to apartheid mutually suspicious and disunited? It seems that when eventually madness took its toll, everyone had the exact change.

There you have it – the mosaic of blame in the Old South Africa: the passive victims, the conniving henchmen and the cruel, calculating masters, all embraced in a symbiotic dance of death, worthy of a Breughel painting. Even if the new South Africa has not succeeded in much, it has provided people with hope for the future where previously there was none.

Put a value on that.

So there was I, off my face, smiling at the blond guy next to me who had the body of a Greek god and a face like a Hollywood star, and yes, inside my head I was already in the Safari Camp, shaking my body to its dusty disco, drum 'n' bush, veld funk, kwaai kwaito, boomtown blues, tent-camp trance, venter-trailer trash, prickly pear pop and cheetah chill choonz, dancing for the Afrikaners in Pretoria, dancing for the Swazis in Mbabane, for Rudy and the gang in St Lucia, for the Zulu and the surfers in KwaZulu/Natal, for the backpackers in the Baz Bus, for the Xhosa kids in Langa, for my lovely hosts in the Cape, for the elephants and the lions and all those plucky denizens of the new South Africa – and guess what?

I did them all proud.

Epilogue

I love those movies where in the end they tell you what happened to the main characters after the film ended. Like in *Animal House* – would you believe John Belushi gets to become a senator?

I did get to meet the Oudtshoorn backpackers again. On that Wednesday, at 9 p.m. sharp, I was at the Hard Rock Café on the Waterfront. I sat down, chose an overpriced polyethylene-burger and shouted my order above the loud music to the smiling, Stepford waitress. I resigned myself to having to finish my burger alone, until I saw the familiar figures of Nicole and Marion come in. All Germans had Ute's travel guide so they ended up at the same hostel, the Sunflower Stop at Green Point, right where the prostitutes flounce about in high heels and hot pants. The ones that were still walking the streets at 10 p.m. were the bruised thorny cactus bunch – the younger more fragrant gardenias had all been picked up earlier. If you ever want to meet a nice streetwalker in Green Point go early; by 8 p.m. they've all gone.

Ute, Herman, Marion, Tanya, Nicole, Daniel, Dirk: they were all there. We got very drunk; my notebook is full of scribbles. I can make out only one entry. Did we all like South Africa? *Oh, yes*, we said in one voice. Would we return? *Oh, yes*. Would we want to live there? *Oh, no*.

Upon my return to London, I found a postcard from Martin waiting for me. Hearing from him reminded me how scared I was when I boarded the Baz Bus in Pretoria and his pivotal role in reassuring me. I sent him a Christmas card.

In that first week back, I had a call from Robert and Wendy. She had found a job as a nanny in fashionable Chelsea and Robert pulled pints in a pub near Oxford Circus. Trip-tired as I was, I had no inclination nor urge to travel and spent a quiet Christmas with them. Next, they moved on to Canada, reaching Vancouver in mid-winter. Yes, that's what I thought, too.

Caz and Callum sent me several e-mails with descriptions of their Latin American trip. They seemed to have followed my advice very carefully, and they had been in peak form: there had been no slope unclimbed, no ravine untrodden, no Inca trail unwalked and, it seems, no local food properly digested.

I lost touch with Piet, Teddy and Vanessa.

I contacted Mohammed asking for permission to use Maureen Jacobs' leaflet for a Chris Hani school web site since she was uncontactable; he answered, slightly surprised, giving me the all clear. I put up a web page quickly and I know for a fact that donations reached the school as a result.

The trial of Dr Wouter Basson, the manager of the South African chemical and biological warfare projects, started in October 1999 with 67 indictments (dropped later to 46) including murder and conspiracy to murder. Thirty months later, after a long-drawn-out judicial process, the judge acquitted him of all charges, saying that the state had failed to prove its case on every count.

In October 2003, the bulldozers moved back into District Six, not to destroy and flatten but to build houses for its uprooted, dispossessed inhabitants so that they could return. A month later, Thabo Mbeki's government made a U-turn on his Aids policy and was pushed into providing retroviral drugs to patients.

Further north, the disgraced President Canaan Banana died, giving rise to obituaries titled 'Dead Banana's Seedy Past'.

And I wrote this.

REFERENCES

Adrian Craven, Stephen *Management Problems at Cango Cave* (University of Cape Town, 1992; also in SASA Bulletin No 34, edited by L. W. Hall, 1994)

Amnesty International, *Amnesty International Report 2003*, AI Index POL 10/003/2003

Ballard, Sebastian *The South Africa Handbook* (Footprint Handbooks, 1998)

Barter, Catherine *Alone Among the Zulus* (University of Natal Press, 1995; originally published in 1866)

Berglund, Axel-Ivar *Zulu Thought-Patterns and Symbolism.* (Indiana University Press, 1976)

Biko, Steve 'Black Consciousness and the Quest for a True Humanity' in *Steve Biko: Black Consciousness in South Africa,* edited by Millard Arnold (Random House, 1979)

Blaustein, Albert P. and Flanz, Gisbert H. (eds.), *Constitutions of the Countries of the World* (Oceana, 1991)

Colenso, J. W. *Pentateuch & Book of Joshua Critically Examined* (Longman, 1862)

Conan Doyle, Arthur *Our African Winter* (Gerald Duckworth & Co, 2001; originally published in 1929)

Deacon, Harriett *The Essential Robben Island* (David Philip Publishers, 1997)

Delegorgue, Adulphe *Travels in Southern Africa Volumes I and II* (University of Natal, 1990; originally published in 1833)

Delmont, Elizabeth 'The Voortrekker Monument: Monolith to Myth' *South African Journal* Vol. 29, 76–101 (1993)

Dorrington, Rob; Bourne, David; Bradshaw, Debbie; Laubscher, Ria; Timæus, Ian M. *The Impact of HIV/AIDS on Adult Mortality in South Africa* Burden of Disease Research Unit technical report (Medical Research Council, 2001)

Etherington, Norman *The Great Treks* (Pearson Education, 2001)

Fourie, P. F. and de Graaf, G. *Kruger National Park: Questions and Answers* (University of Pretoria, 1992)

Guy, Jeff *A Propensity of Sitting on Stones: A Dialog on Shaka Zulu*, NUAfrica list (1996)

Haggard, H. Rider *Diary of an African Journey (1914)* (Hurst and Co, 2001)

Hamilton, Carolyn *Terrific Majesty: The Powers of Shaka Zulu and the Limits of Historical Invention* (Harvard University Press, 1998)

Heymans, Riana *The Voortrekker Monument Official Guide* (1986) and (unattributed) *The Voortrekker Monument Pretoria Official Guide*, 1st edn, Pretoria Board of Control of the Voortrekker Monument (1954)

Jenkins, Roy *Churchill* (Pan Macmillan, 2002)

Laband, John *The Rise and Fall of the Zulu Nation* (Arms and Armour Press, 1997)

Maartens, Maretha *Marike: A Journey Through Summer and Winter* (Carpe Diem, 1997)

Mandela, Nelson *Long Walk to Freedom* (Abacus, 1994)

Mangold, T. and Goldberg, J. *Plague Wars: A True Story of Biological Warfare* (Pan Macmillan, 1999)

Martin, S. J. R. *Images of the Zulu, ca 1820–1879* (University of Cambridge, 1982)

Mossop, T. *Stellarbosch* (*Decanter* magazine, December 2003)

Murray, Jon et al *South Africa Lesotho and Swaziland* (Lonely Planet, 1998)

Nixon, Rob *Dreambirds* (Doubleday, 1999)

O' Brien, Rory and Curtis, Craig *The Donkin Heritage Trail*, SA Institute of Town and Regional Planning, Eastern Cape and Border branch (1979)

O' Meara, Dan *Forty Lost Years, the Apartheid State and the Politics of the National Party, 1948–1994* (Ohio University Press, 1999)

Olivier, Willie and Sandra *Exploring the Natural Wonders of South Africa* (Struik Publishers, 1996)

Peires, J. B. *The Dead Will Arise, Nongqawuse and the Great Xhosa Cattle Killing Movement of 1856–1857* (Currey, 1989)

Ritter, E. A. *Shaka Zulu* (Penguin, 1955)

Rissik, Dee *Culture Shock! South Africa* (Kuperard, 1994)

Sampson, Anthony 'Peace At Last' (*The Sunday Times*, 23 May 1999)

Schonstein Pinnock, Patricia *Xhosa, A Cultural Grammar for Beginners* (African Sun Press, 1994)

Shaw, Gerald, 'Frances Ames' obituary' (*The Guardian*, 22 Nov 2002)

Taylor, Stephen *Shaka's Children: A History of the Zulu People* (Harper Collins, 1994)

Thomas, Antony *Rhodes: The Race for Africa* (Penguin, 1997)

The Reader's Digest Association *The Reader's Digest Illustrated History of South Africa*, 3rd edn (1994).

Tyler, Humphrey *Life In the Time of Sharpeville* (Kwela Books, 1995)

Tel, Christine *The Intrepid Backpacker's Guide to South Africa* (Coast-to-coast, 1998)

Troup, Freda *South Africa: An Historical Introduction* (Penguin, 1975)

(Unattributed) *Castro Hlongwane, Caravans, Cats, Geese, Foot & Mouth and Statistics: HIV/Aids and the Struggle for the Humanisation of the African* ANC monograph, (circulated to ANC branches March 2002)

United Nations, General Assembly, Official Records: *Eighth Session*, Supplement No. 16 (A/2505 and A/2505/Add.1 'Report of the United Nations Commission on the Racial Situation in the Union of South Africa', Annex V (1952)

van Zyl, Mikki et al *Human Rights Abuses of Gays and Lesbians in the South African Defence Force by Health Workers During the Apartheid Era* (Simply Said and Done, 1999)

von Kapff, Ulrich *Zulu, People of Heaven* (Holiday Africa Publications, 1997)

Werner, Alice *Myths and Legends of the Bantu*, e-text at www.sacred-texts.com (1933)

Wylie, Dan 'A Dangerous Admiration: E A Ritter's Shaka Zulu' *South African Journal* Vol. 28, 98–118 (1993)

Young Pelton, Robert; Aral, Coskun; Dulles, Wink *The World's Most Dangerous Places* (Fielding Press, 1997)

Other materials

Addo Ele-Facts and *Flightless Dung Beetle* leaflets published by
the Addo Elephant Park
'The Art of African Fortune Telling' from the leaflet *Roots*
(10PRO169008A)
Contact magazine report about Sharpeville (2 April 1960)
KWV: A Major Driving Force (company booklet)
Outeniqualand Preserved Railway brochure
Safari Camp brochure
The Greater St Lucia Wetland Park Eastern Shores Trails (the
KwaZulu/Natal conservation service)

Websites

Firstly, of course, my own website about the Chris Hani school:
http://www.scroll.demon.co.uk/za/ch.htm

and then:
http://www.amnesty.org – Amnesty International site.

http://www.bazbus.co.za/ – Baz Bus site.

http://www.birdingafrica.net/index.html – Birding Africa site.

http://www.fitzpatrick.uct.ac.za/ – African Birds site.

http://www.africanvoices.co.za/ – African Voices site, including an article on circumcision ceremony by an anonymous author on the *Online Mail and Guardian*, 19 July 2002.

http://www.districtsix.co.za/frames.htm – District Six museum site.

http://www.sil.org/ethnologue/countries/Sout.html – Ethnologue language site.

http://www.times.co.sz/064.html – Incwala site.

http://www.logcabin.co.za/Attractions.asp – Klein Drakensberg site.

http://www.mrinfo.co.za/sa/Mpumalanga/history.htm – Mpumalanga Parks Board

http://www.ecoafrica.com/krugerpark/main.htm – Kruger Park site.

http://www.madamandeve.co.za – *Madam and Eve* site.

http://www.ecit.emory.edu/worldclasses/safrica/
Makulekehistory.html – Makuleke History site.

http://www.saps.gov.za – South African Police Site.

http://www.doj.gov.za/trc/ – Truth and Reconciliation
Commission Archives site.

http://www.ostrichesonline.com/ – Ostriches Online site.

http://protea.worldonline.co.za – a site on Protea facts.

The Marike de Klerk story was pieced together from many sources:
http://www.suntimes.co.za/2000/06/11/news/gauteng/
njhb03.htm

http://news.bbc.co.uk/1/hi/world/africa/1693954.stm

http://www.suntimes.co.za/specialreports/marike/

http://www.suntimes.co.za/2001/12/09/news/news01.asp

http://www.suntimes.co.za/2001/12/09/news/news02.asp

http://www.sabcnews.co.za (several news items)

http://iafrica.com/news/sa/237036.htm
Chris McGreal in the *Guardian*, 6 Dec 2001

Swaziland documents:
http://www.observer.org.sz/ – *Swazi Observer* online.

http://www.sas.upenn.edu/African_Studies/Country_Specific/
Swaziland.html

http://www.swazi.com/government

http://www.times.co.sz/067.html – site on urban scene in
Swaziland.

Zena Mahlangu and King Mswati:
http://www.news24.com/News24/Africa/
(several news items)

Other books by Summersdale

Brazil
Life, Blood, Soul

john malathronas

summersdale *travel*

Brazil
Life, Blood, Soul

John Malathronas

£8.99 Paperback

'In Brazil the motto seems to be: if you've got it, flaunt it, and if you don't, flaunt it even more…'

Brazil: an eclectic nation that evokes images of vibrant carnivals, crowded shanty towns and football on the beach. Shaped by its many cultures, the Portuguese, African, Native Indian and European communities have ensured the evolution of a colourful, diverse population.

John Malathronas fell prey to Brazil's seductive allure in the early eighties, a fascination that continues to this day. His odyssey through the adrenaline-fuelled, chaotic city bars, the extravagant and exotic *Carnaval*, the lush vegetation of the Amazon rainforest and the destitute shanty towns reveals the throbbing heartbeat of this remarkable country.

'like Alex Garland's *The Beach*, dog-eared copies are sure to be falling out of backpacks in airports the world over.' FHM

THE GRINGO TRAIL

a darkly comic road-trip through south america

MARK MANN

summersdale *travel*

The Gringo Trail
A Darkly Comic Road-trip Through South America

Mark Mann

£7.99 Paperback

'… there I was in the middle of Bogotá, coked up to my eyeballs, in a hallway holding two machetes, while some drunk Colombians argued about whether or not to blow up a bar with a live hand-grenade…'

Asia has the hippie trail.
South America has the gringo trail.

Mark Mann and his girlfriend Melissa set off to explore the ancient monuments, mountains and rainforests of South America. But for their friend Mark, South America meant only one thing… drugs.

Sad, funny, shocking. *The Gringo Trail* is an *On The Road* for the Lonely Planet generation. A darkly comic road-trip and a revealing journey through South America's turbulent history.

Drama and discovery.
Culture and cocaine.
Fact is stranger than fiction.

'like Alex Garland's The Beach, *dog-eared copies are sure to be falling out of backpacks in airports the world over'*

FHM

'Darkly comic, ultimately shocking, and packed with astute observations'
Geographical Magazine

'Mark Mann plunges us into the drugs culture of the gringo trail. Great new paperback'
Wanderlust

John Wassner

espresso with the

HEADHUNTERS

A JOURNEY THROUGH THE JUNGLES OF BORNEO

summersdale *travel*

Espresso with the Headhunters
A Journey Through the Jungles of Borneo

John Wassner

£7.99 Paperback

The indigenous people of Borneo use blowpipes and poisoned darts. They wear 'pan handle' haircuts, live in communal dwellings and some tribes have mastered the art of making themselves 'invisible' in the jungle. But above all, they have a reputation as fearsome headhunters.

Having cast aside his Armani jeans and bought up all the jungle equipment he could find, John Wassner sets off to experience and explore the wilds of Borneo, one of the last relatively unknown places on earth. His only concern: whether he would be able to find a decent cup of espresso in the jungle.

But life in the wilderness turns out to be quite agreeable – with wonderful (if unusual) food, all-night longhouse parties, drunken natives and breathtaking surroundings. In a journey that took over twelve months of planning and preparation, John takes on the mighty Rajang river, travelling up its many tributaries into the heart of Borneo – visiting remote longhouses, isolated frontier towns, government outposts, logging camps and nomadic tribes deep in the jungle.

Interspersed with lively descriptions of places and people are anecdotes, glimpses of history, local legends, occasional lies and healthy doses of humour.

'Wassner's account of his time in the jungle makes for an eye-opening read'
FHM

www.summersdale.com

John Malathronas is a seasoned traveller, photographer and writer, and the author of *Brazil: Life, Blood, Soul*.